THE RELIGION
OF THE PRIMITIVES

THE MACMILLAN COMPANY
NEW YORK · BOSTON · CHICAGO · DALLAS
ATLANTA · SAN FRANCISCO

MACMILLAN & CO., Limited
LONDON · BOMBAY · CALCUTTA
MELBOURNE

THE MACMILLAN CO. OF CANADA, Ltd.
TORONTO

THE RELIGION OF THE PRIMITIVES

BY

MOST REV. ALEXANDER LE ROY

SUPERIOR GENERAL OF THE FATHERS OF THE HOLY GHOST

TRANSLATED BY

REV. NEWTON THOMPSON

New York

THE MACMILLAN COMPANY

1922

All rights reserved

Press of
J. J. Little & Ives Company
New York, U. S. A.

𝔑𝔦𝔥𝔦𝔩 𝔒𝔟𝔰𝔱𝔞𝔱

    ARTHURUS J. SCANLAN, S.T.D.

                Censor Librorum

𝔍𝔪𝔭𝔯𝔦𝔪𝔞𝔱𝔲𝔯

   ✠ PATRITIUS J. HAYES, D.D.

            Archiepiscopus Neo-Eboraci

New York, September 20th, 1922.

AUTHOR'S PREFACE

My career as an African missionary, interrupted by a short sojourn in Europe and another in India, began in 1877 on the eastern coast. I brought with me all the current ideas as to the black populations: fetichist peoples, without religion or morality, with no family life, stupidly adoring animals, trees, and stones.

It was the period when by the gate of the Zanzibar coast their "mysterious continent" was opened, with Livingstone, Samuel Baker, Speke, Grant, Cameron, Stanley, Emin-Pacha, and Victor Giraud as the first explorers of the International African Association, and the heroic pioneers of the Catholic and Protestant missions. All set out from Bagamoyo or passed through it. There also, from the distant interior, caravans arrived daily after the rainy season with 500, 1000, or 2000 men. These brought to the coast ivory, copal, skins, and slaves, especially the last named, showing the attentive observer such varied types of that strange world, that on this shore, so little known to the white man, in the course of a year he might see filing before him representatives of all the Bantu tribes, from the Ba-ganda of the Victoria Nyanza to the Wa-yao of the Nyassa, the Ma-nywema of Upper Congo, and the distant inhabitants of Katanga. Bagamoyo was, therefore, an incomparable field of observation.

Moreover, until 1893 the functions entrusted to me obliged me to make numerous journeys with more or less prolonged sojourns from Somaliland to Mozambique, from the Tana to the superb masses of the Kilimanjaro, from the islands of Zanzibar, Pemba, and Mombasa to the Massai plains and the interesting mountains of Taita, Pare, Nguru, Usambara, and Uruguru.

In 1893 I had to pass to Gabon on the opposite coast where, under cover of the great equatorial forest or along the shores of rivers and lakes or on the sunny plains, there mingled other black populations, alike in many respects but so different in appearance, habits, and language as to offer a curious field for study.

In this world thus revealed to me, a world that may be considered primitive in many of its characteristics, everything was an object of observation and study for me; and I can truly say that, during the twenty years I lived there, scarcely a single day passed without bringing me some new element of instruction, correcting an idea, clearing up a doubt, modifying an hypothesis, furnishing an explanation, verifying a fact, disclosing a clue, removing an error, or revealing a new discovery.

How often these observations, made and controlled on the spot, were found to disagree with the generalizations of well-known authors who are cited as oracles, whom one dare not contradict and who, with theories to sustain, have, perhaps unconsciously, too often solicited premature testimony in their favor! How often I regretted having no book to guide me! Since none existed, how often I desired later on to begin this study on the religion of the primitives so as thereby to aid other missionaries by enlightening them in their apostolate, helping them avoid serious misunderstandings, and cooperating to this extent in their admirable task!

If there be an elementary principle for every one proposing to lead his fellow-men to his own faith, it is first of all to know what they believe. There may be some points of contact where the beliefs of both will meet and perhaps, instead of arguing in endless and always somewhat irritating controversy, it will suffice to explain one's self in order to be accepted.

But there is a still better reason. The study of the beliefs of these primitive populations is in itself extremely interesting, not only because it forever nourishes the curiosity of those who like the exotic, not only because it is a new and attractive exploration into the depths of the human soul, not only because it is one of the necessary elements of ethnography, history, and philosophy, but also and especially because it reveals such astonishing points of comparison with the highest religions that we may indict the theologian unacquainted with it as ignorant of a part of theology.

What are these resemblances, how are they to be explained, and what do they prove?

While our Christian scholars appeared uninterested in these questions, others took hold of them and soon found means of profiting thereby. Imagine them, in their first enthusiasm, announcing to us that, being more fortunate, more competent, more able (they might have added, better supported) than Voltaire and the encyclopedists of the eighteenth century, they have at last found the key to the "religious phenomenon" and all that relates to it. The gospel of this new revelation has been taught for a long time in the universities of our capitals. They have been asked to disseminate their doctrine, and apparently the moment has come for putting this teaching into the form of a catechism, placing it in the program of our primary schools, and imposing it on the minds of children, thus forcing positive religions to be replaced by non-religion or "the religion," i.e., "the aspiration toward the ideal and the unlimited perfection of man apart from all supernatural basis and sanction."

The Third International Congress of the History of Religions, held in Oxford (1908), showed that the new evangels were far from being in accord. This was so evident that some disrespectful journalists, in reporting its sessions, called it a "new Tower of Babel."

However, it is advisable to examine the assertions of these scholars and investigate the soundness of their great hopes.

The eminent rector of the Institut Catholique of Paris, Monsignor Baudrillart, encouraged by Pius X and aided by the intelligent and generous initiative of others, decided that Catholic science should have its word to say in these matters; to meet the new needs he founded a new professorship: the chair of the history of religions. The following study constituted the inaugural lectures in that course.

Suddenly called to realize an idea long cherished in my mind, without having had time and means for a suitable immediate preparation, I feel how much I need the reader's indulgence. Already my hearers have given me kind and touching proofs of that indulgence; I trust my readers will do the same.

I dedicate these pages first of all to the numerous Christian missionaries scattered among the primitive peoples still living. If these pages prove useful to them, I will thank God for permitting me to be thus associated in their apostolate; but I hope these earnest workers will profit by them especially to complete them, perhaps to correct them, to work in turn and contribute to clearing the ground where, as I believe, I have recognized the very foundations of that religion to whose service they, choosing the better part, are devoting their lives.

Will theologians, ethnologists, and Christians desirous of enlightening their faith, find here some new data, explanations, and solutions? I venture the hope.

And lastly, among those doubting spirits looking for the truth, not with the preoccupation of surprising Christianity at fault—for such are usually rebellious to all demonstration—but with sincere and humble desire to find the truth and follow it, are there some to whom these studies will bring light? I wish so, and this, I confess, would be my best reward.

CONTENTS

THE RELIGION
OF THE PRIMITIVES

THE RELIGION OF THE PRIMITIVES

CHAPTER I

THE SCIENCE OF THE HISTORY OF RELIGIONS APPLIED TO THE PRIMITIVES

I. THE SCIENCE OF THE HISTORY OF RELIGIONS. Its aim: to verify and explain the "religious phenomenon." Its precursors and founders. The discoveries of the nineteenth century. In England, Germany, and France. For and against Christianity.

II. ITS ACTUAL TENDENCIES. 1. Prejudice in the matter of religion. The denial of the supernatural. Appeal to evolution. The new method. 2. Incompetence: conventional savages; theories and illusions.

III. OUR METHOD. Not *a priori*. On the adversaries' ground. The "Primitives": Negrillos and Bantus. The value of their testimony. Sources of information.

IV. RELIGION AND MAGIC. 1. Definition of religion. Its elements: belief, morality, worship. 2. Superstition, mythology, and magic.

V. PLAN AND SPIRIT OF THIS STUDY.

The religious question is either wholly unworthy of consideration or it is the first of all those problems that man must face in this world.

It is meaningless if it have no objective validity. But how, in such event, can we account for the real, enduring, universal presence of those strange manifestations of man's beliefs, apparently so unnecessary for the development of his physical, intellectual, even, we are assured, of his moral life? Why these temples; some modest, like the little fetich-hut of the African forests, others splendid edifices, such as those erected by the ancient civilizations of the Euphrates and Nile valleys, in the Khmer country, in India, China, Japan, Europe, and America? Why these ceremonies, prayers, sacrifices, priesthoods? Why that extraordinary production of literary works, inscriptions, rituals, hymns, poems, and—at the very hour when they tell

1

us all religion is disappearing—why so many books, reviews, memoirs, articles, lectures, and discussions? Above all, why that faith, often consecrated by martyrdom and strong enough to resist persecution, trickery, jealousy, hatred, injustice, and hostile legislation? In fine, why do we find religion everywhere, among all peoples, in all times?

A strange thing! Behold a conception that corresponds to nothing and yet is universal, outliving everything else. Destroy it? The more you strive to rid yourself of it, the more it declares itself a living reality and, like an indestructible obsession, forces itself on the attention of humanity with a power that can no more be overcome than can the voice of conscience.

I.   The Science of the History of Religions

Its Aim; Its Precursors; Its Founders

Perhaps you have said to yourself: If we were to study one by one the different forms of religion to which man has been attached, if we sought out their relations one to another, if we discovered the reasons for their existence, and especially if we could trace them back to their origin, then perhaps, by the study and methodical criticism of beliefs rather than by philosophical theories, we could throw new light on the great religious problem that dominates the world.

This investigation, and its importance can fail to impress neither friend nor foe, is the object of the history of religions. It is a new science, becoming more and more precisely separated from ethnography; it is a science whose special purpose is to verify a universal fact, ancient as man himself, characteristic of human nature and, despite the predictions of some doubtful prophets, apparently destined to disappear only with man himself.

In former ages the importance of religious questions, the interest aroused by them, the diversity of beliefs and forms of worship, even the very origin of religions provoked numerous and often remarkable studies. These works, however, did not embrace, properly speaking, the history of humanity's religions, with the lessons and conclusions that can be derived therefrom to-day.

Thus in the thirteenth century Roger Bacon in his *Opus Majus* (1266), in the fifteenth century Nicholas of Cusa, then in the seventeenth and eighteenth centuries Daniel Huet,[1] Bishop of Avranches, Dr. John Spencer of Cambridge, and two Protestant ministers, Samuel Bochart[2] and Pierre Jurieu,[3] tried to present a synthesis of the religious knowledge of their times. Later on, a seven volume work with magnificent engravings, written by J. F. Bernard and Bruzen de la Martinière with the collaboration of Antoine Banier, was published by Bernard Picart under the title, *Cérémonies et Coutumes religieuses de tous les peuples du monde.*[4] Still later the spirit of the age inspired different "philosophical" works on the subject, which are now considered out of date. Such were those of Fontenelle,[5] Bayle,[6] Vico,[7] Voltaire,[8] J. J. Rousseau,[9] C. de Brosses,[10] Court de Gébelin,[11] Dupuis,[12] Lessing,[13] Kant,[14] Herder,[15] Creuzer,[16] Benjamin Constant,[17] Hegel.[18] Auguste Comte, in his *Cours de philosophie positive* (1830-1842), established a basis which many still regard with favor. According to him, civilization—and with it religion—has everywhere sprung from the meanest beginnings; its different degrees are

[1] *Demonstratio evangelica* (1679).
[2] *Géographie sacrée* (1646).
[3] *Histoire critique des dogmes* (1704).
[4] The work appeared at Amsterdam from 1723 to 1727.
[5] *The history of oracles and the cheats of the pagan priests* (1688).
[6] *Dict. historique et critique.* 2 vols. (1695-1697).
[7] *Scienza nuova* (1725).
[8] *Dict. philos.* (art. *Religions*); *Essai sur les mœurs et l'aspect des nations* (1756).
[9] *Emile* (1762).
[10] *Dissertation sur le culte des dieux fétiches* (1760).
[11] *Le monde primitif.* 9 vols. (1775-1784).
[12] *Origin of all Religious Worship* (1872).
[13] *Erziehung des Menschengeschlechts* (1780).
[14] *Geschichte.*
[15] *Outlines of a Philosophy of the History of Man* (1800).
[16] *Symbolik und Mythologie der alten Völker.* 6 vols. (1819).
[17] *De la religion* (1824); *Du polythéisme,* etc. (1833).
[18] *Lectures on the Philosophy of Religion.* 3 vols. (1895).

to be found even to-day among the different peoples of the earth; and any one wishing to unite all these stages has but to study these various peoples one after another.

But the later discoveries and progress of linguistics, philology, and ethnography—the unearthing of ancient civilizations not only in Egypt, Assyria, and Chaldea, but also in Palestine, Phœnicia, Syria, Greece, Carthage, India, Cambodia, China, and America, in fact everywhere—the reconstruction of pre-historic ages, based on discoveries in a world seemingly des-tined to be forever unknown to us, and at the same time the progressive exploration of the whole earth, with the different nations that inhabit it—all this, together with new means of utilizing countless documents (among which photography is of first importance) should enable investigators to make a state-ment of religious data that we would never have been able to attempt otherwise and to systematize them in works of a general nature.

"Nobody," says Chantepie de la Saussaye, "has a greater claim to be called the founder of that science (i.e., of compar-ative religions) than F. Max Müller.[19]   He was the first who succeeded in convincing a large public of the importance of the subject, and was able to persuade the best oriental scholars of Europe to combine in a translation of the Sacred Books of the East, so that the general public might be able to read them. His call for a study of the science of religion has been obeyed by almost every nation, nowhere more quickly than in Holland, where Tiele devoted his great powers to this subject, and among many works published the first compendium, in which he gathered together the results of the study of the history of religion.[20]   In Holland the science of religion has now taken its recognized place amongst academic studies.   In Paris,

[19] This honor has been claimed by others (Cf. L. H. Jordan, *Comparative Religion*, 1905, pp. 161 sqq.).   The new science grew, in fact, from 1800 to 1850 under the impulse of several founders: we have cited the chief ones. Besides *The Sacred Books of the East*, F. Max Müller (1823-1900) wrote many other works on religion: *Comparative Mythology; Hibbert Lectures on the Origin and Growth of Religion; Introduction to the Science of Re-ligion; Selected Essays; Natural Religion; Physical Religion; Chips from a German Workshop*, etc.

[20] *Outlines of the History of Religion* (1905).

THE SCIENCE OF THE HISTORY OF RELIGIONS 5

Brussels, and lately in Rome also, chairs have been founded for the science of religion." [21]

In Germany and especially in England since Max Müller's time, the science of religions has given rise to numerous remarkable works, besides special reviews such as *The American and Oriental Literary Record, The Journal of the Royal Asiatic Society, The Encyclopedia Britannica (Anthropology), The Hibbert Lectures, The Gifford Lectures, The Man, The Journal of the African Society, etc.*[22]

[21] Chantepie de la Saussaye, *Manual of the Science of Religions* (1891). The author gives an abundant bibliography of the subject. He studies religions to the exclusion of Christianity.

[22] To mention especially the works of Sir John Lubbock (*The Origin of Civilizatiòn*, 1870); Edward B. Tylor (*Primitive Culture*, 2 vols., 1872; 4th ed. 1903); Herbert Spencer (*The Principles of Sociology*, last ed., 3 vols., 1914); Andrew Lang (*Customs and Myth*, 1884; *Modern Mythology*, 1897; *Myth, Ritual, and Religion*, 2 vols., 1887; last ed., 1899); A. H. Keane (*Ethnology*, 1901); James G. Frazer (*Golden Bough*, 1890; last ed., 1900); F. B. Jevons (*Introduction to the History of Religion*, last ed., 1904); J. and E. Caird, Morris, W. Robertson Smith, A. M. Fairbairn, etc.
In Germany we must cite R. Lepsius (*Uber den ersten Ægyptischen Götterkreis*, 1851); W. Schwarz (*Der Ursprung der Mythologie*, 1860); A. Kuhn (*Die Herabkunf des Feuers und des Göttertrankes*, 1859); E. H. Meyer (*Indo-germanische Mythen*, 2 vols., 1883-1887); Bastian (*Beiträge zur vergleichenden Psychologie*, 1865); Gerland and Waitz (*Anthropologische Beiträge*, 1875, and *Anthropologie der Naturvölker*, 1900); O. Peschel (*The Races of Man*); F. Ratzel (*The History of Mankind*, 3 vols., 1898); Frobenius (*Die Weltanschauung der Naturvölker*, 1898); O Gruppe (*Die griechischen Kulte und Mythen*, 1887); Wundt (*Völkerpsychologie*).
In Germany we also find the following reviews: *Zeitschrift der deutschen morgenländichen Gesellschaft; Zeitschrift für Völkerpsychologie; Archiv für Anthropologie; Globus; Zeitschrift für Ethnologie; Archiv für Religionswissenschaft*, of T. Achelis.
In Austria, *Mitteilungen der Anthropologischen Gesellschaft in Wien*.
In Italy, *Giornale della Società Asiatica italiana*. A. di Gubernatis in Italy echoed the English orientalists.
In Belgium, Count Goblet d'Alviella (*Lectures on the Origin and Growth of the Conception of God as Illustrated by Anthropology and History*, 2d ed., 1897, being the Hibbert Lectures for 1891); and in Holland, G. A. Wilkens (*Het animisme*, 1885); but chiefly C. P. Tiele, Abraham Kuenen, and Chantepie de la Saussaye along with Monsignor de Harlez represent the science of the history of religions. Note also in Belgium *Le Muséon, Etudes philosophiques, historiques et religieuses*.
In the United States, *American Anthropologist, Anthropological Papers*, etc.; *The American Antiquarian and Oriental Journal*, etc. Mention should also be made of: J. W. Powell (*Mythologic Philosophy*, 1880); J. H. King

France has done much for general anthropology, "the natural history of man," for ethnography, "the study of the material manifestations of human activity," [23] and for ethnology, which, according to Dr. Verneau, "treats of the formation and physical characteristics of the different human races." These recent sciences whose domain has been steadily enlarged, comprising physiology, sociology, and linguistics, extend also to psychology and thereby to religion and morality. Hence the "religious phenomenon" has been touched upon, sometimes happily but more often with deplorable ignorance of the subject, by such ethnographists as A. de Quatrefages,[24] Broca, Topinard,[25] Letourneau, and Deniker; by linguists such as E. L. Burnouf,[26] Bréal, and Hovelacque; by philosophers and sociologists, notably A. Comte, already cited, Guyau,[27] R. de la Grasserie,[28] Durkheim, H. Hubert, and Mauss; historians such as A. Maury, [29] G. Boissier,[30] and Fustel de Coulanges; [31] orientalists like J. Darmesteter,[32] and G. Maspero;[33] erudite scholars like Solomon Reinach,[34] or simple partisans such as A. Lefèvre.[35] Unfortunately the open profession of atheism and materialism by some of these writers, who claim to represent the "French school," has sadly discredited it abroad. The

(The Supernatural, 1892); and especially D. G. Brinton (Religions of Primitive Peoples, 1897).

In Switzerland there is Conrad von Orelli, of Geneva.

[23] Definition of Dr. Hamy.

[24] Armand de Quatrefages: Unité de l'espèce humaine (1861); Les Polynésiens (1866); The Natural History of Man (1875); The Human Species (1881); Hommes fossiles et hommes sauvages (1884); The Pygmies (1895); Histoire générale des races humaines (1889).

[25] L'homme dans la nature (1891).

[26] La science des religions (1872).

[27] The Non-religion of the Future, 4th ed., 1890.

[28] Les religions comparées au point de vue sociologique (1899).

[29] Histoire des religions de la Grèce antique (1857-1859); Croyances et légendes de l'antiquité (1863).

[30] La religion romaine, 4th ed., 2 vols. (1892).

[31] Aryan Civilization (1871).

[32] Etudes iraniennes (1883).

[33] Histoire ancienne des peuples de l'Orient.

[34] Cults, Myths, and Religions, a partial translation of Cultes, mythes, et religions, 4 vols.

[35] Religions et mythologies comparées; La religion, etc.

American scholar D. G. Brinton observes this fact; [36] while W. Schmidt, writing in the *Anthropos,* points out the striking contrast between their frivolous and crude treatment of the subject and the respectful, dignified attitude observed in England even by the foes of religion. [37] This remark is well founded but, to be quite just, it should be extended to materialists outside of France; for no French writer has surpassed the ignorance and animus of the author of *The Riddle of the Universe,* Ernest Haeckel.

However, the "science of comparative religions" [38] tended more and more to establish its own special domain. In 1880 Albert Réville, [39] a Protestant professor, driven from the chair of theology at Montauban, Paris, and Geneva, because of the radical nature of his ideas, was deemed to have the necessary qualifications for inaugurating the chair of "history of religions" at the Collège de France. His son, Jean Réville, succeeded him and served until his own death in 1908. Later on, at the Ecole pratique des Hautes Etudes of the Sorbonne, a section for "religious sciences" was created under Léon Marillier.

This official teaching of religions will undoubtedly be extended to schools outside of Paris. It is now given at Lyons, where Virolleaud has revealed to the world that the life of Christ is but the allegory of Mithra, the sun god, put in the form of history by the so-called "evangelists."

Even before A. Réville gave his first lectures under the title of *Prolegomena to the History of Religions,* A. Lichtenberger [40] had begun to publish an *Encyclopédie des sciences religieuses* (1876-1882) in which, despite many interesting articles, grievous errors are to be found. [41] The Musée

---

[36] *Religions of Primitive Peoples,* p. 45.

[37] *Anthropos,* 1908, I, p. 148.

[38] In 1872 E. Burnouf published a work entitled *La Science des religions.* According to Father Weiss, O. P. (*Le péril religieux*), the expression is Renan's.

[39] Born at Dieppe in 1826.

[40] Born at Strasburg in 1832, died in 1899. Founder and dean of the Faculty of Protestant Theology of Paris.

[41] In the article *Adoration,* by J. Monod: "The Virgin (in the Catholic Church) is the object of a special adoration, called *perpetual adoration* (!)."

Guimet, first opened at Lyons (1878), was soon transferred to Paris (1888). It published its *Annales* and its *Bibliothèque d'Etudes* in which considerable material is gathered. Since 1880 there has been published a *Revue de l'Histoire des Religions* under the direction at first of Maurice Vernes, who was succeeded by Jean Réville. The *Année Sociologique* of Durkheim (founded in 1897) devotes one study annually to the religious question. Lastly, other reviews, v.g., the *Bulletins et Mémoires de la Société d'Anthropologie de Paris,* the *Anthropologie,* the *Journal Asiatique,* the *Revue des Etudes ethnographiques et sociologiques* of A. van Gennep, the *Tour du Monde,* the *Missions Catholiques, La Nature, Le Cosmos,* etc., all contain articles in ever increasing number upon religious matters of world-wide scope. The new science has finally become fashionable.

But most of the names and works just cited require at once a qualifying remark: up to the present this "science" seems to have been conducted in a deliberately anti-Christian spirit. The theories thus set forth could not fail to provoke replies. On the Protestant side, the liberal school has a simple and original way of closing its opponents' mouths—by admitting their conclusions. The following seem to belong to this school in different degrees: O. Pfleiderer,[42] H. Preiss,[43] W. Bousset,[44] in Germany; E. Caird,[45] F. J. Gould,[46] and F. K. Ingram,[47] in England; and in France, A. and J. Réville, A. Sabatier, etc. Conservatives, on the contrary, clearly defend the traditional positions in works that are often of great worth. W. Schmidt, from whom we gladly borrow nearly all these interesting data,[48] cites as worthy of note, J. A. H. Ebrard,[49]

[42] *Die Geschichte der Religion,* 1869; *Religions-philosophie,* 1878; *Religion and Historic Faiths,* 1907.
[43] *Religions-philosophie,* 1888.
[44] *What is Religion?* 1907.
[45] *The Evolution of Religion,* 3d ed., 1899.
[46] *Concise History of Religion* (1893-1897).
[47] *Outline of the History of Religion,* 1900.
[48] W. Schmidt, S.V.D., *L'origine de l'idée de Dieu,* in the *Anthropos,* number 2, 1908.
[49] *Apologetik,* 1875.

E. G. Steude,[50] P. Gloatz,[51] C. von Orelli,[52] H. W. von Walt-hofen,[53] M. Söderblom,[54] S. H. Kellog,[55] W. W. Peyton,[56] L. Jordan,[57] and especially A. Lang,[58] of whom he makes a particular study.

To these names we should add those of several exegetes who discuss the question from the Biblical point of view.

Catholics are likewise showing interest in the subject.   In Germany, for example, Dr. W. Schneider, Bishop of Paderborn, published two remarkable works in 1885 and 1891.[59]   The work of Christian Pesch, S.J., on "God and the gods," is well known.[60]   A. Borchert[61] made a special study of animism and the theories relating to it; H. Schell likewise treated the question in his *Apologie des Christentums* (1901).[62]   Finally, let us not forget to note the laudable initiative of W. Schmidt, S.V.D., in founding the *Anthropos* at Vienna, an international review of ethnology and linguistics: it contains numerous studies relative to the religions of non-Christian nations, and is written in German, French, English, Italian, and Spanish.

In France, we may recall the names of Daniel Huet,[63] Rollin,[64] Bossuet,[65] Abbé Bergier, and those who came later, Chateaubriand,[66] Lamennais,[67] Bonald,[68] Bonnetty, and still

[50] *Ein Problem*, 1881.
[51] *Spekulative Theologie*, 1883.
[52] *Allgemeine Religionsgeschichte*, 1899.
[53] *Die Gottesidee*, 1903.
[54] *Die Religionen der Erde*, 1906.
[55] *The Genesis and Growth of Religion*, 1892.
[56] *Anthropology and the Evolution of Religion.*
[57] *Comparative Religion, Its Genesis and Growth*, 1905.
[58] *The Making of Religion*, 2d ed., 1902.
[59] *Die Naturvölker, Missverständnisse, Missdeutungen, Misshandlungen,* 1885; *Die Religion der Afrikanischen Naturvölker,* 1891.
[60] *Gott und Götter*, 1890; by the same, *Der Gottesbegriff in den heidnischen Religionen des Altertums* (1886-1888).
[61] *Der Animismus*, 1900.
[62] At Friburg (Switzerland), Rev. Zapletal has made a particular study of totemism: *Der Totemismus.*
[63] *Demonstratio evangelica.*
[64] *Histoire ancienne.*
[65] *Discours sur l'histoire universelle.*
[66] *Génie du Christianisme.*
[67] *Essai sur l'indifférence en matière de religion.*
[68] *Législation primitive.*

more recently, Rohrbacher, whose *History of the Church* contains some remarkable views on the subject, and Monsignor Gaume who, in his treatise on the Holy Ghost, repeats the thesis of St. Augustine (*De Civitate Dei*). We are happy to cite in addition such orientalists as Charles and François Lenormant,[69] Félix Robiou, Révillout, de Rougé, Scheil, Monsignor de Harlez,[70] and such exegetes as Vigouroux, Lagrange,[71] etc.

Abbé de Broglie, of the Institut Catholique of Paris, possessed true initiative. His intellectual work still remains most productive; one of his friends and colleagues rightly said of him "that there are few men in our age of investigators, who have established so large a number of new and sane ideas in the realm of religious and moral sciences." [72]

At the Institut Catholique of Paris in 1879 he treated this subject in lectures that were later published under the title of *Problèmes et Conclusions de l'Histoire des Religions*. After setting forth the different systems concerning the origin of religion, and examining traditional polytheism, Buddhism, Judaism, and Islam, he decides in favor of the transcendence of Christianity, asserting that its special characteristics proclaim it without a peer and that only a superhuman action can explain it.

Later, and from another point of view, Fernand Nicolay wrote a history of the beliefs, superstitions, habits, usages, and customs of various nations, grouping them about the Decalogue, the "law of laws." After an extensive and conscientious

[69] *Histoire ancienne de l'Orient; Histoire des peuples orientaux et de l'Inde; Les premières civilisations; Les sciences occultes en Asie; Les origines de l'histoire.*

[70] *Védisme, Brahmanisme et Christianisme.*

[71] *Etudes sur les religions sémitiques.*

[72] C. Piat, in the preface of *Religion et critique* by Abbé de Broglie. Besides this work and his *Problèmes et conclusions de l'histoire des religions*, Abbé de Broglie has published a whole series of articles or pamphlets referring to our subject: *Religion de Zoroastre et religion védique; Le Bouddhisme; Les religions néo-brahmaniques de l'Inde; L'Islamisme; La vraie définition de la religion; La vraie religion; La transcendance du Christianisme; Vue d'ensemble de la religion d'Israel; L'histoire religieuse d'Israel.* Abbé de Broglie was born in Paris in 1834. After having been a student at the polytechnic school and a navy officer, he received holy orders at the age of thirty-two. He was assassinated in 1895.

inquiry, he concludes that "respect for science in the realm of its prudent and hence legitimate affirmations, i.e., confidence in the results of rational investigation, strengthens, enlightens, and definitely confirms the reasons of faith in a decisive and victorious manner." [73]

Abbé A. Bros, professor at the seminary of Meaux, was justly alarmed because of the efforts being made to draw anti-Christian arguments from these subjects which are so little understood; he judged it was time to become initiated in these problems.   Unfortunately he began by regarding with surprising docility as "henceforth established" the authenticity of facts presented by Tylor, Réville, Lang, and Marillier.   With the same obliging condescension he admits most of their theories as to the rôle of animism among "non-civilized peoples," as to their ignorance of God, their lack of morality, etc.; he regards all religions of savages, with their various manifestations, as having their origin and explanation simply in the nature of man; and he concludes that these studies can be of service in Christian apologetics only by showing the innateness of religious needs and the wonderful manner in which Christianity has met those needs.

We are happy to acknowledge these labors and good intentions.   Desirous, as we are, of taking our stand exclusively on the basis of scientific observation, as our adversaries challenge us to do, we can not, however, accept with the same easy docility and, so to speak, without examination, the assertions and conclusions opposed to us.   But Abbé Bros, while giving his foes this mark of confidence, proves that the Catholic scholar is not obliged to follow one only method and a single system—reproaches to the contrary notwithstanding.

In any case, whether to the advantage of friends or enemies of Christianity, the science of the history of religions has been born.   The problems that it raises must be solved by facing them squarely.

"Of course," writes Chantepie de la Saussaye, "this has met with some opposition, partly from philologists and special-

[73] Fernand Nicolay, *Histoire des croyances*, 3 vols., Vol. III, p. 451.

ists who fancy that such a general study will lead to empty dilettantism, and partly in the interests of Christianity, since people are afraid that these studies will only increase skepticism and indifference." [74]

II. ACTUAL TENDENCIES

Prejudice and Incompetency

Churches, philologists, and scholars in general might reply to the worthy professor of the Leyden University that they are not the only ones who have a right to complain, not of the researches and discoveries due to the history of religions, but, as I have already remarked, of the spirit which has generally inspired those investigations, as likewise the method that has guided them. Science itself has a right to utter its reservations and protests. It has this right chiefly for two reasons:

1. Hitherto the study of the history of religions has not, generally speaking, been carried on with the requisite impartiality;

2. Nor, we make bold to say, has its treatment been marked by the competency to be desired in matters concerning the primitive or non-civilized peoples that are its object.

Need we add that, in making this double assertion, we have no intention of calling into question the good faith of our adversaries? None of our philosophical, political, social, or religious convictions is purely intellectual. The apparent reasons one may have for not believing, as well as those for believing, are nearly always mingled in various proportions with other reasons more or less obscure and subconscious. First of all, there is ignorance of the subject—*ignorantia elenchi* in the language of the Schoolmen—whatever study one may have made of it and however much one may be satisfied with one's knowledge; added to this are personal dispositions, intellectual or moral, the environment in which one lives, education, association, interests, passions, etc.; all acting on man's spirit with an accumulated force from which he can scarce free himself: a

[74] *Manual of the Science of Religion*, p. 7.

bath, as it were, in which the whole soul is immersed. Proofs that are sought find ready acceptance. Palatable to one, they are easily believed acceptable to all and, however little such a protagonist may be influenced by the spirit of proselytism, he finds satisfaction none the less in the noble mission of enlightening mankind.

Fortunately this disposition is not equally shared. In non-Christian religions, unbelief is not aggressive. The fetichist, the Buddhist, the Mussulman, who has lost his faith, is not the least desirous of making others lose theirs: he simply goes his way, leaving his neighbors to go theirs. On the other hand, the attitude of those professing Christianity, and especially Catholic Christianity, is notably different. Why? For the fundamental reason that, in the case of Christianity, the direction of one's life must be determined according to the solution adopted. And it seems that the *infidel*—using the word in the strict sense of its double root (*in-fidelis*)—not being able to arrive at an absolute, incontestable conviction, unconsciously seeks, while communicating his disbelief to others, to secure for himself sufficient support to reassure his troubled spirit and calm the vague apprehensions of his conscience. For a contrary reason, one of the faithful, sure of possessing the truth, can not keep it to himself, nor does he wish to, for he is prompted to play the missionary by the double desire of assuring himself of the triumph to which he has a right and of putting on the path of eternal salvation his "brethren" endangered by ignorance. Hence the conflict. It had been predicted: *Do not think that I came to send peace upon earth.*[75]

But to return to our historians of religion.

We repeat that, in general, they have lacked impartiality. After collecting the beliefs, practices, myths, traditions, superstitions, forms of worship, and magic of all peoples and all times, the purpose intended and even openly avowed by many of these is, in brief, to show that all religions resemble and explain one another, and that no one of them is justified in imposing itself as a supernatural expression of the truth. Thus

[75] Matth. 10:34.

united and mingled in a sort of museum, each with its proper
label, they can serve as a subject of study for those interested
in matters of psychology; but in practice, the various religions
ought to be gradually replaced by the Religion, which will
remain, if you wish, an august aspiration towards the ideal.
It will even be much better than present-day religions, for
an ideal without dogma or moral code, with neither obligation
nor sanction, can really inconvenience no one. Guided by this
hope, our explorers, lamp in hand, may be seen following their
own footsteps in long and painful circuits, seeking in the night
of the past an ideal theory that will deliver them from a positive,
obligatory, and sovereign religion.

According to some, the "religious phenomenon" can be explained as the product of primitive ignorance, fear of the
unknown, troubles of conscience, the magnitude of atmospheric
phenomena, or the self-seeking fabrications of priests:

> *Primus in orbe deos fecit timor, ardua coeli*
> *Fulmina dum caderent . . .*[76]

Another school replies: this is a deplorable misconception
and degradation of religion and humanity, since there is something here besides emotions and impressions. The religious
phenomenon is a social fact, explained and justified by the
necessity of life in common, though varying according to environment, country, population, and degree of civilization, but
imposing itself nevertheless upon all human aggregations. Such
is the solution of the sociologists.

An inadmissible hypothesis, objects a third school: for the
religious phenomenon *precedes* the social pact, it does not
follow it. "It is necessary to look for the origin of religions
in psychology." [77] Psychology explains it all to us: from his
own inner depths, man has drawn his beliefs, his practices,
his morals, his religious organization, from the simplest form

---

[76] "The gods in the world were at first born of fear, when the terrible
thunder fell from the sky." The verse is from Stacius (*Thebais*, III, 360),
who borrowed it from Petronius. The same thought is developed at greater
length in Lucretius (*De natura rerum*).

[77] Solomon Reinach, *Cults, Myths, and Religions*, p. v.

to the most complex evolution; and as human nature is everywhere identical, so, too, its religious expression is forever repeated, "reproducing itself indefinitely like the images reflected back and forth by two mirrors face to face." [78]

Many other theories have been advanced: but up to the present, none has been received with any marked favor.

Such methods form what A. Réville more than thirty years ago called the *a priori* elements of the history of religion. And after rejecting such of these *a priori* elements as he judged unacceptable, he set forth his own theory. First of all, he eliminated from the study of religions not only "the hypothesis of a primitive revelation of religious truth to mankind," but also that of a tradition or "regular and continuous transmission of recollections going back to the origin of the species and serving as a criterion for the interpretation of parallel traditions."

At bottom, this philosophical dogmatism, while severely reproaching the dogmatism opposed to it—viz., theology—insists on a similarly intransigent system. Such a "natural" dogmatism results from an unwillingness to acknowledge the supernatural. No supernatural in history and no supernatural in religion; no miracles, no mysteries—is the law which, according to the entire materialist and rationalist school, must dominate the science of the history of religions, as all other sciences.

It is evident that if everything in the world were matter, we would be mistaken in looking for the supernatural. But is everything matter, and what right has any one to make such a philosophical hypothesis the foundation of a science that should, like every other science, loyally search for facts, group them, and try in explaining them to draw logical conclusions?

As to the rationalist school, since it admits the possibility of the supernatural, does it not see that it is thereby obliged to admit, as well, the possibility of supernatural manifestations and consequently of their control? In fact, as Brunetière well said,

[78] H. Hubert, Introduction to Chantepie de la Saussaye's *Manual of the Science of Religion*.

"to deny the supernatural is, according to all appearances, to deny the law of history; and to deny the supernatural in nature is, without any shadow of hesitation or doubt, to deny the liberty of God. History, moreover, has only to record facts duly testified by witnesses. To inject therein a gratuitous principle of Kantian and naturalistic metaphysics . . . that can not be done without contradicting reason itself and precisely 'the law of history.' " [79]

If the supernatural be eliminated—for that is the necessary and preliminary operation—what will replace it? Here evolution comes to the front. "Evolution," says Reinach, as an axiomatic conclusion to one of his lectures, "is the great law in the study of humanity because it is the law of humanity itself." [80]   In fact, the idea of evolution, introduced by Lamarck and Darwin into the natural sciences, has gradually penetrated other realms—physics, biology, philosophy, history, and even theology.[81]

Let us not, then, be surprised to find it here in its most absolute and amazing application. First, it must be admitted that man has come from animal life which, slowly evolving, little by little acquired self-consciousness, became intellectually perfected and, at some period impossible to ascertain even approximately, began to show religious preoccupations. Initial religion under these conditions must have been extremely vague and crude; for, as the type of primitive humanity is found, so far as it can be found at all, in the savages of to-day, so the religion of our savages must necessarily be crude and vague. And that is just what they show us by gathering numberless facts, grouping and explaining them.

We, too, will do the same. For the present, however, let us make this simple comment—on which we will dwell later—that,

[79] Brunetière, *Discours de combat: les difficultés de croire*, pp. 212-214.
[80] Reinach, *op. cit.*, p. 209.
[81] Scholars are far from being in accord as to the import of this law. Dr. Quinton wrote: "Does evolution result, as Darwin and especially Lamarck would like, from a tendency towards indefinite progress? I reply positively: No. Evolution has for its purpose to maintain the vital intensity of the origins, and it has no other." It is a point of view and a tendency, as we see, quite different from that generally proposed.

by making the evolutionary hypothesis an *a priori* law which rules all the rest, they seem to begin where they ought to finish. The principle of evolution in religion, so seductive and convenient, should not be a directing principle: and it can be admitted as a conclusion only when the facts support it.

Will its advocates reply that these very facts have been carefully gathered in great numbers by such men as Tylor, Spencer, Frazer, Bastian, Réville, and many others? If so, we beg to ask these authors whether science really consecrates this strange proceeding that consists in placing in relief such facts as support a theory while carefully removing those which contradict it. This reproach, the gravity of which can escape no one, is unfortunately the very one made against all the historians of religion whom we have just mentioned. It is the accusation presented with rare independence of spirit by Andrew Lang, whose authority is beyond question.

"Anthropology," he says, "while fixing its gaze on totems, on worshiped mummies, adored ghosts, and treasured fetiches, has not, to my knowledge, made a comparative study of the higher and purer religious ideas of savages. These have been passed by, with a word about credulous missionaries and Christian influences." [82]

In this clever art of grouping facts, Herbert Spencer has particularly distinguished himself. Although, in the accounts of travelers, he sometimes found on the same page equally authentic and cogent testimony in favor of more elevated as well as lower religious forms, he passes over the former in silence, noting only "the rabble of gods and fetiches."

Tylor and Frazer do practically the same thing. To the latter, Lang puts these embarrassing questions:

"Why does Frazer neglect to cite and refute the reports of witnesses who are so fatal to his theory, whereas he does make use of other passages in their works? Why does he ignore them on these points? I can not understand such a method. Whenever an historian has a theory, he is always in search of facts that may be opposed to it; the chemist or biologist also

[82] A. Lang, *The Making of Religion* (ed. 1909), p. 256.

does not overlook cases that may not be favorable to his system." [83]

In a most admirable spirit of frankness Andrew Lang continues:

"Our science ought above all to be scientific. It should not close its eyes to facts just because these facts do not fall in with its hypotheses concerning the nature of things or of religion: it ought to attach equal value to the facts that contradict its theories and to those which support them. Not only is science never permitted to ignore unfavorable evidence, but it should even examine it with care, investigating what Bacon calls the *instanciae contradictoriae*: for, if there are such, any theory is vain that fails to take account of them."

These just and characteristic reproaches seem to have received a hearing on the other side of the Channel. They are scarcely noted on the continent, where Christianity—i.e., positive, obligatory, and absolute religion—continues to be used as an attractive target by the new science.

To-day we need to know what method to use and how to employ new means. Observe what one scientist tells us. He is one of the best armed, most expert and ardent.

"The strife of insults and raillery," he says, "undertaken by the eighteenth century against an oppressive past has been in vain; but social paleontology, if it wishes to renew the strife with the calmness and dignity proper to science, will find the history of religions the most useful of historic studies and will incidentally discover that it has more spirit than Voltaire." [84]

Urged on by his zeal, Reinach adds:

"The rationalism of the eighteenth century is a shabby doctrine, made up of impertinences and rash negations"—let us remember that—"pretending to suppress religion without understanding its essence, without having any clear idea of its genesis and development. Thanks to philology, anthropology, and

[83] A. Lang, *Magic and Religion*, p. 56.
[84] Reinach, *Cults, Myths, and Religions*.

ethnography, we are now raising the veil that still conceals
from most men the origin and inner significance of their beliefs,
without having recourse to hypotheses so absurd as those of a
Dupuis, so insipid and inadequate as those of a Voltaire. *If
we can do it, we must.* Deeply penetrated with this truth, I
address myself to Jews as well as Christians, to ignorant atheists
as well as to learned believers, in order to herald the good news
of religions brought to light." [85]

To such dogmatic preoccupations of propagandism as have
so frequently inspired and directed religious studies, there is
too often added a lack of acquaintance with all that especially
concerns the primitive peoples who constitute the object of our
researches in this work.

Surely I am most ready to pay sincere and loyal homage
to so many investigators and learned men who, particularly
in England, but also in France, Germany, Holland, the United
States, and elsewhere, have gathered enormous quantities of
material for use in the history of religions. They have devoted
themselves to most fruitful research; theirs has been the first
initiative; with patience and sagacity and even with admirable
tact they have endeavored to throw light on a multitude of
obscure and too often neglected questions.

But religious questions are extremely delicate. And they are
precisely the only ones, besides political questions, that every
one thinks himself competent to treat without preparation.
What misunderstandings are begotten by this unfitness, what
hazardous interpretations, what far-fetched analogies, what systems possessing no advantage but that of destroying one another
and thus facilitating the work of the critic!

Should we be astonished at these results? Here, for example,
is the Christian religion or, to be more specific, the Catholic
religion. The study of it is seemingly easy: it has representatives, official treatises, approved rituals, external manifestations,
in a word, sources of information open to every comer. And
these are not at the equator or the poles, not in prehistoric
ages, not in a domain accessible only to the initiated, but here
in Europe, at Rome, at Paris. The more you question Chris-

[85] *Ibid.*

tianity, the more pleased she is and, as in the time of Tertullian, she asks merely not to be condemned without a hearing (*ne ignorata damnetur*). Read such and such writings reputed to be learned : you will find therein on the subject of the Catholic religion a vast quantity of dogmatic assertions which are, in fact, nothing but inexcusably stupid and absurdly ridiculous mistakes.[86]

But if all these misconceptions are possible in regard to a belief so easily accessible, how many errors are we not exposed to in the study of religions so vague, strange, incoherent, and obscure as those of primitive races? If, moreover, we must depend upon incomplete or inexact accounts, never living in the midst of these peoples, never able to question them in their own language, or to breathe, as it were, the atmosphere of their social, moral, and religious environment, with no means of knowing this so-called savage except through photographic specimens or exhibitions in museums and fairs, how far shall we be led astray?

Personal study, undertaken on the spot, is plainly lacking in most of the accepted historians of primitive religions. Moreover, with strong prejudgments, they take pains to compose a type of religious savage or of savage religion whose most prominent quality is agreement with their own conceptions.

One who is frankly a materialist and atheist makes of the non-civilized man a dull brute, barely emerged from animality,

---

[86] Here is a simple example. In an article devoted to "evolution in theology," Solomon Reinach calmly writes: "Catholic apologetics for centuries has lived on a transparent sophism: the authority of the Church founded on that of the Scriptures, and that of the Scriptures on the authority of the Church." (*Op. cit.*)

Since Reinach, celebrated scholar and member of the Institute, wishes to treat of Catholic theology, how does it happen that unhesitatingly and without examination, he attributes such a vicious circle to it? How does it happen that, when writing of theology, he does not know the first principles of theology and is ignorant of its most elementary treatises (*De vera religione, de locis theologicis*, etc.), where this "transparent sophism" is precisely refuted? By uttering such gross errors as axioms in so important a matter, does he not see that he is seriously compromising his reputation as a safe and impartial scholar? The authority of the Church is founded first of all on the divinity of her origin, and the divinity of her origin is based on historical facts and proofs of reason. (See Tanquerey, *De vera religione*.)

and resembling closely enough the man whom certain classical manuals describe as our first ancestor, "a frightful monster, with long teeth, the face of a beast, arms and legs covered with hair" [87]; all of which, by the way, would tend to prove to enthusiastic evolutionists that if man evolves, he evolves very slowly.

Another, who appreciates the lofty character of the "religious phenomenon," and who feels obliged to give a reason for everything, unconsciously substitutes himself in place of the primitive and attributes to the latter sentiments, ideas, and conceptions contained in our latest philosophical systems. By this process a Hottentot finds himself (without knowing it) quite at home in the difficult mysteries of Kantism and modernism! What illusion and simplicity!

Meanwhile scholars, publicists, and sociologists advance theories, group facts, interpret institutions, point out origins, transform themselves into "seers," reading with ease the most remote past, telling us the mentality of unknown peoples, unveiling every mystery and revealing how man, as he emerged from the beast, began by "adoring" stones, plants, animals, and stars. Then they tell us how naturism produced animism, how from animism was born fetichism, and in like manner polytheism, theism, religions, and finally the Religion. Such is the naturist theory which seems to be that accepted by A. Réville. At any rate, he keenly combats the system that places fetichism at the base of religious evolution, which seems to be definitely abandoned to-day. It was the theory of Auguste Comte, Lubbock, Schultze, and Girard de Rialle.

According to Herbert Spencer and his disciple Grant Allen, religion began with venerating the spirits of the dead. But this opinion, in support of which the celebrated philosopher used a great amount of material collected by other hands, is no longer accepted as "scientific."

Max Müller, the distinguished Indianist, thought that if primitive man had a belief in higher divinities, it was in consequence of an error due to a "corruption of language"; since the ancient Indo-Germanic tongues have a termination to express

[87] Vilain, *La lecture du jour*, p. 6.

the gender of nouns, the words *heaven, earth, sea, rain,* etc., soon passed for living beings and were classed with one or the other sex.

This theory no longer has any partisans. The chief objection against it is that it does not apply to a great many languages in the world.

According to J. G. Frazer, primitive man was under the sway of two fundamental impressions, one of which came to be expressed in magic, the other in religion. This idea was taken up with some modifications in France by Hubert and Mauss, then by A. van Gennep. It is a statement, not an explanation.

With W. Robertson Smith, F. B. Jevons, and Solomon Reinach, totemism becomes a religion. In the sacrifice of the animal totem and by participation in the flesh of the victim, we have at length the source of the Christian mass and communion.

According to Usener and many German ethnologists, religious notions are derived from the depths of conscience by the production of the mythical image, whence came the concrete and allegorical representation of the gods.

Astral mythology especially, which must have spread from the valley of the Euphrates, should be considered, according to A. Jeremias and H. Winckler, as the first revelation of the power of divinity.

But all or nearly all these systems presuppose the theory of primitive animism, advanced by Tylor [88] and more or less adopted by Tiele.

We shall frequently find the chief data of this system in our path: so it may be well for us to summarize them here. To this end we can not do better than profit from the study devoted to the subject by W. Schmidt.[89]

1. Considering, on one hand, sleep, waking, sickness, death, and on the other, dreams and visions, man at an early date must have formed the idea that there exists in him something distinct from his body, viz., the soul. In the first category of these phenomena, he sees the body more or less abandoned by its

[88] *Primitive Culture.*
[89] *L'origine de l'idée de Dieu* (in *Anthropos,* 1908, p. 139).

vivifying principle and, in the second—visions and dreams—this principle seems to manifest itself as isolated from the body. From this first idea comes belief in the survival of the soul, in metempyschosis, and the worship of the dead. The theory of a reward in the other world is of a later date.

2. Moreover, primitive man imagines that the different beings surrounding him are of the same type as himself. On them all he bestows a vivifying soul; and thus between man, animals, plants, and all the rest, a vast relationship is formed.

3. The worship of ancestors begets the idea of pure spirits. These spirits being able in their turn to take possession of this or that body, according to their fancy, we have, as a consequence, the conception of sickness and death being produced by invisible, hostile intervention, belief in diabolical possession, veneration for the objects of nature, fetichism, and lastly idolatry, properly so called.

4. Soon all the elements of nature are regarded as animated, and we have the cult of celestial phenomena, of water, rivers, the sea, trees, groves, mountains, animals, totems. The culminating point of this evolution is the species-divinity, which is no longer a concrete deified object, but an entire species.

5. Then is born the loftier polytheism of half-civilized or civilized races, with gods of the sky, rain, thunder, wind, earth, water, fire, sun, moon; after that, the gods who preside over diverse phases and functions of human life, birth, death, agriculture, war, and finally above all these, the father of the gods.

6. Even in the lower degrees of this religion we find traces of a dualistic system; but the terms *good* and *bad* signify rather *useful* and *injurious*. To this conception is generally added that of a good and a bad power often represented, as in the Zend Avesta, by light and darkness.

7. Above souls or manes, local divinities, and spirits overseeing the elements, we can distinguish in the theology of savages, sometimes disfigured, again majestic, certain shadowy notions of a supreme Being, that increases in vigor and glory in its course through the history of religion.

8. Monotheism could have been produced in different ways: by the elevation of a polytheistic divinity to supreme rank,

whereby he became the first father of the gods or the most powerful divinity of nature; by constituting a sort of "pantheon," the king of which was the supreme divinity; or by the elaboration of a doctrine which considered the entire universe as animated by an all-powerful divinity, the *Anima mundi*.

This theory, although coherent and well constructed, has found but few followers. The American ethnologist, D. G. Brinton, for example, shows how one can admit the same facts as Tylor and arrive at a system quite opposite.

"This universal postulate," he says, "the psychic origin of all religious thought, is the recognition or, if you please, the assumption, that conscious volition is the ultimate source of all force. It is the belief that behind the sensuous, phenomenal world, distinct from it, giving it form, existence, and activity, lies the ultimate, invisible, immeasurable power of Mind, of conscious Will, of Intelligence, analogous in some way to our own; and—mark this essential corollary—that man is in communication with it." [90]

Thus we see that each system is opposed and destroyed by its successor; and in this incoherent multitude of theories presenting themselves one and all as the expression of the truth, we find at length nothing left except the fact that the "religious phenomenon" is discovered everywhere, and that it remains unexplained.

III. Our Method

Not a priori; on the Adversaries' Ground

May we expect to fare better? Such, at least, is our hope. First of all, let it be noted that, while our predecessors in the history of religions have often been influenced by anti-Christian preoccupations and in consequence have begun by removing the supernatural from their scheme, such a display of bias is no reason for us to adopt our dogma as a predetermined principle, in opposition to theirs.

Certainly, we intend to disguise, dissimulate, minimize, or

[90] *Religions of Primitive Peoples*, p. 47.

denaturalize not the slightest parcel of our faith. But we believe that, although this faith could often illuminate the dark path on which we are setting out, it is not desirable for us, in view of our proposed method, to make it the point of departure.

In the preface to one of the first works dedicated to these studies, Sir John Lubbock wrote:

"Fully satisfied that Religion and Science can not in reality be at variance, I have striven in the present publication to follow out the rule laid down by the Bishop of London, in his excellent lecture delivered last year at Edinburgh. 'The man of science,' says Dr. Tait, 'ought to go on honestly, patiently, diffidently, observing and storing up his observations, and carrying his reasonings unflinchingly to their legitimate conclusions, convinced that it would be treason to the majesty at once of science and of religion if he sought to help either by swerving ever so little from the straight rule of truth.' " [91]

This rule we adopt as our own.

We will go still farther. With that simplicity of spirit which is considered one of our Christian virtues, we, who invoke the Gospel, will permit ourselves to be enticed upon the ground which our adversaries have chosen and where they have already taken the precaution to dig our tomb.

We are pleased to cite the words of Reinach because of the authority he enjoys on this subject.

"Man, everywhere and at whatsoever period we observe him, is a religious animal; *religiosity,* as the positivists say, is the most essential of his attributes, and no one any longer believes, with Gabriel de Mortillet and Hovelacque, that quaternary man was ignorant of religion. Unless we admit the gratuitous and puerile hypothesis of a primitive revelation, we must seek the origin of religions in the psychology of man, not of civilized man, but of man the farthest removed.

"Of this man, anterior to all history, we have no direct knowledge, beyond what we glean from the implements and artistic products of the quaternary period. True, these teach us some-

[91] Sir John Lubbock, *Prehistoric Times, as Illustrated by Ancient Remains, and the Manners and Customs of Modern Savages,* 1865, Pref., p. 8.

thing . . . but far less than we could wish. To supplement our information, three other sources have to be tapped:
the psychology of the present day savage, the psychology of
children, and the psychology of the higher animals." [92]

Let us leave to Reinach a task too delicate for our feeble
means of information, the interrogation of gorillas on their
religious convictions; let us spare the children, and content
ourselves with the savages.

As a matter of fact,

"the existing savage," Reinach writes, "resembles a bed of limestone cropping out in an alluvial country. If we dig to a
sufficient depth under the gravel, we strike the same limestone
again; and analogously if we delve far enough into the history
of civilization, from three to five thousand years before Christ,
we rediscover our savage's articles of faith.

"Thus the twentieth century savage enables us to catch a
glimpse—or more than a glimpse—of the opinions of our far-
off ancestors, members of races that ripened earlier into civilization, but nevertheless passed through the phase in which the
savage still remains." [93]

Savages and primitives. If there are any representatives
of humanity that well deserve this name, they are certainly,
in the opinion of all, those Negrillos and Negritos of whom
ancient travelers wrote and whom modern explorers have lately
rediscovered, living, to the great astonishment of the world of
scholars, in the same countries and the same conditions as of
old. Possessing nothing, acquainted with no industry, ignorant
of grazing and farming, they live only by gathering natural
products, by the hunt, and by begging. They dwell in temporary encampments and, in a word, are, as far as possible, true
children of nature. [94]

[92] Reinach, *Cults, Myths, and Religions*, Introd.
[93] Reinach, *op. cit.*, p. 30.
[94] The following may be consulted: A. de Quatrefages, *The Pygmies;* Mgr.
A. Le Roy, *The Pygmies.*

De Quatrefages has applied the word *Negritos* to the Pygmies of Asia,
Malasia, and Melanesia; Hamy gives the name *Negrillos* to the Pygmies of
Africa.

Surely, if it were possible to point out the ensemble of these primitives' religious ideas, we could satisfy the *desideratum* expressed not only by the scholar whose words we have quoted, but by all those who conscientiously seek to throw light on the origins of humanity.

This is the attempt we are going to make.

During the twenty years that I passed in Africa (1877-1896) on both coasts, on the desert frontiers of Tana and in the great equatorial forest of Gabon, I had the pleasure of visiting several encampments of the Pygmies. I was their guest, I talked with them and learned all that could be drawn from them. Since then, I have been able to increase these data by information from other sources. If this inquiry has not been complete, I can at least vouch for its sincerity.

Because of the difficulty of access to our little men and the necessary limitations to the study of their "theodicy," I can not flatter myself with having seen clearly to the depths of their obstinately closed souls. We will complete our investigation, determine the details, and facilitate the control thereof by extending our study to neighboring and kindred tribes. These are better known and have already been studied in their chief representatives—the Bantus. Since the time of Bleek they have been called Bantus (personal prefix *Ba-* and the radical *-Ntu,* "men"),[95] which designates the linguistic group occupying the greater part of inhabited Africa, since it extends from one ocean to the other and from the upper valleys of the Nile and the Tchad to the Orange. From the physical point of view, the Bantus present a great variety of types coming from ancient mixtures: in the north the Negrillos, the Nigritians, and the Hamites, in the south the Bushmen and Hottentots. But we can discern a special characteristic that distinguishes them from the Nigritians.[96]

Comparing with our life, the material, social, political, intellectual, moral, and religious conditions in which these and kindred peoples live, we note many important differences in our

---

[95] Dr. Bleek, *Comparative Grammar of South African Languages,* 1867.
[96] J. Deniker, *The Races of Man,* 1900.

favor, and accordingly divide mankind in two groups: the *civilized* and the *non-civilized, i.e., barbarians, savages, primitives.*

Let us remark at once that we have preferably adopted this last word, not because we consider it a perfectly just use of the term. In reality, history furnishes us no precise indication as to the *primitive* state of humanity, and we nowise intend to supplement the data of history by any hypotheses whatever.

As Dr. Fairbairn writes, "savage races are as ancient as the civilized ones"—let us not forget this: it will be useful for our conclusions—"and they no more deserve the name of primitives than we do." [97]

We know that several of these peoples have degenerated; while, on the other hand, several of them have known days when, materially at least, they were less supplied with tools than at present.

So we are far from pretending that, in their present condition, the Bantus or even the Negrillos represent the primitive state of the species. May we not conceive humanity advancing, since its infancy, towards an ideal which we will call integral civilization and which, alas, appears somewhat like the rainbow toward which children stretch their hands without ever reaching it? But in this long procession of mankind through the ages, families, clans, tribes, peoples, and races do not present a straight front; some march ahead and others follow, some stop, some retreat, some seem scarcely to move at all.

These last we call the "primitives." On the march toward the ideal, they set out from the point of departure long ago, as long ago as the others; but on the route some untoward occasion, some obstacles, some misfortunes have delayed them; they have lost their direction and perhaps they will never overtake us. Undoubtedly they do not represent humanity exactly as it was at the time of its origin; but of all the peoples composing the human race, these are, nevertheless, the ones who seem to give us the most reliable image of the past. [98]

[97] Academy (quoted by A. Lang, *Myth, Ritual and Religion.* 2 vols. 1899).

[98] A nation may have lived two thousand years before another and yet

What is our conclusion? It is by turning to these "backward" people that, in all probability, we have the best chance, perhaps not to discover in their beliefs and practices the original religion, but at least to extract therefrom certain elements that will aid us toward this discovery. At any rate, we shall be on the very ground taken by our adversaries.

Sources of Information

We can not count on written documents of the primitives, for they do not write.

Nor do they build for posterity: no ancient temple, no tomb, no wall, no ruin attests their activity or transmits their thought. Like bands of running antelopes behind which the clumps of tall grass close in, their generations succeed one another, leaving no mark of their passage. When man abandons the little spot he has cleared for the erection of his shelter, hut, or village, African nature soon takes its place, one season sufficing to cover it with a young, all-conquering vegetation.

We must understand that the most ancient documents relative to the civilization of Egypt, Babylonia, Phœnicia, India, and China are many centuries subsequent to the formation and dispersion of the nations. In the remote ages when, on the banks of the Nile and the Euphrates, man traced the first written characters on stone, brick, skin, or papyrus, the Negrillos and the Blacks had long since been roaming in the African forests in a condition not unlike that of to-day, with the same conception of life and doubtless with the same religion. We can, then, draw from these ancient inscriptions only scattered information and a few points of comparison.

There remain:

1. The oral testimony of the primitives themselves, gathered

represent a more advanced stage of civilization. Take an Australian savage of the present day, and compare him with one of those Greeks who, twenty-five hundred years ago, created the beautiful monuments of Athens. Which of the two is the primitive man? Which of the two would have the more rudimentary—the more primeval—notions on religion? The savage, obviously. The savage, then, is our principal witness. (Reinach, *op. cit.*, p. 30.)

directly from their lips during a sojourn of twenty years in various localities. This is a testimony easily controlled and complemented by similar inquiries on the part of authoritative residents worthy of belief.

2. The indigenous languages whose expressions reflect more or less adequately the new or ancient religious ideas of those speaking them.

3. Their various practices—without speaking of possible monuments, objects, and institutions—which are related to religion, commanded or inspired by it, practices whose primary and true sense at times escapes the natives themselves. After comparison and induction, these often throw a clear light on the obscure object of our studies.

4. Lastly, let us note the texts, more or less well preserved by memory and handed down from age to age: ritualistic formulas, sacred songs, legends, and mythologies.

What is a myth? It is not a legend, but, as A. Réville says, the two closely resemble each other.[99] By "legend" we here mean particularly "a traditional, popular, and marvelous account, more or less imaginary, and not claiming serious acceptance by enlightened men."[100] A myth or mythological tale is considered rather as giving a real but marvelous explanation of the origin of the world, of the divinity, celestial phenomena, and so forth. In addition, we may add that myths and legends are often intermingled and are to be found everywhere, at times with astonishing analogies: this is partly what constitutes the new science of *folk-lore*. Naturally they bear the impression of each people's particular genius. Very poor and simple among the Negrillos, more or less incoherent among the Blacks; in Polynesia their developments are not lacking in grace, grandeur, and poesy.

---

[99] *Prolégomènes de l'histoire des religions*, pp. 145, 162.

[100] *Ibid.*, p. 162. This name legends (*legendæ*) was first given to the lives of the saints that had to be read in the monasteries. The word was subsequently extended to popular narratives without serious authority.

The word *myth* comes from the Greek μῦθος, whose primitive and general meaning is *word, utterance,* and the derived meaning *fiction, poetry, fable.* Mythology (μυθος, λόγος) is the collection of the religious myths of a people, with their origin and interpretation.

Therein we surely find interesting indications, precious allusions, traces of beliefs and ancient practices, from which we can derive much advantage. But, after all, this element of information is very uncertain.

Who will separate religion from the magic, history, science, poetry, story, and fancy in these accounts that have been retouched again and again? For all this is or can be found in them. Besides, we would really be taking the primitives for spirits too naïve if we supposed them to accept these fantastic stories as articles of faith. In the evening, about their fires, they like to hear them, as children like to hear stories; they entertain themselves by them, they find their own mentality in them, they gratify their taste for the marvelous, they enjoy them as one enjoys tales of the past, and by them delight their imagination.

But it is not the expression of a *Credo:* their true religion is much less than that, and much more.

IV. RELIGION AND MAGIC

It is particularly in the first sources indicated above that we must seek the constituent elements of the religion of the Negrillos and the Blacks.

But what is religion? It is commonly defined as "the service of God." It is, no doubt, by referring to this simple yet sublime and beautiful notion that travelers and missionaries, seeing the Blacks do not "serve God," have written that they are without religion. We need, then, a more comprehensive definition corresponding to the order of thoughts, aspirations, and practices of our savages.

On the other hand, recent philosophers and historians of religion, Kant, Fichte, Schleiermacher, Hegel, Auguste Comte, Feuerbach, Max Müller, Tiele, Réville, and others, have given us various definitions. Each one thinks that his definition should replace the others, whereas none of these efforts, according to Abbé de Broglie, succeeds in "defining its object." [101] In fact, by an *a priori* exclusion of the supernatural from the

[101] *Religion et critique,* p. 12.

world, by conceiving an ideal religion that can do without it, while obliged to face existing religions, none of which is indifferent to the supernatural, these scholars leave a baffling problem to be solved. "Consequently we have these definitions which burst, so to speak, since they are unable to hold a mass of dissimilar objects which they would like to embrace:"[102] philosophy, magic, and anti-religion.

We shall experience none of these embarrassments.

If there is any fact most certain and universally acknowledged, though formerly held in dispute, one over which we have no occasion to pause, it is that in the minds of these primitive peoples there is another world distinct from this tangible and experimental world of the senses, this world which we touch, hear, and employ in every way: there is a supernatural world. "There are more things above us," an old African chief once said to me with an air of mystery, "than all the books of the Whites contain." What a strange and faithful echo reverberating from the depths of the black continent, of Shakespeare's lines:

"There are more things in Heaven and Earth, Horatio,
   Than are dreamt of in your philosophy."[103]

There is an invisible and supernatural[104] world mingling with our visible and natural world, penetrating it with its influence, dominating and ruling it. Is it possible, useful, necessary for man to enter into relations with that world?

Without prejudging the basis of the question, we can henceforth affirm that man has always believed in it and acted

[102] *Religion et critique*, p. 29.
[103] *Hamlet.* Act I, scene 15.
[104] By "supernatural" Catholic theology means, properly speaking, the world of revelation and grace existing outside of and above the exigencies and possibilities of our nature. In historic studies on religions, the expression "supernatural world" must take a broader meaning; in the proper and theological acceptation indicated above, it implies an invisible, suprasensible world distinct from our world, where real, living, personal, free beings exist, with whom all historic religions place man in relation. For the sake of the precision of language, we may regret this extension of a word's meaning; we can not neglect it in an historic study, inasmuch as our language has no exact equivalent. Cf. Abbé de Broglie, *Religion et critique.*

accordingly: to establish this fact we have only to cast a glance over the inhabited parts of the earth.

From this double conception is born religion and its counterfeit, magic.

We can define religion, considered subjectively, as *the ensemble of beliefs, obligations, and practices by which man recognizes the supernatural world, performs his duties towards it, and asks help from it.*[105]

This definition, while showing us the nature of religion, indicates the essential elements that compose it.

Everyone, however, does not thus understand it.

In the first place, we are told, this definition does not conform to pantheism, which has no form of worship, nor to magical practices nor to totemism nor to the practice of "envoûtement";[106] for in these cases man does not recognize the supernatural or invisible world for the purpose of performing duties to it, but to make it serve him.   To this we reply: Granted!   But pantheism and the different philosophical theories assimilated to it are not religion; they are philosophy. And likewise superstitious beliefs and practices, charms, sorcery, etc., are not religion; they are magic.

While some wish to extend religion to what it is not, others take from it precisely its constituent elements.

"Religion," writes Marillier, "is not a collection of dogmatic affirmations nor of moral precepts; it is a totality of emotional states, of feelings and desires . . . which we can profitably compare with esthetic emotions."[107]

Without fully discussing this singular theory, let us say simply that it nowise applies to authenticated reality. "Religious emotion" is not and can not be a primary sentiment: for one to be moved, there is needed a cause moving him; if human-

---

[105] Religion, from the old Latin word *religio* or *rellegio,* its uncertain etymology refers it to *re-ligare,* "to rebind," or to *re-legere,* "to reread," or to *re-eligere,* "to rechoose."   Cf. I. L. Gondal, *Religion,* p. 1.

[106] The practice of doing harm to a person by inflicting injuries on his effigy.   See also p. 230.

[107] A. Lang, *Myth, Ritual, and Religion,* Pref.

ity in its ensemble, at all times and places, has experienced religious emotion, this is really because it has felt itself dominated by a supernatural world inspiring this emotion in it: it is what we call *dogma*.[108] Belief has preceded sentiment.

Religious beliefs do not remain, like algebra or geometry, purely speculative: they impose a certain direction upon human life, they prescribe, forbid, and counsel. By them, we know that some things are forbidden and others permitted. This is *morality*.[109]

In fine, the same supernatural world wishes that man should externally manifest his deference to it by prayers, rites, and ceremonies: i.e., by *worship,* for the public exercise of which certain objects, places, and ministers are needed, whence a *priesthood*.

Dogma, morality, worship, and sacerdotal organization are the constituent elements of the great religions among civilized peoples: if we find them among the primitives, we shall be obliged to recognize them as a religion.

But we shall be exposed to irreparable misunderstanding if we do not first clearly separate religion from what we have already pointed out as its counterfeit: *superstition, mythology,* and *magic*.

Superstition,[110] under a certain religious appearance, supposes only beliefs without an object, and vain practices. It can have, consequently, no result.

Mythology is of a speculative order: its purpose is to satisfy a people's curiosity by giving them, sometimes mixed with more or less deformed traditions, marvelous explanations of unknown things: the theogonies, the origin of man, the beginning of the tribe, the earth, sky, cosmic phenomena, animals, discoveries, and so many other things. In mythology there is,

---

[108] This expression, generally applied to Christianity, must be here extended in the most general sense to designate the sum total of religious beliefs. The word *dogma* (δόγμα) comes from the participle δεδογμένον of the verb δοκέω : what is authoritatively decreed as the expression of the truth.

[109] Morality is the rule of manners, *mores*, and the science of life.

[110] From *super-sto.*

indeed, a little of everything: theology, history, story, legend, and poetry. Hence the difficulty of deriving anything of serious value from it.

Magic [111] has an essentially practical character. It is an art, the art of using the forces of nature by certain occult observances with a religious appearance, or of courting the influences of the invisible world. Hence it follows that magic is the perversion of science as well as of religion.

Between all these elements and religion properly so called, there are fundamental distinctions which the continuation of our study will make more evident. Because of failure to make these distinctions, a number of philosophers, historians, and other scholars, as also travelers and even missionaries, have so often confused these matters. Besides, we must understand that in the savage world these very elements of religion, superstition, and magic are ordinarily so mingled as to make it difficult to separate them clearly. Shall we ourselves succeed? Not always, perhaps, and this can not fail to make us indulgent towards others.

V. Plan and Spirit of This Study

What is our plan?

In the realm of the history of religions, what characterizes the spirit of the naturist school, partly and in different proportions, is, as has been said, the appeal to the evolutionist theory to explain the varied forms of the "religious phenomenon"; and also the constant pretension of having recourse only to the historical, experimental, and comparative method, proceeding solely in the light of facts. [112]

Making our reservations on the theory, whose appreciation belongs to philosophy and which we will have occasion to notice later, we frankly accept the method offered us.

We will study the question sincerely and loyally, not avoiding but rather invoking our adversaries' criticism, not making

[111] From μαγεία, science of the magicians.
[112] Abbé C. Piat in the preface of Abbé de Broglie's *Religion et critique*, Pref., p. 8.

a clever choice of facts that suit us, but setting forth the ensemble of beliefs, morality, and worship, not theoretically grouping fragmentary data taken here and there from the reports of persons unknown to us, but devoting ourselves to a direct, personal inquiry, dealing with those primitives we have known and visited : the Negrillos and Bantus.

Among these primitives we will gather sufficient notions to enlighten us in regard to their religion, if it be true that they have one, and compare them with those furnished by other similar peoples, whether in our own times or in remote ages of the past.

If, in very moderate proportions and with a reserve suited to our knowledge, which is manifestly inferior to the task thus outlined, we conduct this inquiry to a successful issue, we should be able to extricate the elements of man's primitive religion.

Will these conclusions—for we must finally reach them— be contrary to Christianity or favorable to it? We shall see: for the time being, we enter upon this study without predicting anything and without fearing anything.

Still another question. In the course of our exploration, as long as the duration of centuries, as extensive as the world, often uncertain, obscure, and difficult, shall we touch the frontiers of that supernatural world on which the humblest religions rest? Neither can we announce that in advance.

If it does not manifest itself to us and if the whole "religious phenomenon" of primitive races can be explained without it, we will say so simply, without concern as to our own beliefs. They are sufficiently solid to maintain themselves without recourse to outside support. Besides, we remain firmly convinced that there are no truths against the Truth.

If, however, it shall appear to us that this same religion, in its ensemble or in one or other of its parts, could not be fully conceived without the supernatural world, we will not hesitate to say so: and thereby will this study be distinguished from certain others. If science has its heroism, it has also its weaknesses; and when, at the end of a painful and obscure journey, it happens all at once upon a glimpse of God's presence, why should it appear embarrassed and ashamed to find itself before him?

CHAPTER II

THE PRIMITIVE IN THE PRESENCE OF NATURE

I. A PRELIMINARY REMARK

When a missionary goes to establish himself in an unexplored part of the black continent, amidst a tribe he does not know, one of his first cares is to learn the language. Generally he has a native interpreter at his side; but in spite of this considerable help, for a while everything seems confused, inextricable, and in the strange sounds that strike his ears, he distinguishes neither phrases, syllables, nor words. From that material, however, he must make a grammar.

Days pass, and weeks and months. Then at last comes an hour when the grammar is made. This language which had seemed a mere succession of inarticulate sounds, turns out to have its parts of speech, its inflections, its rules, its philosophy, its beauty. But the natives, who speak it with surprising correctness, are unable to explain how it is constructed. It is the missionary who must now teach it to them.

Somewhat the same process takes place in acquainting oneself with their religion.

The Christian, or more exactly, the Catholic possesses a *Credo* with sharply defined limits, and he has the priceless advantage of knowing at each stage of his journey towards eternity whether he is on the right path or astray. But notice this curious fact—the further we depart from Catholicism, the more do the limits of belief appear effaced; they are quite so with the primitives.

There we find no religious system properly so called, no dogmas imposing themselves, no defining authority, in a word no obligatory "truth," given and received as such: hence there are no discussions, no heresies. Religion, with our savages of Africa, is mixed and identified with everything: with their laws and traditional customs, feasts, joys, griefs, work, business, the incidents and accidents of life. It is even hard at times to distinguish it in practice from medicine, science, superstition, and magic. That is why we have no word to designate it in its entirety. We call it by the general name, *customs,* meaning what has been retained from ancestors, what has always been believed and always done, what must be practiced to maintain the family, the village, the tribe, and if neglected would lead to certain evils—as has often been observed.

We also understand that this element of uncertainty in beliefs affects various individuals or groups unequally: there are some very religious tribes where the ancient traditions are relatively well preserved, others with very little zeal, and some with none at all. In fact, each one takes what he likes: nowhere in the world does "free-thought" seem more sincere than in the "savage" country.

But on certain occasions such and such practices are to be observed, such initiations, dances, ceremonies, sacrifices. Whether or not the natives have any ideas corresponding to these external rites is of little importance; they must be performed, and rarely is there any inclination to neglect them.

Religious instruction is likewise transmitted by custom and example, especially since religion is intimately associated with the family and social life, with the laws and with the necessities of daily existence. Religion is not a series of lessons imparted by way of instruction, but an institution by which one lives. Exactly this explains its permanence; for lessons are forgotten, while institutions remain.

Particularly at the initiations of youth are the tribal and family traditions recalled. Undoubtedly on this same occasion religious instruction has its part along with all the rest. We must say the same for the instructions, ceremonies, and trials of candidates in the secret societies, of the aspirants to sacerdotal functions—understood in the widest sense—of the "schools of fetichers," and so forth. But, outside these special cases and periods of initiation, there is in the black country no religious instruction, properly so called, no authorized religious system.

If, then, in this study, we distinguish dogma or belief from morals, worship, and other religious elements, it is for the sake of logic and clearness, for the sake of presenting religion in its ensemble. Our primitives, less exacting, are not acquainted with these differences and are often incapable of giving an account of them. It has been very well said that "what these tribes most lack, at least the lowest of them, is some resoluteness and firmness in the imagination itself, a certain solidity of spirit,"[1] on which a doctrine might rest.

II.   Evolution and Religion

Though often asserted, is it exact to say that man is the product of one or more pairs of apes; that the primate resulting from this union, even after evolving in the direction of new progress, has been intellectually and morally susceptible to religious ideas; that these religious ideas have been very crude; and that, as evidence confirming these theories, we still find the elements of this primitive religion in the religion of our present day savages?

Is all this exact? And must it necessarily be admitted as a definitely ascertained postulate, before beginning the study of the primitives and their religion?

We have briefly answered this question already.

[1] Renouvier, *Philosophie analytique de l'histoire*, p. 3.

1. Though some scholars understand evolution thus, others understand it differently. Some admit it only for the lower species; others declare its sole aim to be, not indefinite progressive development, but "the maintenance of the vital intensity of origin"; and still others deny even this. In any event, no one has proved it: evolution remains an hypothesis. As our opinion in such a matter is not that of an authority, let us shelter it behind that of a scholar who can not be suspected, viz., Virchow. In 1890, when presiding over the congress of German anthropological societies at Vienna, he made this declaration:

"When we met at Vienna twenty years ago . . . we shared the general expectation that man's descent from the ape or some other animal would soon be proved. . . . Up to the present, Darwinism has not fulfilled that hope. All to no purpose have we had pointed out to us animals that were to connect the human species with the ape: they failed to prove their relationship. The *Pro-anthropos,* that pretended ancestor which was to bridge the gap, has not yet been found. No real scholar claims to have seen it. . . . Someone may have caught a glimpse of it in a dream, but once awake he can not say he has met it. Even the hope of its future discovery has quite crumbled: in fact, you scarcely hear it spoken of any more. For we do not live in an imaginary world of dreams, but in a real actual world that has shown itself extremely exigent. . . . At present, all we know is that among the archaic types of man, none has been found more closely related to the ape than the types now existing. . . . To-day it is clear that among non-civilized tribes, there is not a single individual any closer to the ape than we ourselves." [2]

This testimony, which is by no means an isolated instance, is sufficient. To base a whole religious theory on an hypothesis assumed as an indisputable postulate, though unproved, and to proclaim this as the only good, scientific method, seems to require of the kind reader a singularly extreme confidence.

[2] Translated from the *Correspondenz Blatt der deutschen Gesellschaft für Anthropologie,* 1890 (quoted by S. H. Kellog, *The Genesis and Growth of Religion,* p. 30).

2. Even if the animal origin of man's body were to be scientifically established, that discovery would leave intact the question of the origin of his higher faculties and his religious and moral conceptions. These two questions are quite distinct.

3. And there is a third difficulty: even if that descent were proved, it would not and could not have, by that very fact, the effect of excluding a supernatural intervention. Another scholar, a confirmed evolutionist, Alfred Russel Wallace, recognizes this. When speaking of Darwin, Wallace says:

"His whole argument tends to the conclusion that man's entire nature and all his faculties, whether moral, intellectual, or spiritual, have been derived from their rudiments in the lower animals, in the same manner and by the action of the same general laws as his physical structure has been derived. This conclusion appears to me not to be supported by adequate evidence, and to be directly opposed to many well-ascertained facts. . . . Because man's physical structure has been developed from an animal form by natural selection, it does not necessarily follow that his mental nature, even though developed *pari passu* with it, has been developed by the same causes only." [3]

After speaking of man's higher faculties, he adds:

"These three distinct stages of progress from the inorganic world of matter and motion up to man, point clearly to an unseen universe—to a world of spirit, to which the world of matter is altogether subordinate." And he concludes that, in order to explain the successive advent of unconscious life, then conscious, and finally intellectual and moral as we see it in man, "we can find an adequate cause only in the unseen universe of Spirit." [4]

4. Let us continue. In transferring the jurisdiction of the law of evolution from one realm to another, from the realm of the physical and material to that of moral things, have these men remarked that these two worlds are essentially distinct, that the principles directing one do not necessarily govern the

---

[3] A. R. Wallace, *Darwinism*, p. 461.
[4] Wallace, *op. cit.*, p. 478.

other? It is very evident that the strongest, the ones best constituted, best armed for life's struggle, are not always the finest and the most intelligent. Similarly, because man at his origin was ignorant of our modern discoveries, built no palaces, wore only rudimentary clothes, possessed little or nothing of what constitutes our material civilization, we can not conclude that he was completely lacking in intelligence, religion, or morality, or that he possessed only very imperfect elements thereof.

5. Moreover, even in the event that evolution has directed and still directs the religious development of the human species by necessary, continuous, and unconscious effort, it is still evident that evolutionists falsely apply the principle by confounding what is *crudest* with what is *simplest*. Between these terms there is an absolute divergence. We understand, for instance, that an oak comes from an acorn; we do not understand that it comes from a pebble. That the first men had or must have had religious notions but little complicated, we do not deny; that such notions were valueless or even very crude, must be proved. And when this belief is imposed on us *a priori*, out of respect for the unproved hypothesis of evolution—unproved at least in this matter—we reply: "So much the worse for evolution; let evolution, thus understood, begin by proving itself!"

III.   Naturism and Animism

The import of these brief reflections is evident. They do not count, however, if the savage of to-day "does not even distinguish the difference that exists between the living being and the inanimate object" [5]; if "all that moves seems to him endowed with life and consequently with will" [6]; if "in all the forces of nature he sees the personality, the will, the conscience of an active and conscious being, similar to his own personality and will" [7]; for we shall then have to admit either that the savage of to-day is a degenerate, fallen into intellectual and

[5] Gustave Le Bon, *Les premières civilisations*, p. 76.
[6] Gustave Le Bon, *loc. cit.*
[7] *Ibid.*

moral brutishness concomitantly with his descent into physical misery, and utterly unable to raise himself, or that in his arrested evolution, he almost represents the dull brute that was our pitiful ancestor.

On this hypothesis, according to Pfleiderer,

"primitive man must have been aware neither of his superiority over other animals, nor of his own personality, nor of his spiritual nature; the original religion must have been a kind of indistinct, chaotic naturism" [8] ;

and the earliest religious phenomena must have made their appearance in the presence of every natural object that could provoke in man a feeling of reverence.[9]   Such is the definition of what it is agreed to call Naturism.

Naturism, the first religion of man, would be seen, for example, in some parts of Africa.   A. Réville says so, along with Allan Menzies and many others.   It is even divided into *small* and *large* according as worship is directed to stones, mountains, caves, bodies of water, plants, animals, or mounts to the stars, the sky, sun, moon, and atmospheric phenomena.   And in the spirit of our modern craze for cataloging, these different forms of worship are called litholatry, hydrolatry, dendrolatry, astrolatry, etc.

Hence man, supposing animation to reside in all objects as he feels it in himself, must himself have placed a living spirit in each of them.   This is a phase of *animism*,[10] a theory brilliantly represented by Tylor in England and by Tiele in Holland which we have summarized above.

Then, desiring to represent his god to himself, to approach him and, so to speak, appropriate him, man became a fetichist [11]; making statues or images for himself in order to place therein the spirits or divinities that he honored.

---

[8] *Encyclopœdia Britannica*, art. "Religions."   (Ed. 1906, vol. 20, p. 379.)

[9] Louis H. Jordan, *Comparative Religion*, p. 536.

[10] From *animare* or *animus*.

[11] From the Portuguese *fetiço*, a natural object divinized, a name given by the first navigators of the African coast and introduced into science by the President de Brosses, author of *Culte des dieux fétiches* (1760).   The Portuguese word is related to the Latin *facticius, facere*.

Another step would have brought him to *idolatry*,[12] which consists in the adoration of the image representing the different divinities of his pantheon: whence we would also have *polytheism*.[13]

At length, as his intelligence became gradually enlightened and his conscience refined, he would have multiplied his gods until they became lost in a universal pantheism,[14] or vanished before the need of a personal, sole, and sovereign God.

Will he stop there? No. By a prodigious advance, science, "the true science," a stranger to everything supernatural, will conduct him in one leap to the material conception of the universe, to the sole adoration of nature, humanity, and self: so that, as Weiss [15] remarks, the history of religions thus understood, could be well represented by the familiar emblem of "the serpent biting its own tail."

Assuredly all this exposition is not to be rejected *en masse*. Presented, as it is, under the form of a necessary process, uniform and constant, it is first of all an ideal, theoretical construction growing out of the European spirit. Without entering into a detailed consideration of the replies that might be made to the naturists and animists, we may simply rely on what Durkheim himself says of their common character and declare that neither is acceptable. Both of these theories seek to derive the notion of sacredness from things and events of immediate experience, at first appearing altogether profane. But, as the sacred can not come from the profane, the laborious mechanism by which it is pretended to trace such a derivation is founded on an illusion, born, as Tylor remarks, of an intemperate imagination, or according to Max Müller, a disease of language (i.e., of thought). In either case, religion would be nothing more than a system of false and hallucinatory ideas. It would be merely the realization of a dream; and we could explain its long duration only by recognizing in its permanence the effect desired by clever priestly policy. Such an idea,

[12] Adoration of graven images (εἴδωλον, λατρεία).
[13] A system that admits a plurality of gods (πόλνς, θεός).
[14] God constituted by the universality of beings (παν, θεός).
[15] *Le péril religieux.*

familiar to the eighteenth century, can not be accepted to-day. It is altogether inadmissible that religious beliefs have no objective value and that sacred objects are but imaginary ideas whose nature and powers are unreal.[16]

We can not adopt these theories. Not, as might perhaps be supposed, because in their ensemble they embarrass us by their opposition to Biblical tradition; the Bible is here outside the question. In fact, if Genesis teaches us that the first human couple were created in a state of supernatural innocence—which their knowledge of duty to God presupposes—it tells us also that they "fell." Through their own fault, they lost that original perfection. Then we, their descendants spread over the earth, are fully justified in thinking that at least certain of these first human groups might have passed through deep physical, intellectual, and moral misery, before reaching the degrees of ancient civilization of which we find traces to-day.

If, then, we do not acknowledge the portraits in question as authentic, it is because the "savages" of to-day, however wretched, are not the ones thus depicted for us. There are some, it is true (and I have met them), who find it difficult to count up to 3, 4, and 5: an embarrassment not experienced by "clever" dogs. Yes: but that difficulty is due to the fact that the intelligence of these poor people was never trained, even a little, in arithmetic. Their minds, less incompetent in other matters, even in arithmetic need only exercise.

IV. THE PSYCHOLOGY OF THE PRIMITIVE

This reflection leads us to a short examination of the primitives' psychology as we ourselves have observed it.

Despite his intense vegetative life, his animal instincts, and his dense intellect, the primitive is first and foremost a man, with all the passions, aspirations, energies, weaknesses, and preoccupations of a man; in short, nothing resembles his soul so closely as our soul. Are not barbarism and civilization, after all, easily interchangeable states?

Our primitive is a man. But he is a man who has kept, in

[16] E Durkheim, in the *Revue de philosophie*, May 1, 1907.

varying quantity according to race, family, and even individual, the infantile characteristics of the species: not only from the physical point of view, but especially the intellectual and moral points of view. He is a *man-child*.

By reason of his plastic nature, the environment in which he lives exercises an undeniable influence upon him: even from the religious point of view, the Black of the vast, almost desert steppes is, for example, different from the Black of the dense equatorial forests; the shepherd, the fisherman, the warrior, the farmer, the nomad, the settler, all differ from one another.

But, in general, regarding existence as he would a cocoanut, the primitive makes use of it from day to day, without preoccupation and without aim. Nothing surprises him, and the inquiry into primary causes is a matter of utter indifference to him. To reason about everything, to analyze and demonstrate everything, to penetrate everywhere, to delve into the earth or mount to the heavens, seem to him quite profitless occupations. Perhaps he, too, addresses many "why's" to himself. But he does not wait long for an answer: the first that comes suits him well enough.

His will is wanting in balance, constancy, and harmony. It is especially for this reason that the Black has remained in the inferior situation where we see him. He lacks what goes to make a man: character. Having no taste for useless effort, he is called apathetic. As a child of nature, he depends largely upon this mother. If she fails him at times, he is not angry at her: no one accepts the inevitable more readily than he.

Credulous he certainly is. But his credulity is like all his qualities, never very deep. He is suspicious, always on his guard; not so naïve as one might suppose—easy to deceive, perhaps, but not for long. In Africa, the social state depends upon mutual exploitation, as everywhere else. Since the Europeans have penetrated his country to bring "civilization" to him, that régime of exploitation has, of course, been shifted, enlarged, and intensified; but, after all, the more exploited of the two is not always the one you might suppose.

The Black loves to laugh and takes things good naturedly. But it would be wrong to suppose him indifferent. He knows how to appreciate a good turn, is faithful, devoted, generous, and loves what he loves. Yet withal he has terrible recurrences of evil instincts. He is quite capable of deep dissimulation, has no pity for weakness, and is subject to fits of abominable cruelty. But contrary to what is sometimes supposed, he is extremely sensitive to injustice, wrongs, humiliations, or injuries to his self-love. On the outskirts of the equatorial marshes, there are certain thorny clumps of sensitive plants that remain unaffected by most severe storms; but let them be hit with the stick of a passer-by, you will see them suddenly draw in their trembling foliage as if they felt themselves bruised and wounded in their innermost delicate nature. The Black is somewhat like these mimosa thickets.

Leaving aside all theories and taking our primitives for what they are, if we try to learn their general attitude towards the "religious phenomenon," it seems to us that the best means of doing so will be first to place them face to face with those two worlds with which we are in relation: nature and the supernatural, united by that mysterious bridge called Death, a bridge over which we all must pass some day.

The study of these two worlds and the conception formed of them constitute the very study of the religion of the primitive.

V. Nature and the Supernatural

First of all, then, what is nature? The primitive is not a philosopher. Very simply he admits what he sees and does not weary his mind by the investigation of causes. He is a positivist in the sense that he observes a fact, finds or does not find an explanation of it, and troubles himself very little with trying to combine theories or abstract the quintessence of things. However, he loves unconsciously perhaps but no less certainly that nature which he approaches the more closely in proportion as he is less civilized; he enjoys it and gladly returns to it if he has been obliged to leave it for a while. Does he, then, deceive himself so much as we say, when he believes that it lives, breathes, sings, sleeps, changes its appearance, is born, develops, suffers, and dies in each of its countless elements?

All this escapes an animal's observation because it is an animal; but it does not escape the observation of the primitive, because he is a man. Why does the wind, that we can not grasp, now so mild and now so terrible, cool our face and make the forest tremble? Why does the seed come forth, here growing into grass and there into a tree? Why does the fire, springing from the stone or the dry wood, warm our body and devour whatever we throw into it? Why do certain fruits nourish us while others poison us? Why all these powers, all these contrasts, why all this that we see?

The primitive answers himself simply: If water flows, if fire burns, if the stone remains in its place, if the spark springs forth from the tinder-box, if such a bark cures and such another kills, if the seed springs up, the bird flies, and the monkey steals, that is because "it is their manner." Everything has its "manner."

In all things there are hidden powers, secret properties, mysterious "manners" peculiar to each of them, that we can utilize, turn to account, neutralize: everything is in knowing how. The Whites have their own methods, the Blacks theirs. Thus it is that, by observations and hypotheses, often incomplete, defective, and ridiculous, the primitive makes a beginning in science; after noticing the action of the immanent forces of nature and feeling himself face to face with them in a variable attitude that makes him now conqueror and now conquered, he has conceived the idea of turning them to his own advantage. His attempts show him day after day that he is not completely mistaken. If strychnos is poisonous, if the cola-nut gives strength for a long march, if coffee keeps him awake, why not suppose an alligator's gall, a lion's paw, or a leopard's beard has specific effects equally powerful?

In our opinion, that is the idea which inspires a great number of remedies, preventives, recipes, amulets, and various superstitions employed in all the exigencies of life and against all the dangers that threaten: sickness, hunger, drought, famine, serpents, the arrows of the enemy, and so forth. Similarly there are omens, auguries, divination by lot, the curative or preventive powers of certain movements and formulas.

All this is based on the view that visible nature, of which man is a part, contains immanent, mysterious, and powerful forces that dominate and at times crush us, but which we can also seize and master.

But is this really a religious conception?

To push our inquiry still further. It seems as if the sight of the sky, the great atmospheric phenomena, storms and lightning, have produced and still produce a profound impression on the mind of the primitive.

We have already hinted at the error here. For the savage, nature in her manifestations, great as well as small, proceeds in a certain fashion: while these manifestations are produced normally, he does not notice them. Of what use would it be?

When a child is traveling in a train, he joyfully lets himself be carried along without wondering how the cars roll by themselves on the long steel rails; but let a sudden stop take place, a crash be heard, an unusual whistle blow like a cry of alarm, he is the first to ask an explanation. It is partly the same with the primitive in regard to the immense machinery of the world. While it works without other incident than the customary alterations, he regards it with confidence and has no other care than to let it go on.

But if something unusual or simply unforeseen happens about him, either on the earth or in the sky, if the sun burns the plants by its exceptional heat, if the sky holds back the beneficent rain, if a comet appears, if an eclipse threatens to cover the sun or moon forever, at such provocation his mind begins to work, he is disturbed, he seeks an explanation and finds it; then, by prayers and sacrifices, he prepares to ward off the impending evils. Yet we would not be justified in saying that these facts reveal a worship of the stars. The appearance of the moon, its contrast with the sun, its changes, its mildness and brightness, the faithfulness with which it measures time, the sort of serene kindness with which it presides for whole nights over his dances and feasts at the sound of the tam-tam, the chance it gives a traveler to enjoy the refreshing coolness along the little footpaths where it casts its light, all that makes it a "friend." And the primitive goes along happily *per amica silentia lunae*.

He does not "adore" it any more than he does the sun or stars; but he is happy to greet its return, he is alarmed at the dangers threatened by an eclipse, and he attests a sort of distant gratefulness to it for all the services it renders to him.

Yet the primitive, like a child, does not want to delay before the numerous "why's" that of their own accord present themselves to his mind. He answers them according to his particular mentality; and he makes up stories about the stars, about the animals, about everything. These stories are repeated in the evening about the common household fire or in the village forum. Among the Fans of Gabon, for example, the story goes that in the beginning the sun and moon were married: the stars are their children. They feed on fire, and that is why they shine. But once the moon was unfaithful and deserted the conjugal fireside. As soon as the sun perceived this, he entered into so violent a rage that the frightened stars fled to all parts of the sky and thenceforth, desperately and untiringly, the sun pursues his family. But the latter, as soon as they see him appear on the horizon, quickly conceal themselves in their huts on high. When the sun has traversed all that part of the firmament which is over our heads, he passes back by the other side without stopping a single day. Scarcely has he disappeared from sight, when you see the moon appear, now here, now there, for she often changes her hiding place to throw her spouse off the scent. As soon as she is free, she hastens to the midst of her children, the stars, like a good mother and visits them one after the other, going from hut to hut. No sooner does the sun appear again at the other side of the earth, than she escapes with all her children except one, always the same, who both morning and evening remains there to act as sentry and warn her. And the pursuit continues.[17]

With these stories and others like them, primitive man relieves the solitude of his evenings and gives a simple and not uninteresting explanation of the phenomena that he can not elucidate. But it would be a mistake to suppose him the dupe

[17] Trilles, *Proverbes, légendes et contes fâns*, p. 123.

of these stories. It is his poetry. Would it not be an exaggeration to call that poetry a religion? Assuredly the most stupid savage does not believe that the sun is *really* a man, the moon *really* a woman, stars *really* their children, the lightning a big bird, the thunder an animal. He says all that, no doubt: but it is a "manner of talking." Have we not also our tales and legends? Do we not always find the unusual and marvelous interesting? When our children ask us to tell them some "stories," are they not manifesting their taste and showing what little importance they attach to the question of authenticity? Very well, the taste of the primitives is quite similar. Although their "stories" are very interesting to such as know how to find what they contain, still from the point of view of language, tribal affinities, a more or less remote past, certain traditions, usages, and even beliefs and religious or magical practices, we can draw nothing serious from the fact that these narratives accidentally personify the beings and objects that enter into them.

These accidental personifications belong to the very essence of such compositions and in themselves have no religious signification properly so called; it is rather the life of the tribe transferred by imagination to the life of the heavenly bodies.

But there is an unconscious expression of a people's mentality, namely their language. Might not this supply some data for us? The Bantu tongues, which belong to the agglutinative [18] type, have no grammatical distinction of gender according to sex. Instead of being divided into *masculine* and *feminine,* the nouns are divided into classes according to the different categories of beings that are found in nature itself; hence the vocabulary of these people resembles a subject catalog of persons and things. These various classes or categories are characterized by prefixes which pass from nouns to all the variable words depending on them, thus marking inflections.

The first class is that of living things, often subdivided into rational and non-rational. Into this class are placed all the

[18] I. e., in which *affixed* elements are joined to a root to form a word or to change the meaning. The other fundamental types are the *monosyllabic,* as the Chinese, and the *flectional,* as Greek, Latin, etc.

names of beings supposed to be endowed with movement and life.

The other classes include all the remaining names of beings, prescinding from this double characteristic. Thus we have the class of common nouns, the class of nouns indicating beings that have increased, another class of diminutives, a class of abstract and of collective nouns, another class of place names.

An example taken from the Swahili (of Zanzibar), but which might equally well be extended to all the Bantu languages, will show how these classes are determined. Let us take the word *mu-toto,* "child" (a living, animated, rational being).

mu-toto a-dya, the child comes (the prefix *mu* with the inflection *a* denotes a living, animated being).

dyi-toto a-dya, the big child comes (the prefix *dyi* indicates the large size, the inflection *a* indicates the quality of being alive).

ki-toto a-dya, the little child comes (the prefix *ki* is diminutive).

u-toto u-dya,[19] childhood comes (the prefix *u* indicates abstraction, and as *childhood,* in so far as it is an abstract noun, is not a living thing, the inflection *u* will not be that of living beings).

Another example:

The good man falls,	*mu-tu*	*mu-zuri*	*a-anguka*
The good bird falls,	*n-ndege*	*n-zuri*	*a-anguka*

(living beings characterized by the prefix *a*).

The good tree falls,	*mu-ti*	*mu-zuri*	*u-anguka*
The good seat falls,	*ki-ti*	*ki-zuri*	*ki-anguka*
The good water falls,	*ma-dyi*	*ma-zuri*	*ya-anguka*

(inanimate objects of different characters specified by their prefixes and inflections).

By the language they speak, it is easy to apprehend with which category of beings the Bantus classify the different elements of creation. But, for them, the sun, moon, stars, as

[19] In fact, they would say *w-a-dya, w* or *u* being the connective, *a* marking the present indicative.

well as the air, the earth, the woods, minerals, are beings without life or movement and classed as such even though, in a marvelous story, they may be personified. All this clearly shows they are not considered in themselves as living, animated beings.

We have another confirmatory sign. Some words are applied equally to both animate and inanimate beings. When designating the latter, they take the inflection of inanimate things; but when designating the former, the inflection changes, becoming that of living beings, and by this very fact changing the character of the thing signified. Such, for instance, is the word *pepo,* which may mean either *wind* or *spirit* (generally a *bad spirit*): when meaning *wind,* it will take the inflection of inanimate things (*pepo i-dya,* the wind comes); but when it means *spirit,* it requires the connective of animate, living beings (*pepo a-dya,* the spirit comes).

We must therefore conclude that, far from considering nature as "organized on the same plan in all its parts," the Bantus, and likewise all the Blacks, regard it, on the contrary, as composed of hierarchical series, placed one above the other. Not only do they know enough to make a difference between "the living" and "the inanimate," but this distinction is the very basis of their language and consequently of their most authentic conceptions.

Nor may we admit under the general and absolute form in which it presented, that other view of Tylor, which Abbé Bros and many others confidently accept, namely that

"to the lower tribes of man, sun and stars, trees and rivers, winds and clouds, become personal, animate creatures, leading lives conformed to human or animal analogies, and performing their special functions in the universe with the aid of limbs like beasts or of artificial instruments like men; or what men's eyes behold is but the instrument to be used or the material to be shaped, while behind it there stands some prodigious but yet half-human creature, who grasps it with his hands or blows it with his breath." [20]

[20] Edward B. Tylor, *Primitive Civilization.* Abbé Bros, *La religion des peuples non civilisés,* p. 51.

These assertions which appear so strange to any one who knows and has studied the Blacks, are due to a false interpretation of the stories, legends, and mythologies reported by travelers.

Finally, were such beliefs or suppositions really those of our primitives, this discovery would advance us very little: for is it not, in fact, scientific rather than religious? And if we wished to show that their religion began in that manner, we would have to prove that religion, at its beginning, consisted and still consists only of these simple factors: but this is not proved and never will be.

VI.   What the Primitive Sees in Nature

In brief, what is the opinion which our Blacks have of nature?

The most exact answer to this question is that many of them, perhaps most of them, do not think about it at all.

However, in the depths of their souls, less simple than we think, are latent ideas, subconscious, unreasoned, which on occasion spontaneously awake, as it were, and translate themselves with surprising accuracy.

In the first place, nature, in the multitudinous manifestations under which it appears to our senses, takes the form of a hierarchy, distinct categories each of which has its place, with its specific qualities and its purpose. It has also, if you will excuse the impropriety of the terms, its families and tribes.

As in the human species, which the primitive unconsciously uses as the type of all the others, each one has its "manner" and its sex.

Its "manner": that is its own distinctive nature, determined for each of the beings constituting the species by a certain *form,* to use the scholastic expression, or, if you prefer, a certain *soul.* But it is an inert soul in lifeless things, a living soul in the plant, a feeling soul in the animal, a reasoning soul in man, a phenomenal soul in the cosmic elements, a terrestrial soul in the earth, a celestial soul in the sky, a universal soul in the universe.

Its sex is its faculty of reproduction in consequence of the cooperation (active and passive) of two elements, one male, the other female. Thus it happens that in Loango the ocean is considered as an active, male principle, for from it comes the rain that falls on the earth which is the passive female principle, and makes it fertile.[21]

So much for visible and material nature. All the "souls" that give things their "manner" which specifically distinguishes them and makes them what they are, all these souls "die" with them—souls of minerals, plants, and animals. But the same is not the case with souls that animate rational beings, i.e., men. These souls survive in another world, the invisible and supernatural. Accustomed to live in a body, these disembodied souls aspire to reënter them: hence we feel their presence or activity at times in children of their family and this is how we explain the convulsions of new-born infants and their resemblance to their parents. At other times, they take their abode in animals related to them by totemic alliance, in certain trees or caves, in a word, everywhere that their destiny determines. This has sometimes been called metensomatosis.[22]

Besides these souls of human origin, there are other spirits or genii, some good, protecting us; others more or less indifferent; still others wicked, wandering in space, favoring such or such a spot, or amusing themselves by producing various phenomena.

There is the invisible mysterious world, distinct from the other, but always concerned in its different manifestations.

Now we can see why the primitives so easily animatize things, attributing to them qualities and feelings more or less human in their tales and stories, in their simple reflections, and especially in their legends and mythologies.

We see, too, why natural phenomena, particularly when they have the appearance of being directed in a conscious manner, as whirlwinds, hurricanes, and cyclones, or when they

---

[21] R. E. Dennett, *At the Back of the Black Man's Mind*, p. 105.

[22] B. de la Grasserie, *Les religions comparées au point de vue sociologique*. From μετά, *with*, εν, *in*, σῶμα, *body* (change of body).

have an unexpected and extraordinary character, are, with the
same facility, attributed to beings of the other world—manes,
genii, or other spirits.

And we see why, in the native belief, these spirits who
abound in the world of the invisible can at pleasure seize upon
all that we see, assume its form, and make use of it.

This idea, which in part is inexact only because it is applied
indiscriminately, coexists with another still more general, more
profound, more intimate, and, I dare say, more delicate.

A child, when it does not feel itself at home, appears at first
timid and reserved.

It is the same with an animal, not only domestic animals,
like the dog, but the wild ones also. When the leopard is surprised in the enclosure that shelters the flock, its first movement is to scamper away like a thief caught in a flagrant act
of plundering.

A like feeling is to be observed in the depth of the primitive's soul in the presence of nature. These deep forests, so
silent, dark, cold, and full of mystery, these majestic mountains where the clouds pass and repass, these immense plains,
these free herds of beasts, these trees, flowers, fruits, plants,
bodies of water, all the world in fact, to whom do they
belong?

To whom? To that spirit of the earth—the *Ombwiri* of
Gabon—whose influence, according to the suspicions of many,
extends over everything here below?   Perhaps.

Or to the spirit of the heavens who organized everything,
who has given life and who takes it away, whose name or sur-
name in many tribes is precisely equivalent to "Master" [23] or
"Father" or "Proprietor"?   Perhaps.

At all events, like a poor child who might awake some beautiful morning in the park or garden of a king, the primitive
here below does not feel completely at home.

One day I asked a chief, "Who owns the land occupied by
your tribe?" "The land?" he replied in astonishment. "Who

[23] *Mweny'ezi* (literally, "He who has the power"); *Reri yajio* (our
Father); etc.

owns the air, the water, the light? It is to Him alone that the land belongs!" And he pointed towards the heavens.

So, when the primitive is about to lay hands on some fruits of nature, he first recalls that this product has an immanent power able to turn against him and that, also, it has an owner in that universal Master whose distant, vague, but certain and dreadful presence is felt everywhere.

What is to be done? Finding himself between these mysterious exactions and the necessity of living, man has felt that he could not make use of nature with unlimited and unrestrained freedom. He will, then, first of all be careful to acknowledge the just rights of the invisible and sovereign Master who keeps himself hid from view behind the visible world, although he does reveal his presence from time to time. Each time the Negrillos establish a new encampment, after clearing the place, they begin by making a fire on which each one puts a branch. If everything passes without incident, it means that the encampment is good; but if, in this first fire, a twig doubles up, it means that the earth protests and that it is futile to camp there: the place is at once abandoned and they go further on.

Nature has her secrets and mysteries. She does not like anybody to take them from her and often avenges herself on the audacious who compel her to give them up. When they clear a forest, when they dig into the earth to get the water or the metals that she is hiding, when they establish their encampment or village in certain places, has it not often been observed that accidents or diseases stop the invader? It is nature defending herself.

It is necessary, first of all, to recognize the rights of nature and nature's Master, and to use his gifts only with precaution and reserve.

This is why, in primitive society, the head of the family and of the tribe makes use of his authority, the character of which is nearly always sacred, to interdict certain products, certain acts, certain places, certain things, certain persons. This interdict can be removed only by the authority that imposed it, after a particular ceremony destined to restore the freedom of usage by a sort of expiation or sacrifice. It is the legal principle of the *sacred interdict* or *taboo,* which we shall have occasion to treat later under the question of morals.

Feeling the need of acknowledging his position of vassal, the primitive offers the firstfruits of whatever he asks of nature—by the sacrifice of a part he will redeem the right to use the rest—he makes a libation before drinking a fermented liquor, casts to the four points of the compass a piece of the wild honeycomb he has just gathered, casts back into the sea the liver of the first fish he has taken, performs various ceremonies before culling a medicinal plant, clearing a corner of the forest, digging a well or tapping a spring, mining or smelting metals that are hidden beneath the soil, and so forth.

Therein we have the explanation of the *sacrifice,* like that of the *taboo.* Thus, passing and repassing about the great table of nature, always served by the care of an invisible and mysterious Master, primitive man, reserved because he is suspicious, cautiously puts his hand to it, murmuring after his fashion formulas of politeness that his simple and troubled conscience suggests to him. Sometimes the Master, perhaps to train this greedy child, has given him a crack on the fingers: this child remembers it and consequently is particular to acknowledge the superior rights and to respect the mysterious will of him who presides over the whole banquet.

VII. The Primitive Data: Science, Religion, Magic

The conception of visible nature general among the Negrillos of to-day and the ancient Bantus, is this:

1. Nature, in the countless elements of which it is composed, is full of secret influences and innate forces, powers, properties, specific "manners," susceptible of being exercised for or against man and directed by what we have called the "souls" of things.

2. Nature in these different elements can be, and often is influenced, governed, and subjected by numberless spirits that are wandering about us; in other words, as we make use of nature, the spirits do also, but with means superior to ours.

The art of magic consists precisely in getting possession of these secrets so as to force the spirits to work for us.

3. Lastly, nature is not given to us without reserve. We have not every right over it, as it often makes us clearly understand. Let us use but not abuse it; let us use it, but at the same time acknowledge the rights claimed by the Master and take the necessary precautions.

According to our opinion, in this sense alone can the primitive be called a *naturist* or an *animist*.

This idea, which perceptibly differs from the views we have set forth of Réville, Pfleiderer, Tylor, and their disciples, perfectly explains the attitude of the primitive in the presence of nature, without making him what he is not, a brute and an idiot, incapable of distinguishing between the animate and the inanimate, putting all on the same plane as himself, and regarding as rational persons even the sun and moon as well as stones or trunks of old trees.

When the primitive thinks there are hidden powers in things, he is right, he is making science. But he often deceives himself, more often than the members of our learned academies— and therein is the difference—in his appreciation of these "powers" and in the means he employs to utilize them.

When the primitive regards this world as not belonging to him and is persuaded that it has an invisible, sovereign Master with whom he must reckon, he is also right, according to our opinion—and this is also the view of many other folk who occupy a sufficiently high rank in human society, as Moses, Aristotle, Plato, Cicero, St. Augustine, St. Thomas Aquinas, Dante, Bossuet, Leibnitz, Newton, Washington, Napoleon, Pasteur. But he differs from them inasmuch as he perceives this Master less clearly and shows himself more "primitive" in the methods he employs to acknowledge him. Nevertheless we here reach the initial *substratum* of belief and religious worship.

When the primitive thinks that outside of this material and visible world in which we live, there is another world of invisible beings, disembodied souls or independent spirits, who can manifest themselves in various ways, act on external objects, enter into communication with us, and through certain practices be made to act to our advantage, then he is performing magic: thereby he makes himself guilty of superstition and anti-religion, but therein he is like a great number of civilized men who, in all times and places, have tried also to fasten magic at the side of religion.

When the primitive translates these different impressions, beliefs, and practices into stories more or less coherent wherein everything is mixed together—poetry, history, science, religion, superstition, and magic—he does as we do, with this difference that we can employ in our productions better established facts, ideas more connected, more sure outlines, more solid judgments, material better divided.

But, after all, we resemble each other much more than we suppose or than we dare say. As the child is found in the mature man and in the old sire, so the primitive might be found in the civilized, and the civilized in the primitive.

Are we so sure that we have best understood existence and have taken the best part for our happiness?

No doubt, when we consider our poor savages from the height of our complicated, rational, proud civilization, their life seems wretched and their ideas seem strange. As the hand of man works at nature and discloses her mysteries, nature seems to become less and less familiar to him until, bruised, disfigured, shrunk, deformed, it no longer speaks to him at all.

It is not the same with virgin nature. When you have lived over again the life of the primitive, when you have tasted the delights of the woods and the charm of solitude, learned to commune with the inanimate world that surrounds you, to appreciate especially the infinite sweetness of liberty, of a liberty to which man has not fixed sacrilegious limits expressed in countless laws, rules, customs, habits, and exactions of all sorts, you understand that everything is not wretched and stupid in the conceptions and the existence of the savage.

CHAPTER III

THE PRIMITIVE AND THE FAMILY

I. The Theory of Primitive Promiscuity

If the primitive had only a general concept of nature to support his religious ideas and practices, these, we could readily understand, would remain extremely vague and inconsistent. As a matter of fact, they are so with a great many. But there exists a natural, permanent, precise, and essentially human organization which determines them everywhere, nourishes and transmits them: it is the family.

The family among the primitives of Africa, as among all others, is the central pillar on which, along with religion, all social life depends. If the family is strongly constituted, the tribe prospers; if its bonds are lax, the tribe grows weak; and if, as happens on the coasts and in the European centers, it is disorganized, the tribe disappears.

The materialist school seems not to have learned this fact, essential as it is. It is true that its system does not leave us any choice as to what our point of departure shall be.

"The example of the animals," says one of its partisans, "shows us what were the first habits of mankind. We see our forefathers roaming through the forest, like big monkeys, in little groups composed of a single man with, no doubt, several women whom he has appropriated by the superiority of strength' over weakness and whom he defends against his rivals." [1]

And further on he adds:

"Local necessities caused considerable variation between different peoples in the rapidity (and the secondary forms) of that evolution (i.e., of marriage and the family). But among all, we find at first general promiscuity, necessarily giving rise to relationship through the women. Then came polyandry, a restrained form of promiscuity. And last of all we have polygamy or monogamy, along with which were developed paternal relationship and the patriarchate, such as it appeared at the dawn of the first civilizations." [2]

That such a gregarious condition existed in some particularly wretched human groups is possible: yet, before transforming such an hypothesis into incontestable truth, it would be wise to establish it by precise facts. This much is certain, that nowhere in Africa do we see traces of this promiscuity to-day—except in the great steppes of the eastern and southern zones, among herds of antelopes. As to the men, in the degree that we descend towards the populations of a general primitive aspect, as the Negrillos and the San, the more the family appears as the fundamental, necessary, and indisputable basis of elementary society.

This does not surprise us when we recall the mentality of these poor children of the steppes and forests. What man seems most to fear in the presence of material nature and the world of invisible beings that dominate him, is isolation. In that savage environment, pitiless towards weakness, an isolated man is a lost man: *Vae soli!* As soon as he is found defenseless by another stronger than himself, he will be seized, reduced to slavery, perhaps eaten. From this point of view an encounter with men is still more dangerous for him than a

[1] Gustave Le Bon, *Les Premières civilisations*, p. 50.
[2] *Ibid.*, p. 59.

meeting with wild beasts. His instinct, his anxiety for self-preservation, without speaking of other aspirations, urges him to seek alliances in the world about him. There is none more reliable, more enduring, and sweeter than that of the family, because there is none more natural. So, in the land of primitive civilization, the more difficult life is because of the dangers that threaten it, the more closely is the family drawn together; the easier life is, the more lax become the family relations.

Among the Bantus, the social crumbling of all the tribes, their perpetual wars, the isolation due to the large uninhabited tracts of land, disease, famine, the fear of ferocious beasts, dangers of all sorts that pursue the solitary individual; the indolence that leads the Black to count more on others than on himself, besides other dispositions natural to man, bring about the same result. Everywhere, their constant preoccupation is to establish a family, to tighten the bonds that unite them under the incontestable authority of a head, to maintain along with the purity of blood, the totality of goods that are found therein, to strengthen it by forming alliances, to make it a place of refuge and a means of defense, to ward off the visible and hidden dangers that threaten it, and for the accomplishment of all that, to assure themselves of the necessary supernatural cooperation.

In Europe, our civic groups, cities, towns, and villages, formed of diverse elements that are often strangers to one another, give us but an imperfect idea of the African groups. There, the encampment (if they are nomads), the village (if they are settlers), is formed solely of relatives united under the authority of a chief; his peoples are his sons and daughters, nephews and nieces, his sons-in-law, cousins, uncles, relatives-in-law, and adopted "children"; these are surrounded by their respective relatives and slaves.

In the same way we may explain the origin of a group of encampments or villages likewise united by kinship, but of more remote origin. Lastly, the tribe is nothing more than an enlarged family.

Let us take, for example, the Ba-vili of Loango, whom R. E. Dennett has studied with remarkable precision.

"The organization of the family or Xifumba is certainly one that the Ba-vili need not be ashamed of, and when compared to that of many civilized peoples, can only be looked upon as a model of logical compactness.

"The family forms part of the higher organization of the tribe. Each individual belongs to a family; each family is under a chief called Kongo Zovo, and this chief is under the prince of the province containing these families. Seven of these provinces hold the people of Loango, called the Ba-vili. The Ba-vili, under their King Maluango, formed a third part of the kingdom of Kongo, or the Fjort people, who are a section of the Bantu race." [3]

We may say it is the same with all the peoples that have constituted themselves into tribes or kingdoms. Others have a more lax and fragmentary organization, under an authority that is often nominal; none of them is altogether devoid of some authority.

No one may leave the village without the chief's permission, and on returning every one must present himself before the chief, render an account of what he has seen and done, speak of his fishing and hunting, his business, his meeting with other persons, and give all the news that can be of any interest. The chief must be obeyed and respected; he has authority to punish delinquents, confine them, deprive them of food, rent them out, and sometimes even to sell them. In general, the right of life and death belongs to a higher dignitary. The local chief may, in all cases, demand the services of his whole family. [4]

Undoubtedly in the long run, journeys, business affairs, wars, invasions, without mentioning the almost universal practice of slavery, lead to inevitable mixture, yet it is true that the tribes are able to maintain a relative purity distinguishing them not only by their features but by an ensemble of institutions and marks of which we shall have to speak.

Love of the village is universal. Although the Black enjoys travel, he never forgets his home, his mother, his brothers. His mother's name often comes to his mind far away in those

[3] Dennett, *op. cit.*, p. 35.
[4] *Ibid.*, p. 36.

gentle songs that he repeats to himself in the evening at the encampments of the caravan, on the little footpaths, and on the big rivers where his canoe glides noiselessly along.

When sick, abandoned, wounded, or dying, there is from one end of Africa to the other, in all ranks and at all ages, a call that comes to his lips, always the same, ever touching: "Mother! Mother!"

So also, there is no insult more grievous, and we must say none more common, than that touching the woman who gave him birth. I am happy to find the following remark from the pen of a judicious and authoritative observer, the Rev. Leighton Wilson, cited by another well-known observer, Miss Mary H. Kingsley:

"Whatever other estimate we may form of the African, we may not doubt his love for his mother. Whether she is dead or alive, her name is always on his lips and in his heart. She is the first being he thinks of when awakening from his slumbers, and the last he remembers when closing his eyes in sleep; to her he confides secrets which he would confide to no other human being on the face of the earth. He cares for no one else in time of sickness, she alone must prepare his food, administer his medicine, perform his ablutions, and spread his mat for him. He flies to her in the hour of distress, for he well knows if all the rest of the world turn against him, she will be steadfast in her love, whether he be right or wrong.

"If there be any cause which justifies a man in using violence towards one of his fellow-men, it would be to resent an insult offered to his mother. More fights are occasioned among boys by hearing something said in disparagement of their mothers than from all other causes put together. It is a common saying among them, if a man's mother and his wife are both on the point of being drowned, and he can save only one of them, he must save his mother for the avowed reason that if the wife is lost he can marry another, but he will never find a second mother." [5]

The blessing of one's parents is a gage of happiness, and their curse is the worst of calamities, one that pursues the

[5] L. Wilson, *Western Africa*, in *West African Studies* by Miss M. H. Kingsley, p. 374.

guilty son everywhere, empoisoning his life and sowing misfortune all about him.   I was a witness of the following scene. With her garments in shreds, her features distorted like those of a fury, her thin body agitated by convulsive trembling, uttering cries that were almost inhuman, an old woman gathered up handfuls of earth and, with her long lank arm, cast it in the direction of a young man who was fleeing in terror.   This sight was most impressive, like that described in the first pages of the Bible, where Cain is cursed by his mother and by his God after the murder of Abel.

The family, as we have said, is generally monogamous among the Negrillos, except in certain encampments affected by the contagion of neighboring example.   The same is true of a few Bantu tribes.

But in most of the black populations polygamy is the rule— by law at least, if not in fact—polygamy organized and regulated by customs having the force of law, customs which, in the spirit of this world, not only do not destroy the family, but strengthen it by giving the chief more ease, more riches, more relatives, more alliances, and especially more authority. However, in the tribes dominated by polygamy there is usually a marked difference between the "first" wife and the others. She commands, has charge of the property and, after the death of the master, it is her duty to see that nothing disappears before the legal assignment.   Naturally there are frequent disputes in these multiple households: the man does not concern himself with them, judging that it is the best way to stop them. Often the first wife is the most zealous in urging her husband to get other wives: for in this way there is a chance to see her authority increased and her work lessened.   Each wife has her own hut, children, slaves, plot of ground, chickens, and goats, her own little domain where her husband comes to see her, in this manner dividing his time between them.

As regards work, the woman plants and cultivates, cooks the food, fetches the wood and water, and takes care of the children; the man looks after the religious duties of the family, sickness, burial, and business affairs, attends the council, takes part in war and commerce. He builds and repairs the hut, and when it is time for planting, it is he who clears the ground.

With the rare exception of a few tribes, as, for instance, the Wa-rundi,[6] the woman never eats with the man and ordinarily does not share his company.

Polyandry is unknown—at least I am not acquainted with any example among the Bantus. But where it does exist, as in Thibet, strange and immoral as it may be, this institution is not a denial of the family: its object is to form about the woman a group of absolute unity and to maintain the property undivided as long as possible: it is the product, not of a primitive state, but of an advanced and perverted civilization.[7]

From the fact that in Africa as elsewhere the family is considered a necessary institution for the maintenance and development of society, it does not follow that this plan works without defects or difficulty. The family institution is involved in most lawsuits for the simple reason that woman and the value she represents are at the bottom of nearly all litigation.

Divorce is everywhere recognized and accepted, in some places more frequently than in others. It is but just to add that it is everywhere considered an evil. Besides, it is subject to certain minute regulations that can not be legally infringed. In case of separation, no one remains alone, neither father nor mother nor children: each returns to his or her respective family or founds a new one. So that in Africa families are destroyed only to be reëstablished; for primitive society, divorce has not all the weakening consequences that it exercises in our civilized communities.

In Africa the patriarchal custom, by virtue of which the father is master of the family, seems to be most ancient: at all events it is so with the Negrillos and with a great number of Bantu tribes.

But we also meet the matriarchal organization in a number of tribes. This system makes relationship, authority, and the

---

[6] Rev. J. M. Van der Burgt, *Dict. franç. kirundi*, 1903 (art. *Femme*).
[7] *Bulletin de la Société neufchâteloise de géographie*, XII, p. 304.

order of inheritance pass on the mother's side. All these rights ordinarily belong to the maternal uncle, who thus becomes the real head of the house or family; on him everything depends, to him everything comes. Hence the more sisters a man has, the more importance will he have: since the woman is given in marriage only for a certain value or "payment," the more dowries he will receive, the more granddaughters he will have to give in marriage in the same manner, the richer he will become, the more alliances he will have, and the more his authority will increase.

What is the reason for this régime, that seems so strange to us, in which the father's rights almost disappear? Such of the natives as can reason a little about their customs—and there are some—reply that its purpose and actual result is to insure legitimate successors to the chiefs of villages and tribes. If the chief has his sister's son for his successor, he is certain to have one of his own blood: whereas, with the son of his wife, "who can tell?" The matriarchate, then, comes from the idea of insuring the unity and purity of the family.

Whatever form it may have, especially on the western coast, the family has such a power that it absorbs the individual and truly remains the constituent unity of the entire community. It is the whole family that shares the goods acquired by its most energetic and most industrious members without the latter being able to hinder this forced liberality. The family is sponsor for all its members whether right or wrong, and on it they all rely to be upheld, assisted, defended, avenged. By contributing to furnish the necessary funds, the family aids the young members to get married; but it likewise profits by giving in marriage (in return for value received) the daughters that are the issue of these unions and by exploiting the strength and cunning of the boys in its interest. We can easily understand what abuse may arise under such a system especially when the European centers are ready to arouse the cupidity and sensuality of the Blacks: then we witness the regular exploitation of children, particularly the girls, by the "ancients," without their fathers or mothers being able to offer effective opposition, since they are only individuals without authority and without power before the head of the family.[8]

Nevertheless, however hard these laws may be for individuals, they express a condition the very opposite of that gregarious and unconscious promiscuity of which we have spoken above. They even bestow an exaggerated unity and power upon family authority.

Other numerous and characteristic regulations take the child from its mother's bosom, follow him until puberty, then establish him in his new environment by a preliminary initiation, rule over his life, cling to him in death, and pass with his manes into the supernatural world where they survive. This will occupy the rest of our studies: let it suffice at this point to remember that all or nearly all these laws, customs, and practices, both social and religious, concern the organization, life, and development of the family, village, clan, and tribe.

But first we must briefly touch upon two questions about the family that have been a great puzzle to scholars: exogamy and totemism.

II. EXOGAMY

First of all, these two institutions must not be considered as depending one upon the other: if, in fact, totemism leads to exogamy, exogamy does not always presuppose totemism.[9]

Exogamy is the rule obliging one to take a wife outside the clan or, more generally, outside his relations. This rule seems to be in force among all primitive societies. It is interesting, in passing, to point this out among the "primates" that are incessantly described as living in bestial promiscuity. In fact, consanguineous alliances within various degrees are severely forbidden throughout all Africa. Incest, the sexual union of individuals who are related within the forbidden degrees, is

[8] Cf. R. H. Nassau, *Fetichism in West Africa.*

[9] Exogamy (ἔξω, *outside*, and γάμος, *marriage*) is the opposite of Endogamy (ἔνδον, *within*). The clan (from Scottish *Klaan,* "child") is an organization whose members consider themselves descended from the same ancestor as their chief or, more strictly, from the same totemic ancestor.

everywhere abhorred and punished: the fruit of such a union is generally destroyed as abominable in itself, dangerous for the family, and fatal to the country.

Why this prohibition?

Many complicated theories try to explain it but, according to Reinach,[10] they have not fully succeeded; it is quite possible these very learned sociologists—Lubbock, Spencer, MacLennan, Morgan, Durkheim—wandered too far off in search of explanation.

As Durkheim and Reinach very justly remark, in all primitive society, woman is the object of a sacred interdict or taboo at different periods of her life; hence the separation of the sexes and the customs dictated, at least partly, by a generally prevalent sense of modesty. In addition to the reasons that have been given for this interdict, referring to the "dangerous" nature of contact with a woman at these periods, there is no doubt in our mind but they had the morality of the family in view.

What? you will say. Savages concerned with morality? Even so; and this is not the only example of such preoccupation furnished by the savages. Thanks to this taboo forbidding consanguineous unions, the sexual instinct is restrained, its exercise removed beyond the circle of relationship, the family morality is assured, and the ever dominant concern for the preservation of the group is satisfied.

It is possible, however, that totemism is not a stranger to this prescription. If, in fact, the husband found himself obliged to send his wife away or if she had to quit her husband —a double case to be foreseen—and if they both had the same totem, this totem would be offended by such a division. In short, when husband and wife belong to different families, both of them preserve a greater liberty for the future. In the black country this perspective is greatly appreciated.

In the maintenance of exogamy there is another reason of very practical import. In Africa and generally in all primitive countries, the head of the family has been able to derive considerable advantage from his daughters. Since they are

[10] Reinach, *op. cit.*

sought after, they have a value, and if they have a value, the most elementary care for his interests urges him to give them only for an exchange or payment. That is what happens. But the head of the family, being already proprietor of all that his family possesses, can evidently derive profit from his daughters only by giving them to strangers. Likewise, in case of divorce, justice requires the return of the "dowry"; but this return would be purposeless if it were made within the same family. In fact, the head of the house would be giving back the dowry to himself, which would be absurd.[11]

According to what we have set forth, one preoccupation of the head of the household is to strengthen himself by alliances, which will permit him and his to travel more easily, to have more numerous relations, to count on more friends in case of war or lawsuits, to traffic on a larger scale, to find all about him an ever ready hospitality. Marriage outside the limits of relationship assures all these advantages.

Are not these reasons sufficient to explain exogamy? At any rate they are the ones that best correspond to the native institutions and the most conformable to the mentality of the primitives.

Once the law is made, admitted, and sanctioned by long usage, it will be enforced, regardless even of hygienic considerations—for which the primitives have more regard than we think—as a social necessity which one may not neglect without arousing the reprobation of his relatives and the punishment of the invisible world.

Yet we may add to these different motives another that may well be the principal one.

In their method of farming, the system of alternation is general in this sense, that they never cultivate the same field twice in succession. They know the ground becomes quickly exhausted in producing the same crops indefinitely; hence, since they generally have unlimited space, they keep changing the place of their farming.

It must be the same, they think, in human crops: under pain

---

[11] Cf. H. A. Junod, *Les Ba-Ronga*, in the *Bulletin de la Société neufchâteloise de géographie*, X, 1898, p. 70.

of impoverishing them, "it is necessary to change the blood."
Whence the practice of exogamy.

III. Totemism

With totemism we touch on another problem to which great
importance is now attached.

J. G. Frazer, who made a special study of the subject, gives
us this definition: "A totem is a class of material objects
which a savage regards with superstitious respect, believing
that there exists between him and every member of the class
an intimate and altogether special relation." [12] And Reinach
says, with more exactness, that under this term are included
"the animal, vegetable, and more rarely, the mineral or
heavenly body which the clan regards as an ancestor, protector,
and a rallying sign. . . . The totem is not an individual, but
an animal clan affiliated to the human clan." [13]

This expression, *totem*,[14] which has been unusually fortunate,
is a barbarism derived from a word of the Chippeway Indians
of North America; for totemism was especially flourishing
among them.

Not only in North America is totemism known. We find it,
though only in a state of partial survival, in all parts of the
world. It may be family, sexual, or individual according as it
is applied to a whole family or tribe, exclusively to one sex of
such a group, or to a particular individual. We also find
totems of secret societies notably in Africa: thus in Loango
there is the "Society of the Leopard," among the Wa-nika the
"Society of the Hyena."

Totemism is both a religious and a social system, or rather
it is a social and family institution based on a magical idea.

---

[12] J. G. Frazer, *Totemism*, p. 1.
[13] Reinach, *op. cit.*
[14] "According to Abbé Thavenet," says Frazer, "the word is properly *ote*,
in the sense of 'family' or 'tribe,' possessive *otem*, and with the personal
pronoun *nind otem* 'my tribe,' *ket otem*, 'thy tribe.'" So that, if one insists on employing this expression which has the advantage of possessing
a mysterious air and impresses the common mind, one should at least say
oteism or *otemism*. Frazer, *Totemism*, p. 1.

It did not create the taboo, the explanation of which comes from another source, but it has been the occasion for the creation of many taboos. Thus generally the members of the family are forbidden to kill or eat the totem which they invoke or whose name they bear—except in sacrifice by way of communion; they are forbidden even to touch it or to look at it.

A *totem* is not a *fetich*.

"The radical distinction between it and the fetich," says Reinach, "is this: the fetich is one individual object; the totem is a class of objects, regarded by members of the tribe or clan as *tutelar*—protective, in the widest sense of the word. Take the case of a clan with the serpent totem: the members will call themselves *Serpents*, claim descent from a serpent, abstain from killing serpents, raise pet serpents, read the future by the aid of serpents, believe themselves immune from serpent bites, and so on indefinitely." [15]

Notwithstanding North America is the classical land of totemism, we find, as we have said, many curious traces of it in Africa. The Negrillos of the Gabon equatorial forest, for example, have the chimpanzee or *kweya*, as totem; whence their name *Ba-kweya* (the Chimpanzees) among the Mpongwes.[16] They do not speak of this species of monkey except by way of paraphrase, nor do they permit any one to pronounce its name in their presence for fear of failing in respect towards it and of provoking its resentment.

To the south, their cousins the San, or Bushmen, have a sort of worship for an insect, the *ngo*, that encloses itself with tiny bits of straw in a case like that of the phryganides larvae, from which only its head and first pair of legs emerge. It is the emblem of the hidden life which our Pygmies affect to seek after. When they go to the chase, they try to find one of these caterpillars; they pray to it that, by helping to conceal them, it may enable them to approach the wild game they hope to bring down by their arrows.[17]

---

[15] Reinach, *op. cit.*, p. 11.
[16] According to one of my Benga informers, of Cape Estérias (Gabon).
[17] Quatrefages, *The Pygmies.*

Among the Bantus, we find the same ideas and practices. The Fans, for instance, have a legend in which the crocodile enters as an ancestor, who, after numerous adventures, is immolated in sacrifice and partaken of by the first family chiefs so that its power passes into them by this strange communion. To recall this ancient alliance, the Fans have their teeth filed to a point like the crocodile.[18]

In Loango there is a practice which greatly complicates the question of matrimonial prohibition. The "son of the family" has four totems, namely, those of the two first ancestors (the first couple that gave birth to the tribe), that of his father and that of his mother.[19]

On the eastern coast, the totem of the Wa-nika is the hyena. When one of these animals has been killed or is found dead, the ancients arrange a funeral ceremony as for one of their own. They beat the sacred drum, and on all sides cries and lamentations are heard. Once the animal is buried, they slaughter an ox or a goat and for three days they eat and drink, stopping only to cry over the defunct "brother." On this occasion every one must shave his head.

The Zulus keep tame, harmless serpents, showing them affectionate respect and cherishing them as relatives.

These examples might be multiplied indefinitely; but we must hurry on to the discussion of the system which has assumed a considerable importance during these latter years.

Though testifying that "no satisfactory explanation of the origin of totemism has yet been given," [20] Frazer offers the following:

"As the attribution of human qualities to the totem is of the essence of totemism, it is plain that a deity generalized from or including animals and plants must, as his animal and vegetable attributes contradict and cancel each other, tend more and more to throw them off and to retain only those human qualities which to the savage apprehension are the common element of all the totems whereof he is the composite product.

[18] P. H. Trilles, *Proverbes, légendes, et contes fâns,* p. 114.
[19] Dennett, *op. cit.,* p. 154.
[20] *Totemism,* p. 95.

In short, the tribal totem tends to pass into an anthropomorphic god." So that "we can detect in the totemic philosophy itself some advances towards the formation of a deity distinct from and superior to all the individuals of the totem species." [21]

Starting from a different point of view, Reinach follows W. Robertson Smith, Jevons, and a whole school of others and tends in the same direction, making of totemism and animism the initial point of man's religious and social evolution. According to this school, the primitive form of zoolatry and dendrolatry must have given way to the cultivation of corn, grazing, agriculture, industry, the use and combination of metals, as well as the constitution of the family. At the basis of all this, Reinach sees religion.

"Primarily," he says, "religion is a system of taboos—spiritual restraints on the brute energies and instincts of man. . . . The taboos applied alike to the human, animal, and vegetable kingdoms, between which the savage—an animist by nature— was incapable of discriminating with precision.[22] . . . Now, so far as the system of taboos centered round the relations of man to man, it formed a nucleus of family and social law, of morality and of politics; so far, however, as it concerned the animal and vegetable world, it constituted totemism." [23]

E. Durkheim really belongs to the same school. But as he is a sociologist, he makes it all come from sociology. According to him, the true primitive was in the state of *passive atheism* spoken of by Herbert Spencer, and he would have remained in that state indefinitely had he not yielded to his instinct of becoming united in society. Theoretically an isolated man is incapable of religion. But the exalting influence exercised by uniting in a crowd gave him a glimpse of a new world: the world of sacred things, which is, after all, simply the more or less vague feeling of social strength. Keen emo-

---

[21] *Ibid.*, p. 88.
[22] Reinach, *op. cit.*, p. 23. Recall that, on the contrary, the language of our Bantu savages is based on the distinction between the kingdoms of nature. It is the same with many other primitive peoples.
[23] Reinach, *op. cit.*, p. 24.

tions, however, like religious feelings, tend to crystallize into a symbol. This symbol, this rallying sign, this banner, was, for the primitives, a *totem*. At first it was created spontaneously without any one being able to foresee the useful rôle it might play. Naturally this emblem would be chosen from the species of beings most closely related to man, first the animals, then plants, then other objects. One general idea dominates the primitive world: the idea of the consubstantiality of things, the interpenetration of all beings, and consequently a sort of moral and physical force spread throughout all. In other words, it is the "totemic divinity" of which the totems are symbols and of which human souls are the fragments. The idea of the soul begets the idea of the spirit, which easily leads to that of a divinity ruling over the entire tribe. Then come the ceremonies, making their beliefs more vivid and precise.

Thus understood, the divinity is nothing else than society itself; its reality, as well as its necessity, coming only from the fact that it is a mode of collective representation.

"Such is the solid foundation that gives value to all religions," Durkheim concludes. And he conscientiously adds:

"There is the 'eternal' of religious worship; it is not necessary for his existence that man should contemplate society under the personified form of gods, nor that he should believe in the material efficacy of ceremonies over physical things. But the moral and social services rendered by a form of worship will be permanent and indispensable so long as there will be men, that is to say, societies. Thus it is that the French Revolution felt the need of substituting a new form of worship for the old one it wished to destroy. When this need for a form of worship is not felt, it is because society and individuals are passing through a grave crisis, for every human being should feel the need of always living a broader and more intense existence and of renewing its life." [24]

What an admirable act of faith, the more meritorious since he holds it all alone, flying such a brilliant kite in an empty sky, a kite fastened to the clever hand of a child by an imperceptible thread! Durkheim's thread is the totemism of a few

[24] *Revue de philosophie,* 1907.

little Australian tribes, such as Baldwin, Spencer, Gillen, and later on Howitt, have made known to us. And when you realize that this universal, necessary, permanent institution, which is religion, has issued from that origin—when you recall that its initial emblem was a toad or a caterpillar, that the human soul, the spirits, God himself are only totemic creations, that it possesses no other reality—and when you remember that religion thus understood is a profound actuality and a social necessity, you ask yourself what is this mystery and what is this miracle unquestionably surpassing the miracles and mysteries of all religions.

Regarding the question as definitely settled, certain popularizers of "modern thought," while announcing a projected encyclopedia "of higher popular instruction," draw some practical conclusions.

"In primitive religious manifestations," they say, "we see no god, properly speaking. Man is dependent on the totem, an animal or vegetable form. Then come the worship of ancestors, local cults, national religions, polytheism, and monotheism. Religions are phenomena that disappear under the influence of material causes." [25]

Extraordinary initiators! Drawing conclusions like these from such premises, one is amazed at the bare and audacious assurance with which, by such simple means, they presume to solve the most delicate and important question that has ever been proposed to the world: the religious question.

It seems to me that I can the more easily attempt the explanation of totems since I myself have a totem, and know perfectly well under what circumstances it began.

[25] *Encyclopédie d'enseignement populaire supérieur publiée sous la direction de J. M. Lahy.* The General Assembly of the Grand Orient dealt with this publication in its session of September 29, 1907: "Conformably to the desire manifested by the last General Assembly, the Council of the Order has been interested in establishing a summary of the history of religions suitable for school children. This work of our F.˙. Lahy has appeared: it is presented in a remarkable fashion. F.˙. Sembat insists that this book be used in the primary schools." *La Franc-maçonnerie démasquée,* no. 23, (Dec. 10, 1907), p. 361.

It was on the Kilimanjaro, in eastern Africa. This is a superb mountain rising abruptly from an immense plain almost on the equator. It raises its calm and majestic head, covered with eternal snows, to a height of 20,000 feet. We were the first French travelers and Catholic missionaries to appear there (1892).[26] There was question of founding a mission station on the mountain. Fumba, the chief of Kilima, greatly desired that we should remain, but he required us, first of all, to proceed to the solemn ceremony of "fraterniza-tion" (in aboriginal America, "totemization"). I was desig-nated for the affair.[27] At the appointed hour, with all the warriors of the tribe present, Fumba and I sat down on the same ox-hide in the great square of the village. Our sponsors successively began to question us and to heap terrible impre-cations upon us in case we should be unfaithful to our alliance. Then a white goat was slain. In Fumba's arm and in mine they made a gash from which the blood flowed. The victim's liver was cut into six pieces that were then smeared with this blood, after which we gave them to each other to eat.

The blood of Fumba was now mine, mine was his, and we were "brothers" (in Swahali *ndugu,* in Chippeway *otem*) : we were united in friendship, counsel, aid, and assistance, our interests were common, our families were sister-families. That was many years ago: in the midst of all the revolutions and wars which the Kilimanjaro has since waged against Euro-peans, Fumba has not violated his word for a single day— nor I mine. My sons, that is the men of my race, the Catholic missionaries present and future, have become his sons, as also the children of Fumba, that is the men of Kilima, have become mine: they are brothers and allies.

If this relationship by exchange of blood is not exactly totem-ism, it is at least very close to it and will help us understand it.

Let us picture primitive man marching ahead and pushing his explorations further into a mysterious world that extends

[26] The expedition was composed of Mgr. de Courmont, Rev. A. Gommen-ginger, Rev. A. Le Roy, and about sixty men. Since then three mission stations have been established there: they are all very prosperous.

[27] See *Au Kilima-Ndjaro,* by Rev. A. Le Roy, p. 231.

wider the further he penetrates it. Nowhere is there any creature that resembles him, that has his way of standing or walking, his features, his language. Everywhere there are different beings, climbing, walking, flying, swimming, digging into the earth, preceding him in the conquest of the world.

If he is their superior in many respects, in others he feels his weakness in their presence. Had he but the monkey's agility, the elephant's strength, the leopard's cunning, the serpent's acuteness, if he were only a little bird!

This idea, which so naturally presents itself to the infant mind, was the idea, also, of the man-child; he has kept it to the present time, and even pretends to have realized it.

We are not here speaking merely of his transforming himself into an animal of his choice through fancy and curiosity. Although primitive man is driven as much by the exigencies of the dangerous surroundings in which he lives as by the instinct of his nature to guard himself against his family, he is equally impelled by all his interests to extend his relations and alliances. The more he has of them, the stronger will be his family.

But what most of all constitutes the family is community of blood. The primitive can, then, with such and such men whose friendship, power, and fidelity he values, make a pact of alliance sealed by the exchange of blood and consecrated by an appropriate ceremony. After that they are of the same relationship—*ndugu,* as they say in eastern Africa; *ntene* in Guinea; *totem,* according to the expression borrowed from the redskins.

Man, however, is not the only being with whom it is possible to make such a pact. Thanks to mysterious practices that are the secret of the initiated but which always involve an exchange of blood, it is possible to summon an animal, the chief of a herd or band, to win his favor, to profit by his powers as well as his secrets, to disguise one's self, to become his "brother," to conclude an alliance with him and his race.

"There are some people," they will tell you at Zanzibar and throughout Africa, "who have an animal for a companion.

Man and beast know each other. They aid each other. When the man has need of the beast, he calls it, and it comes." [28]

But let us not deceive ourselves. By this alliance, the man's purpose is not to win over the animal merely as such and to associate its family to his, but rather that animal as reënforced by the presence and action of a spirit of the invisible world—the soul of the animal itself, the spirit of its ancestors, or the tutelary genius of extra-human origin. Consequently this pact *by means of a visible creature is a pact with the invisible world.*

After living a long time under the favor of a magical pact, in close and friendly relations with some animal, a chief is about to die. If he gathers about him those of his children who can understand, and communicates his secret to them, if he orders them to maintain this pact and gives them to understand that his spirit, on leaving its human abode, will like to come back among them under the appearance of his animal-brother, we can see how *totemism* or *animal relationship* will be formed for his descendants. As this family spreads, multiplies, and scatters, its representatives will take with them, if not the precise recollection, at least the trace of this origin, manifested by the different interdicts or *taboos* that will be established in regard to the family of the beast, now become sacred: this beast will become their "relative"; they will often take its name, bear its mark, and pay homage to it, they will believe that after death their souls will have a place in its mysterious society: and this belief will sustain the piety of their descendants.

Such would be, according to our opinion, true totemism. But it is possible and even probable that in many cases this institution, once accepted, might be traced back through assimilation to other origins.

If, for example, an ancestor, respected or feared as a famous sorcerer, announces or in some way makes known, that at his death his soul will pass into a certain creature, this declaration will suffice to create the totemistic worship among his descendants.

[28] The words of a native literally translated. (Note of Father Sacleux.)

If someone has remarked the friendliness of a particular animal, the assiduity with which it frequents a certain place, its manner of appearing, and a thousand similar incidents, the "seer" will be consulted; and finally it will be decided that these manifestations come from a particular supernatural sympathy with which one must correspond.

Under such circumstances, a newly formed secret society, a family just founded, or an individual who wishes to succeed, chooses a totem that becomes an emblem and a symbol.

We might multiply these examples. A totemic alliance always supposes at its base an explicit or implicit pact, and a pact implies reciprocity of respect and services. As a matter of fact, the allied animal, accustomed to the assiduous cares of his human family, is, so to speak, "domesticated" among them and often shows astonishing friendliness, thereby impressing these simple people and confirming them in their faith.

If you wish to follow totemism in its multitudinous manifestations, as pointed out by Tylor, Frazer, Durkheim, and Reinach, you will see that our interpretation, based on the mentality and the data of the natives, gives us an explanation of all that confuses these scholars.

It is because of relationship ritually obtained by community of blood, that the totem animal is neither killed nor eaten nor abused, but on the contrary often treated with care, as a member of the family.

That explains the mourning when they find one dead. It is the reason why they bury it with the same honors as a relative and why, if they kill one under the stress of urgent necessity, they offer excuses and by various artifices try to attenuate the offense.

That is why they weep after sacrificing it for the purpose of renewing the ancient alliance with it by an exchange of blood and communion; why they clothe themselves in its skin for certain religious ceremonies; why they take its mark, carry its name, dance and sing after its fashion; why members of the same totemic group often in their legends call themselves related to the animal totem by the bond of a common descent;

why these members recognize one another as relatives by the mark and name they bear and why they do not intermarry; in fine, why, because of a just reciprocity coming from a pact concluded by the other party and faithfully observed, the animal relative, when it is a dangerous beast, spares the members of its human family, i.e., only those who belong to it by birth, by blood. A member of this group who is attacked, bitten, or killed by this animal, is evidently not truly one of the family or else, because of some public or secret crime, he no longer deserves to belong to it.

Hence, in a general way, the totem animal, plant, or other object aids and protects its own, announces the future to them, guides them, cures them of certain diseases, and warns them of imminent dangers.

All these solutions, which now appear so simple to us, answer the difficulties of those scholars who have been occupied with the question of totems, in particular Frazer and Reinach.[29]

But this is not all. Besides the need man has felt of having allies in the mysterious world about him and of assuring himself of their services by a religious pact with reciprocal transmission of blood, he has another instinctive need: that of forming himself into a separate community, distinguishing himself from neighboring groups, often jealous, rival, and hostile, maintaining himself with his own, according to his special temperament, ideas, needs, and "manner." That is why we see all men, even the most primitive, form themselves into families and groups, taking a name to distinguish them. Often the best they find is that of some animal whose strength, cunning, agility, or beauty they have remarked, or a plant that was useful to them and peculiar to their country, or some object or phenomenon that struck them. Thus arose the use of the ancestral eponym,[30] to whom a family, a clan, a phratry, or a tribe traces its origin and name.

This method of distinction was also one of recognition. It

---

[29] Frazer. *Totemism;* Reinach, *op. cit.*

[30] Eponym (from ἐπί, and ὄνομα, *name*), the hypothetical person from whom a race, a kingdom, or a city is supposed to have taken its name; also the name so derived.

was important for them to follow their genealogy carefully so as not to mingle the blood of relatives, in obedience to the severe prohibition against consanguineous marriage. Thus, by means of the name that distinguished them, they readily maintained the family according to the established rules; the "leopard," for instance, would not contract marriage with another "leopard," the "hare" with a "hare," etc. In those countries where there is no writing, each one carries his certificate of citizenship about with him.

Because of this same preoccupation, they determine for each social group certain characteristic dances, ornaments, mutilations, tattooing, etc., often recalling the totem. Their manner of life, of amusements, of fighting, the arrangements of the encampments and villages, their mutilations, dress, ornaments, etc., all these are intended to affirm the line of descent to which they belong.

But it is especially the wars carried on by surprises, treachery, and terrible confusion, that have forced on relatives and allies the necessity of recognizing one another. Hence we see that each social group has, not only its war costume, but its special kind of arrows, bows, spears, cutlasses, missiles, drums, horns, and particularly shields which often bear veritable coats-of-arms. Consequently every black man of Africa can tell the tribe and family of any other who passes through his village or whom he meets on the road or with whom he enters into combat.

So the need both of distinguishing himself and of allying himself, has urged man to the practice of totemism. Which of these two natural instincts preceded the other? It is hard to say; and it is useless to try to find out. Let it suffice for us to note the resemblance and the reality.

We will not insist on the preference given to the animal kingdom in the totemic alliance. In the surrounding world, the animal approaches nearest to man. In the eyes of the primitive it has also certain mysterious powers; it has fascinating charms, it can make itself invisible, and foretell the changes of weather, accidents, good fortune; it always manages to live even where man starves to death, it is in relation with the world of spirits; most important of all, it alone has that element which by its exchange establishes alliance or relationship, namely blood. All our interests, then, induce us to unite ourselves to an animal, and by it to the mysterious beings with whom it is in relation.

The vegetable, mineral, and other totems are merely an extension of the former, and man can derive the same advantages from them. It all depends on the nature of each. Recognizing the services they could expect from a carnivorous animal, for example, a reptile, or a bird, so too, following other inspirations, they have made a sacred alliance with a tree or other object remarkable for some special property. The ancestor has designated it as being his "ally," and it is received as such: thenceforth it is a national tree or the national object.[31]

The totem is not always a free choice. It is imposed either by an inspiration that it sends or by a manifestation of the advantage that it brings or by a series of circumstances that cause its acceptance.

Once the principle is adopted, each one is obliged to apply it to himself or to his children. This is why in America, where the institution is much more developed or better maintained than elsewhere, each redskin has his totem that he bestows on himself or that has been given him by another, generally after a revelation in the form of a dream. "Usually he carries a mark or symbol of it on his body, his armor, his clothes. He marks it on his hut and on his canoe. He regards as relatives the animals having the same name, abstains from killing them, and invokes them in danger." [32]

In Africa the father, the mother, or the head of the family generally gives these individual totems to a child at the time of his initiation, on the advice of the sorcerer. But they bear rather the character of taboos, i.e., names one must not pronounce, animals or objects one must not look at, etc., under

---

[31] Of five hundred cases noted, there are forty examples of totems relating to inanimate things, and only four or five relating to the heavenly bodies. This great scarcity is an argument against naturism. (From E. Durkheim.)

[32] Réville, *Les religions des peuples non civilisés*, I, p. 223.

pain of death or sickness. Of these we shall later on have
occasion to speak.

We now have the necessary elements to form an exact idea
of the origin, of the *raison d'être,* and of the philosophy of what
it has been agreed to call totemism.

In a general way totemism rests on the idea that man not
only can enter into relation with the invisible and supernatural
world, but can also conclude a pact of allegiance with it, valid
for himself and his posterity.

As the representatives of the supernatural world can not be
reached directly and as they have ordinarily no immediate relations with us, it is necessary to treat with them through
visible beings to whom we address ourselves and whom we
make our allies. This result is obtained by magical ceremonies,
implying, in their primitive essence, a pact, with exchange of
blood, a sacrifice, and a communion. The community of blood
establishes community of life: and as animals are the only
beings able to furnish this element of the first importance, it
is especially with animals—transformed and, if I may say so,
supernaturalized by the presence of a spirit—that such alliance is made. Other beings will be taken only if particular
circumstances show that the protecting spirit will manifest
itself to such a family or individual through them.

The ancestor, having advantageously employed the totem,
bequeathes its name, remembrance, and worship to his descendants, to the family which is the continuation of his person after
he has disappeared. The family receives it as a sacred testa-
ment. Thereby the members of a family are grouped under
a common name for their mutual recognition and to distinguish
them from strangers as also to assure the purity of their blood
—united by a sacred pact to the blood of the totem—by regard
for the prohibitions that have been imposed on them. They
also make use of it to maintain the ancient alliance, to renew
it at times, and to welcome its mysterious blessings.

As soon as the children of the family reach adolescence and
may be considered men, elaborate initiations reveal to them this
mystic relationship, the advantages it confers, the obligations

and prohibitions it imposes, and the penalties exacted from those who despise it.

Then, generally, a special ceremony assures the renewal of the pact with the newly initiated. The special marks of the family are given him, which consecrate this initiation and become his rallying sign. New prohibitions are imposed on him; and others, that he has had to keep until then, are removed. His childhood is over: now he is a man, a man of the "family."

Undoubtedly the institution is not everywhere found in the totality and purity of its primitive phases. But we can entirely reconstruct it by the survivals that remain, all of which refer to identical conceptions.

After this exposition, does totemism keep the fundamental importance that many have tried to give it? We do not think so.

Totemism is a means employed by primitive man to unite, distinguish, strengthen, and extend the family, through a magical pact.

It *creates* neither the religious conscience nor morality nor belief in spirits nor sacrifice nor communion: on the contrary, *it supposes all these as already existing,* and uses them to perpetuate itself. To make an alliance with an invisible being, it is necessary to believe that it exists: you do not ally yourself with nothing.

It is, then, not the primitive religion, it is not even a religion nor even a part of religion. It is a family and social magical pact.

In conclusion, we will offer a definition of totemism: "an institution consisting essentially of a magical pact, representing and forming a relationship of a mystical and supernatural order, by which, under the visible form of an animal and, by exception, of a vegetable, mineral, or astral body, an invisible spirit is associated with an individual, a family, a clan, a tribe, a secret society, in view of a reciprocity of services."

In considering the different works relative to the history of religions in their origins and transmission, one is surprised to note that the importance of the family in the conservation of beliefs and worship, does not seem to have been noticed.

It is true that the sociological school notes, even exaggerates, the influence exercised on religion by tradition, education, suggestion, authority, etc. But it goes too far in making society the generative cause of all religion.

If this doctrine were true, the isolated man would have remained the *passive atheist* that it makes him at the beginning, as we have already remarked. But the Negrillos, who live in a state of dispersion in Africa, have a religion and morality perfectly well defined. And do we not also know from the example of the anchorites that solitude is, on the contrary, very conducive to the nourishing of religious thought?

Moreover, for society to exalt the religious phenomenon, the latter must, evidently, exist previously to the individual conscience.

When a religious man obeys an exterior force, in which he believes and to which he submits, he feels that this force is not society, nor even the sacerdotal authority considered in itself; this "compelling power" comes from above: it comes from the Invisible.

In the first ages of humanity, society was no doubt for a long time without any effect on religion, for the simple reason that it was a long time in the process of formation, in a world where there were no frontiers, where men, dispersing in all directions, nowhere formed large groups. But the family is probably an institution of all times; this is the conclusion reached by E. Crawley in a study of his on primitive marriage:

"It may be confidently assumed that individual marriage has been, so far as we can trace it back, the regular type of union of man and woman. The promiscuity theory really belongs to the mythological stage of human intelligence . . . these myths are interesting but of no scientific value." [33]

The primitive family after it had received religion under conditions that remained still to be determined, preserved it and assured its transmission while incorporating itself in it in

[33] E. Crawley, *The Mystic Rose, a Study of Primitive Marriage*, p. 483.

such a way that no notable phase of family life could dispense with religion and no important manifestation of religion could be produced outside the family and without it.

In its own way, exogamy has beyond question had a moralizing influence on the family; that is why it was maintained.

But we can not say the same for totemism. Totemism became attached to the institution of the family and the clan, as everywhere magic became attached to religion. As its action was of a superstitious nature, it has been able to disappear not only without inconvenience but even with profit. Religion alone suffices to maintain the family.

CHAPTER IV

BELIEF

The Invisible World, the Soul, Manes, and Spirits, God

The Three Planes of the Invisible World

I. THE HUMAN SOUL. Its nature. What the Bantu languages tell us. Some reconciliations. The different forms of the soul. Materialization. Whence comes the idea of the soul? Death and funerals: their teaching.

II. THE MANES. Where do disembodied souls go? The shade. The *Mzimu*. Toward higher regions. Ghosts. Survival.

III. SPIRITS. Tutelary spirits. What language teaches us. Bad spirits. No "Prince of evil." Genii. New examination of naturism and animism.

IV. GOD. Belief in God shown by his name. New appeal to the Bantu languages. Some misunderstandings. A sign of regression. Other remarks. Where is God? Who is he? Whence does he come? The reply of scholars; the reply of the primitives. What are his attributes? Two competent witnesses. The religious faith of the Bantus.

However little we may have, up to this point, entered into the primitives' general conceptions of beings and things, yet we have noted that for them this visible, material, and experimental nature of which we form one element—the living, animated, and rational element—is only a part of the universe. There is another part: as the full day comprises two parts, one dark and the other light, so the present life is prolonged into a further life where, so to speak, the visible world is duplicated in an invisible world.

But of what does this invisible world consist? What are its elements? If we were not constantly afraid of altering the beliefs of our natives by trying to put them in order, we would say that for them, the invisible world is formed of three degrees, the first of which would be made up of the manes of

90

the dead, the second the spirits of extra-human origin, the
third would be that sovereign Being whom we have already met
as the mysterious Master of nature. We find no juster name
to give him than "God."

I. THE HUMAN SOUL

On the lowest plane, are the *manes,* that is to say the human
souls disengaged by death from the bonds of corporeal matter
and continuing to live their life in the "over there." It is
almost in this sense that the Latins use the word "manes." [1]

This belief in the manes and the worship paid them are so
characteristic among our Blacks that their religion has sometimes been designated by the name of *manism.* A good observer,
an English major, Arthur Glynn Leonard, in a work on the
natives of the Lower Niger, wrote these words that we can
apply to all the human groups of the African continent,
Negrillos, San, Hottentots, Bantus, Negritians, and even the
Hamites.

"Among the Ibo and other Delta tribes, the belief in the
existence of the human soul is universal. To them it is an active
principle that is awake and about when the body is asleep.
Further, it appears as a something indefinite and indefinable,
an invisible and yet to some extent tangible essence apart from,
and of different texture to the material body, which leaves the
latter during sleep, or for good at dissolution." [2]

According to the teaching of philosophy, the human soul
is a simple spiritual substance, and hence immaterial, intelligent, free, and immortal. But to attain to this idea and
preserve it intact, according to St. Thomas, much study and

---

[1] The difference is first of all that the Latins placed the "manes" in the
underground world, while the Blacks give them a more extended dwelling-
place. Moreover, the word "manes" (from the old Latin word *manus* or
manis, "good," which we find in the compound *immanis*) means, strictly
speaking, the "benevolent spirits" as opposed to *larvæ* and *lemures,* "malevolent spirits," ghosts, phantoms. Cf. Freund's *Latin Dict.* Thus primitively, *manis,* pl. *manes,* was an adjective that was added to the word *dii,*
taken in the sense of *spirits: dii manes.*

[2] *The Lower Niger and Its Tribes,* p. 139.

penetration are necessary: *There is required a careful and subtle inquiry.*[3] We can easily understand that poor savages, without intellectual culture, have very confused ideas as to the nature of the soul. What astonishes us more, however, is that their ideas have such a firm and broad foundation. Let us try to understand them, first interrogating their languages and inquiring into the sense of words used by them which correspond to those we employ.[4]

There is the Bantu radical *-ima,* signifying *to be straight, to stand up,* and by extension *to be alive.* It has given birth to a concrete noun *heart,* employed both literally and figuratively, and to several abstract nouns: *life, the principle of life, conscience, human soul, manes,* according to a gradation that we can easily grasp.

The following abridged table will give an idea of these formations.

Root -IMA, literally *to stand up;* figuratively *to be living.*

umu-tima (Rundi) principle of life, soul	mo-dimo (Duala, Subu) manes	mo-limo (pl. ba-) manes (Tchwana)
m-tima (Nyungwe) heart, soul	go-djimu (Lolo) spirit	mo-limo (Ngala) soul
m-tima (Y-ao) heart	umu-dzimu (Rundi) manes	m-limu (Teita) manes
m-tima (Bemba) soul, manes	umu-zimu (Zulu) manes	e-limu (Lolo) soul
n-tima (Sena) heart, soul	mu-zimo (Makua) soul, spirit	
m-rima (Makua) heart, soul	m-zimu (Swahili, Nika, etc.) manes	
	n-rimu (Sena) soul, manes	

[3] *The Summa Theologica of St. Thomas;* literally translated by Fathers of the English Dominican Province, p. 1, q. 87, art. 1.
[4] The linguistic data that follow were furnished by Father Sacleux, C.S.Sp., former missionary in Eastern Africa. Father Sacleux may be considered as the one at present best acquainted with the Bantu languages.

A larger number of other languages have ingrafted the same ideas on the idea of *breath, wind,* the regular phenomenon of breathing having been more generally considered as the indication of life in animate beings.

Root -OYA (Tonga of the Upper Zambesi) *breathe.*

mu-oya (Tonga)   onw-oyo (Ganda)   m-otyo (Pokomo)
air, wind   heart (seat of life)   heart, life, soul

m-onyo (Vili)   m-oyo (Swahili, Nika) bo-moto (Yanzi)
life, soul   heart, life, soul   soul

omu-inyo (Herero)   m-oyo (Shuna)   Etc.[5]
life, soul   heart, soul

omw-enyo (Nyaneka) m-oyo (Teita, Nyandjya, etc.)
heart, breath, soul   life, soul

in-ina (?) (Mpongwe) um-oyo (Dyonga)
soul, manes   soul

In still other languages, the word signifying the *human shade* is used also to designate the *soul:* such is the case with the Fan word *nsisim,*[6] whether it be that in the native thought the soul and the shade have a common nature or that the one is the manifestation of the other.

It is interesting to compare these different expressions with those that have been transmitted to us by the Hebrew *nepheš* and *rûaḥ,* the Sanskrit *atman,* the Slav *duch,* the Greek ἄνεμος, πνεῦμα and σκιά, the Latin *animus, anima, spiritus,* and *umbra.* The Bantu languages appeal to the same figures as ours to express that something *unrepresentable* which the primitive, like the civilized man, considers as the "principle of life" in us, that seems to reside in the heart, that shines in the eyes, that disappears with the last breath and seems to be identified with it, that is projected without in a moving shade, and which, at the same time, reveals its presence in us by a will, an intelligence, and a conscience.

[5] The verb *Oya* is given here merely as an example. In other languages, other verbs having the same meaning (*to breathe*) have similar derivatives, meaning *breath, principle of life, heart, soul.*

[6] *Nsisim,* "shade, soul," by reduplication from *Nsin,* "form, image."

What is this mystery?

Is the human soul all that at the same time, or do these different manifestations require several substances? In reality, the Blacks know nothing at all about it. They have no consistent theory on the subject; their psychological ideas do not retreat in the presence of grave incoherencies; and you may say of all the Bantus what Dennett writes about the Ba-vili of Loango:

"Even in the country in which I have lived, although the white man has been there over four hundred years, I doubt if there are many who could enter into this subject with any great hope of giving you a definite idea of the difference a native draws between life, shadow, breath, and intelligence on the one hand and ghost, soul, and spirit on the other." [7]

The ancient Egyptians have rendered us a service in leaving behind them monuments, paintings, and inscriptions that permit modern scholars to reconstruct the Egyptian theory of the soul, with a precision of outline in which perhaps the ancient philosophers of the Nile valley would not recognize themselves but against which none of them could protest. A double (ka) airy projection of the body is repeatedly found in the tombs; a more completely separated substance (Bi or Bai) which they considered as the essence of human nature, flies towards the "other-land," like a bird, and is able at pleasure to leave the tomb or reënter it. Another luminous principle (khou) abandons the world and joins the procession of the gods; there is also the *heart* that is manifested as *conscience* during life and a *witness* after death. [8]

But, aside from this precision of doctrine, which perhaps belongs less to the philosophers of the Nile valley than to those of the Seine or Thames, we are struck by the curious analogy to be observed between the beliefs of the ancient Egyptians and those of the Bantus of to-day.

In the case of the latter, whether the human soul has several distinct forms or several manners of manifesting itself, it is

[7] Dennett, *op. cit.*, p. 79.
[8] G. Maspero, *Histoire ancienne des peuples de l'Orient*, p. 43.

the soul that beats in the heart and arteries, that breathes, that shines in the eye: it is the soul that is the principle of life and, as such, disappears momentarily when a man falls into a swoon or lethargy and definitely when he dies. Thus it is a sort of ethereal substance which, during the sleep of the body, is visited by other spirits; it sees them, talks with them, it "dreams." It is an interior voice speaking to us, inspiring us with good or wicked feelings, urging us to do good or evil, causing us joy or remorse. Lastly it is represented by that materialization of our person, which is called a shadow, more striking and more living in sunny countries than in ours; they have not arrived at explaining it as the interception of light by an opaque body: it rests in a man while he sleeps and follows him in death.

The Black, a scholastic of the good school without knowing it, attributes a "form" or "manner" to everything that exists, mineral, plant, or animal, instinctively recognizes in man a "something" by which man lives, moves, is self-conscious, governs himself, reasons, talks, dreams, and survives.

This "something" is distinct from the body, and is not so inseparable that it can not leave it for a time. So it happens that many persons, thanks to a particular charm they possess in their entrails, often without their knowledge, a charm that can be found by an autopsy, wander about during their sleep, occasioning disease and death, and vampire-like sucking the blood of sleeping men, carry off the heart of their neighbors, and cause endless calamities. Besides these, there are voluntary sorcerers who use this power of exteriorization and displacement, who also find stolen property, pass wherever they wish, enter into animals to find out their evil purposes, go at night to be present at diabolical gatherings, or conceal themselves under the form of vapor, balls of fire, glow-worms, nocturnal birds, and many other such objects. But, thanks to counter-sorcery, if you attack these spirits under the material form which they have assumed, if you strike them, if you kill them, it is the sorcerer that suffers and dies. That is why some people who go quietly to sleep in the evening, never awake again.

This first point is disputed by no one. Our African primitives believe in the existence of the human soul, even though
forming a conception of its nature that may appear strange
to "sane" philosophy. This should not surprise us. How
many systems of psychology have already succeeded one another
in the schools without any one of them being definitely
accepted!

Whence comes the primitive's idea of the soul?

It comes, reply the theorists of animism, from the observation
of sleep, dreams, death, and from the erroneous explanation
of those states or natural phenomena for which the savage can
give no other reason.

This assertion seems to us gratuitous and undemonstrable.
It is, in fact, impossible to determine whence the first men
derived the idea of the soul; as to the primitives of to-day, who
can say whether in their mind this notion arises from the observation of these phenomena or whether, already existing, it serves
to explain them?

This latter would seem to be the true hypothesis. H. Schell
has good reason to write:

"It is evident that by the soul, one has always meant to signify
something else than the breath, vital heat . . . dreams, a
shade, or an image reflected in a mirror. All these phenomena
together are not sufficient to produce the idea of the soul. This
idea has no need of so many detours in order to be born. Without all that, man has recognized and does recognize this something interior and living, unique and elusive, persistent and
invincible, that perceives, judges, inquires, doubts, feels and
wills, loves and hates, fears and hopes, determines and is determined, in which all his impressions are concentrated and
mingled, from which proceed all that he does and all that he
thinks. It is not in coming to the knowledge and concept of
the soul that the breath, the fire, the shade, the reflected image
are of value, but in furnishing, by analogy and comparison, an
image and a name." [9]

The immediate perception of the acts of the inner life,
noticed at every instant and in relation to everything, is for

---

[9] *Apologie des Christentums*, I, p. 59 (quoted by Schmidt, *Anthropos*,
1908, p. 360).

all men, civilized or savage, the real primordial basis of the concept of the soul. But this perception, more or less distinct in each individual, is confirmed by a large number of phenomena, some of which concern life, others the after-life, either well or poorly controlled and interpreted. These phenomena have established everywhere in the primitive world the absolute conviction that man is animated and intellectualized by a substance which, while still himself, is distinct from his body.

That is a question of the philosophical, psychological, and profane order. It is related to religion and to magic also, but neither of these *necessarily* finds its starting-point therein.

Before determining this starting-point, we must continue our examination, following the soul into the mysterious beyond, whither it passes at the dissolution of the body that it inhabited.

Death! What is death in the eyes of the Bantus? It is the excorporation of the soul, the principle of life. Whether God calls it or the spirits oblige it to depart or the charms of sorcerers break the bonds that fasten it to the flesh or itself aspires to be gone—for all these are different causes of death— the soul, at that last hour, *wishes* to be separated from the body. In fact, if we watch the effort of a dying man, the convulsions of his body, the contractions of his features and limbs, his agitation, dejection, anguish, in a word what we ourselves call his *agony*,[10] that is his last struggle, does it not seem that something is there *wishing* to depart, something powerfully attached to the material body while yet painfully striving to separate from it?

Once disembodied, the soul bears a new name, but it remains substantially the same; herein the Bantu languages remain faithful to their genius that employs distinct expressions for the same being which passes through different states.

Naturally the ceremonies that accompany death, and the subsequent funeral, vary in the different tribes. But we may say that everywhere they appear as the most important in the course of life, as well as the most characteristic and indicative of a belief in certain survival.

[10] From the Greek ἀγωνία, ἀγων, "struggle."

In the visible world, the Black keeps his family close about him; they have every claim on him. That same family having entered the invisible world under the form of manes—*mi-zimu, abambo, koma* [11]—is perpetuated in a sort of indefinite prolongation that binds it to the most recently deceased, and binds this latter to the primitive ancestor. Between these two worlds, the funeral rite is like a mysterious bridge that leads the soul to its destination. If the ceremony is properly performed, the soul will reach there and will leave the survivors in peace; if not, it will feel itself abandoned by its own, wretched, out of place; and there is every reason to fear its vengeance.

These ideas explain the differences of treatment employed according to the qualities and social rank of the deceased.

Criminals, condemned persons, those convicted of sorcery, are pursued into the beyond by public reprobation and receive no funeral honors. In most of the tribes, they are burned in a little fire on a funeral pyre of ebony, their ashes are abandoned, and their miserable garments are hung on a near-by tree. In other places they are thrown into the water. Sometimes they are killed and their bodies left a prey to beasts and ants that very soon reduce them to nothing. These are truly excommunicated.

Slaves are generally not the object of any funeral ceremony. Whether they were born in servitude or fell into it, does not this show that their guardian spirit has no power? They are people of no importance; the slave has no family.

Children, if they die young, have no right to special honors.

It is otherwise with freemen, with the head of a family, especially with the head of a village, and still more so with the head of a tribe: they are more honored at their funeral than they were at any period of their life.

When one of these important, rich individuals falls dangerously ill, the first thing to be done is to consult the physicians, seers, and conjurers, to administer medicine and offer sacrifices. Then, when the last hour arrives, all the relatives are called. The sick man makes his last wishes known, names those who are indebted to him, recalls business matters not yet

---

[11] Different expressions with the same meaning, according to the different languages.

concluded, charges his children with vengeances not yet satisfied, and tells where his hiding places are.

The agony begins. His nearest of kin are present and, in certain tribes, an exorcist is called to drive away the evil spirits. Here is one of the songs employed on such an occasion among the Fans of Gabon. You will notice that the poet, instead of saying things openly, employs allusions and figures; it is the style of all ritualistic compositions.

Song of Exorcism at the Last Hour [12]

(Turning towards the dying person)

The son [13] has gone to the field, to see whether the trees are ripe.[14]

Response 1. The trees are ripe. The spirits are wandering.[15] The time has come. The night begins. The prisoner is free! *Refrain:* The son has gone, etc.

2. The prisoner is free. He passes to the opposite shore without looking back, without looking back. *Refrain:* The son has gone, etc.

3. The shadow has touched the fireside of the hut. (*Very slowly*) I see a spark that passes like a lightning-bug, that turns, that flies around a palm tree. Yes. *Lamentations of the women:* yi! yi! yi! yi! . . .

Here is another song by way of example.

O father, alas! alas! why, father, do you abandon your home?
A man has slain you, O father.
You will seek [16] vengeance for his death.
Your shade will pass to the opposite shore.
O father, why do you abandon your home, father?
The sky has brightened; and the eyes have grown dim.
The water (the life) falls from the tree drop by drop.
The rat (the soul) has gone forth from its hole.
See! It is my father's house.
Gather the funeral herbs, sprinkle to right, sprinkle to left.
A man now sees the things invisible!

[12] These chants are sung by the women.
[13] The eldest son, the heir.
[14] I. e., to see if the life of the father is ripened.
[15] The spirits of the ancestors who come to look for him.
[16] The women are addressing the men present.

These two songs deserved to be reproduced: their inspiration lacks neither movement nor ideas nor beauty.[17]

As soon as death is ascertained, an outburst of characteristic cries, weeping and shrill laments rise and spread through the village; then silence returns. The relatives come to identify the dead man. They prepare the body, close the mouth and the eyes, wash it, empty the stomach and intestines by pressure; in some places they smear the body with a paint made of red wood powdered and mixed in palm oil, they wrap it in a prodigious quantity of cloth and, if they have not the practice of waiting for it to desiccate, they bury it at once with various ceremonies.

In Urundi (northeast of Tanganyika) they perform the following ceremony. The body is carried out of the house and deposited near the open grave. After the head of the defunct is partly uncovered, his wife approaches, weeps, kneels near him, and anoints his head with butter, saying:

> "Be you well! You were a man hero.
> Go in peace, farewell!"

She anoints a second time and continues:

> "Be you well! This for your wife.
> Go in peace, farewell!"

Then, after a third anointing:

> "Be you well! This for your child N . . .
> Go in peace, farewell!" [18]

And the ceremony is repeated for each child of the deceased. This is a touching expression of an idea revealing a belief in man's survival and even in a certain reward. In recommending to the spirit of the deceased "to be well," the woman recalls her husband's qualities, wishing him a happy voyage in the beyond, and taking leave of him successively in the name of the village, of his wives, and of each of his children.

---

[17] These two songs were furnished me by Father Trilles, C.S.Sp., missionary in Gabon.

[18] Rev. Van der Burgt, *Dict. franç. kirundi*, art. "Enterrement."

In many places the dead are interred in their hut or beside it. In other places their remains are deposited near the village; some have veritable cemeteries, formed by sacred groves where the dead are placed either on the ground or on a kind of mat; or they may be left in deserted places near a river bank; sometimes they are abandoned to the hyenas, who thereby become sacred animals; or they are cast into the water; or else they are eaten! This last manner of sepulture, however, is practiced in such manner that these "dear" deceased are absorbed only by neighbors not related to the family: bodies of the dead are exchanged. Women and children are not admitted to these strange feasts: only the ancients are worthy enough to take part. In 1894, when ascending the Upper Ogowe in Gabon, we encountered several bodies floating down stream. They had been caught by a tree branch or were circling about in some little corner. Frequently in the trees on the bank we saw men (Fans) holding long hook-like sticks in their hands, trying to gather this disgusting prey.

Where the custom is to bury the dead, the body is placed in a sitting posture or in the reclining attitude of sleep or in the position of an infant in the mother's womb, as if for a second birth.

But the mourning is not over. From the time of the death, the women's lamentations have ceased only at stated hours. They will continue morning and evening for a more or less prolonged period, generally a month.

Mourning requires a special dress—white—the color of the manes; then the position of the things in the house is changed, sometimes they even abandon the hut or the village, offer sacrifices, perform lustrations, wash and purify themselves, and shave their heads.

Eight days after the burial, the family again assembles. Then come the exercises at the end of a month. For the anniversary, there has been time to gather provisions; a great sacrifice takes place, they have a big dinner, drink and dance—for the dance is a part of a great many ceremonies: thus the soul at length is laid at rest and the mourning is ended.

At the anniversary exercises, in many Bantu districts,

especially toward the western coast, the head of the deceased
is cut off, cleaned, painted red, and enclosed in a box made
of bark which is then set in a little niche of the hut, where it is
surmounted by a wooden statuette.

At times the statuette is made of clay and in it they place
relics of the deceased, bones, eye-lashes, hair, finger-nails, and
such like. Sometimes the skull is placed in a cave, in the
trunk of a tree, or in a sacred grove. Or they may be satisfied
to build a miniature hut where the disembodied shade will come
to rest.

But however diverse may be the ceremonies of mourning and
the funeral exercises, the purpose is always the same: to
assure rest to the departed spirit, to fulfill one's duties towards
it, particularly to perform the rites that are due it and, if
there be need, to avenge it; to prevent it from coming back
by tracking it, by gratifying it with sacrifices, by scaring it
with shouts, enchantments, and even insults; and lastly to
purify one's self from the influences that might have been
contracted on this occasion.

Throughout this ceremonial we have clearly in evidence the
idea of man's survival after death.

II. The Manes

Where do the disembodied souls go and what do they become?
This is a very perplexing question, especially if you want a
theory that will apply equally well to all the Bantu tribes.
Neither the data that the ordinary natives can furnish nor the
numerous details that we find in the reports and studies of travelers allow us to form what might be called a complete and
rational theory of the survival of souls. To unravel this
capital question a little and to avoid misunderstanding, contradiction, and incoherence, into which both Blacks and Whites
ordinarily fall, we must return to the distinctions already
indicated in the concept of the soul. Let us take as an example
a people that has been well studied, a people whose ancient
traditions seem to have been sufficiently well preserved: the
Vili people of Loango.

1. We will find at first that this *something* whose existence the Blacks have noticed as associated with corporeal matter and as constituting the human being, has a perishable part and a permanent part. The former is that human *shade,* the *forma corporis,* with that living breath and vital principle of which there has already been question. It is attached to the body and follows it in its mortal ruin. This is why sometimes certain statements of the natives have led to the supposition that they believe nothing of us remains after death has reduced our body to dust. In fact, these miserable remains "which have no name in any language," have neither shadow nor breath nor movement. And in so far as that is concerned, we shall die quite completely.

2. But it is not this essential part of the soul (speaking according to Bantu philosophy) that constitutes, properly speaking, our individual and distinctive personality: this latter is formed by what is called, especially in the languages of eastern Africa, *m-zimu, n-simu, n-simo, mu-zimu, umud-zimu, mo-dimo, mo-limo* [19] which we can translate by *manes.*

This is what really survives the dissolution of the body and forms, under the appellation of ancestor-worship or *manism,* the chief object of the Bantu's religion and, we may likewise say, that of nearly all ancient peoples. These manes have a right to our respect, homage, offerings, and sacrifices. Since they have lost their mortal bodies, we ought also to prepare a dwelling-place for them to replace their former bodies. In western Africa it is the skull of the deceased that is carefully preserved in the family hut or in a sort of niche in the remotest corner of the common house of the village or in a veritable little chapel that certain tribes erect beside their huts. Formerly the manes were thought to dwell under the floor or near the fireplace.

As we advance toward the east, we find minute structures either at the entrance to the village or in the village itself or at the crossroads: these are the huts of the *mzimu.*

Or again, these manes are supposed to remain near their tombs, in the cemeteries, or at the very spot where the man

[19] From the root *ima,* "to be alive."

fell.   Hence along the caravan routes we often see heaps
of stones, twigs, or even leaves that are piled up in the form
of a mound (*tumulus*) to which each passer-by adds something,
a pebble, a little twig, or a handful of grass.

But these disembodied souls long to enter again into objects
to which they were attached, living animals and even human
creatures, notably into their relatives' children.

One day, Kingaru, a village chief on the eastern coast, whom
our missionaries had visited, came to Zanzibar and urged us
to settle with him at Mandera.   One of us had given him a
large medal, and Father Sacleux asked him to wear it.   "This
present," he replied, "is very precious to me.   I will wear it
all my life, and at my death I will leave it to my son; for my
mzimu will enter it and rest there."

At Mombasa, the founder of the Christian colony, known
by the name of *Shehe wa Mvita*,[20] often appeared, the natives
said, under the form of a serpent, especially at New Year's,
during the dances performed near his tomb.   Among the Wa-
rundi, when the king dies, his body, wrapped in a black ox-
hide, is mummified by drying it near a big fire, then exposed
in the open air on a platform, where it continues to receive
funeral honors until the catafalque crumbles of its own accord.
The remains are wrapped in matting and buried on the spot.
Then, the first worm that comes from the putrefying body
receives a hearty welcome and is fed on cow's milk.   Soon, they
say, this worm changes into a python or a leopard or a lion
or some other beast.   It is therein the spirit of the deceased
resides: this animal is thenceforth sacred; they feed it and
offer sacrifice to it.[21]

The people of Taïta [22] have, on one of their mountains, a lake
around which a number of little huts are built where their
wa-rumu (manes) come and rest.   All the ducks and other birds
as well as the fish of this lake are equally sacred.

We have already observed that the Wa-nika have a great
veneration for the hyena.   Their neighbors, the Wa-kamba,

[20] "The ancestor of Mvita" (Swahili name of Mombasa).
[21] Rev. Van der Burgt, *loc. cit.*
[22] Eastern Africa, between Mombasa and the Kilimanjaro.

and higher up the Wa-kikuyu, in imitation of the Massai, eat no birds, because all these tribes leave the bodies of their dead on the surface of the soil under some branches; the spirit of the dead passes into birds, hyenas, and jackals that devour the body in which it dwelt.

Yet, whatever be the dwelling-place of the manes, they are in a world not ours, that has not our sun, that is dark and cold. Each takes with him his passions, affections, preferences, hatreds, and grudges. The people of no account, children, slaves, and miserable wretches, remain what they were, and their *mi-zimu* soon fall into a sort of torpor from which they never emerge. The same is not true of the chiefs, the "seers," those who were distinguished by their supernatural powers. These had within them an intensity of life that permits them to remain active and powerful even when they are discarnated. They are interested in those whom they knew, share their afflictions, take part in their feasts, in a word, live the family and tribal life. Besides, they have powers superior to man, over the winds, the rain, the crops, the game; they can appear to the living; they like to pick out certain favorite places, as groves, hills, caves, or tombs, where their activity will be more efficaciously manifested and where they will receive the homage of mortals with greater pleasure; they also take possession of men, particularly when they have been neglected, and they quit them only after long ceremonies and large offerings.

3. Certain populations catch a glimpse of another life for the shades of their dead, a higher life where, though not completely separated from human interests, they are not entirely absorbed therein. The Fans, for instance, think that, although there is in man an obscure principle that is lost in the night, there is also a luminous principle that shines in the crystal of the eye and goes to join the light of the sun. That invisible world where souls go that are in condition to be happy and powerful, is, in the thought of these peoples, the world of God. Listen to the words of an authoritative observer speaking of the beliefs of the Nyandjya (or Nyassa):

"The *mzimu* remains alive when the man dies; the soul flies, flies; it goes there where the souls of all men who are dead have gone; they fly like the wind; they live in some way like there where God lives; they know all; if someone complains to the *mzimu,* the *mzimu* hears him; the *mzimu* comes in my dream; if someone falls into danger, he will make him return; if someone is possessed by the *mzimu,* it is to make him tell everyone to listen to him."

4. But there is also another side to this matter. As the Latins had the manes whom they honored and from whom they expected favor, they also had the larves and the lemures, ghosts, phantoms, and specters who were capable only of doing evil. It is the same with our Blacks. In their mind, these specters are apparently disembodied souls that "have turned bad": those of sorcerers, criminals, all those who do not deserve the place, honors, and privileges reserved for the manes. The appearance of these specters, which everywhere arouses great fear, signifies, in the eyes of him who sees them, the proximate death of himself or of someone belonging to him. By clever enchantments, the sorcerers are supposed to summon these specters to their service, make them take the form of a leopard, an alligator, a hippopotamus, and thus carry out their wicked designs by killing a great many persons. In short, nothing good can be expected from these damned souls. Especially is it to them that magic makes appeal.

Let us take the Nika people at the opposite side of Loango in eastern Africa. In a painstaking work, Krapf and Rebmann have brought together, around the word *koma* (spirit of the dead, manes) some native texts that will enlighten us as to its meaning.[23]

"There are spirits of the left side and of the right."

"The spirits of his ancestors have entered into him that he may be a sorcerer (seer)."

"The spirit produces dreams: what he sees, will happen. If such a one dreams that some person dies, he will die indeed."

"The spirit announces what is going to happen; if it is war, if it is famine, he makes it known to you."

"A storm arose to-day: it passed by with a troop. Ah, well,

[23] Dr. L. Krapf and Rebmann, *Nika-English Dict.,* art. "Koma."

they are the ones from the home of Him-on-high, they are taking a walk at home."

"The storm passed with the spirit; night visits the earth."

"Is he possessed by some spirit? He is possessed by his grandfather's spirit."

"Do not moan so (to a child), you will make the spirits come; the spirit will come to torment him because of his father's anger."

"When people eat rice, they must put aside a little ball of it for the spirit; thus he receives his part on the road."

"What is that? It is the spirit's thing."

These extracts, though merely a summary, enable us to make it evident that our Blacks firmly believe in the survival of souls. But must this survival be considered eternal?

This new and difficult question is too fine and theoretical to become a subject of speculation with men essentially practical. Yet, in general, it seems that the degree of survival after death is measured by the force of life contained in the soul of things and living beings. Thus the soul of material objects, plants, and animals, essentially depends on their elements and disappears with them.[24] It is almost the same with the soul of little infants who do not know enough to answer to their name; older children, slaves, people of no account, have souls that do not persist very long after them. The manes of ordinary free men eventually fall into a certain torpor from which they never awake. But there are others, both good and bad, souls of great chiefs and famous sorcerers, whose activity seems to continue indefinitely; for you hear certain spirits of families and tribes mentioned as still powerful that once occupied such and such a place but have long since disappeared.

Philosophical and theological notions of immortality and reward, such as we understand them, seem beyond the capacity of intellects so little suited to speculation. The natives scarcely take note of these questions and pause very little over them.

[24] Exception must be made in the case of certain animals that are considered superior: thus on the island of Pemba (near Zanzibar) the natives honor the *mzimu* of the cat.

In fact, their minds do not follow the soul into the beyond
of the invisible world except in so far as its activity interests
them in their own persons or in the persons of those belonging
to them. The rest is not their affair. Although they believe
firmly in the survival of souls, as firmly as if they had seen
them with their own eyes, what do they know of their condition
in the mysterious world where they have gone? The Fans of
Gabon echo the thought of all their Bantu brethren, when they
repeat in a sort of powerless anguish: "Death is like the moon;
who has seen its other side?"

III. Spirits

Among these disembodied souls that keep, along with their
passions, their power for good and evil, some become gradually
freed from human weaknesses and imperfections until they
take their place in the ranks of true spirits and are no longer
distinguished from them; for there are some spirits that seem
to have nothing in common with man, either by their origin
or their nature.

Such seems to be the case of the *Ombwiri* (pl. *Awiri*) in
Gabon.

"As it is used in the plural as well as in the singular form,"
says J. L. Wilson, "it no doubt represents a class or family of
spirits. It is regarded as a tutelary or guardian spirit. Almost
every man has his *ombwiri,* for which he provides a small house
near his own. All the harm that he has escaped in this world,
and all the good that he has secured, are ascribed to the kindly
offices of this guardian spirit. *Ombwiri* is also regarded as the
author of everything in the world which is marvelous or mysterious. Any remarkable feature in the physical aspect of the
country, any notable phenomenon in the heavens, or extraordinary events in the affairs of men are ascribed to *ombwiri.*
His favorite places of abode are the summits of high mountains,
deep caverns, large rocks, and the base of very large forest
trees. And while the people attach no malignity to his character, they carefully guard against all unnecessary familiarity
in their intercourse with him, and never pass a place where he
is supposed to dwell except in silence. He is the only one of

all the spirits recognized by the people that has no priesthood, his intercourse with man being direct and immediate." [25]

"*Ombwiri* is fine and admirable in aspect, but is very rarely seen; it is white, like a white person." Dr. Nassau adds that, as criminals' souls can become evil spirits, "souls of distinguished chiefs and other great men turn to awiri." [26] This confirms what we have already said.

This idea that man has a guardian spirit interested in him and his home becomes more precise in certain tribes. Among the U-rundi, for example, the foundation for the popular belief would seem to be that the human soul has a sort of patron spirit associated with it and, as it were, welded to it: it is his familiar "demon." This solidarity persists after death and thus we understand the power of disembodied souls for good or evil. [27]

However tutelary these spirits may be, the Blacks do not trust themselves completely to their humor, for other spirits—and they seem indefinitely more numerous—have a quite well determined evil character.

What is the nature of these beings?

Here the native language again comes to our aid. We have stated that, to designate the human soul, expressions are used, borrowed from words signifying *to live, breathe,* etc. This same soul, this principle of life, once freed by death, takes another name that is, however, connected with a root of the same meaning: *m-zimu,* for instance, with its many related forms, is evidently connected with -*zima,* meaning *alive,* which in turn is related to the root -*ima, to be erect, to live.*

But when there is question of designating other spirits that are, by their nature, strangers to us, the Bantus seek an image in the exterior world. They will select, for instance, this breeze that springs up in the silence, passes in the trees whose leaves it moves, touches our faces, and although invisible, has a perceptible, mysterious, and disturbing effect on the things

---

[25] J. L. Wilson, quoted by Nassau, *Fetichism in West Africa,* p. 67.
[26] *Ibid.,* p. 68.
[27] Rev. Van der Burgt., *op. cit.,* art. "Manes."

of visible nature.   The same word *Pepo*,[28] *Peho, Om-pepo, Om-bepo,* literally meaning *wind,* figuratively signifies *spirit.* But let us not be misunderstood: the one is not the other, for whereas the word *Pepo, wind,* takes the prefix of inert things, the word *Pepo, spirit,* takes that of living beings.

The evil spirit, of which we are now treating, seems not to be everywhere designated by a term exclusively its own, like that of *pepo,* opposed to *m-zimu* (manes), that we have just cited.   In Tchuana, for instance, the plural word *ba-dimo* (evil spirits) comes from the same root as *m-zimu;* but then we have another expression to designate the manes.   Likewise in Rundi the words *imi-tima mi-bi* (wicked spirits) and *mu-dzimu* (manes) come from the same root but form two words of very different meanings.[29]

Many of these spirits have a specific name by which they are known.   Each one also has his character, his manner of being, his powers, functions, and exigencies, and his ordinary sorcerers.   Note this curious fact: throughout Bantu Africa several of these demons—for we are here in the depths of demonology—are designated by the names of neighboring tribes and are supposed to appear under the form of animals, particularly when they are evoked in the secret societies consecrated to them.[30]   According to Rev. W. E. Taylor, such are the following in Giryama (eastern coast):

Nyama Mbarawa, literally, the beast of Brawa (Somaliland).
Nyama Mugala,   "   "   "   of the Gallas.
Nyama Mkamba,   "   "   "   of the Wa-kamba.
Nyama Mtaita,   "   "   "   of the Wa-taita.
Nyama Mkwavi,   "   "   "   of the Wa-kwavi.

There are others which appear in human shape, sometimes deformed and bizarre.

"A *jinn* or demon called Katsumbakazi," says Taylor, "is

[28] *Pepo* in Swahili (Zanzibar) and in a great many languages; *Peho* (Nika, Nyamwezi, etc.); *Om-pepo* (Nyaneka, in Angola); *Om-bepo* (Herero).
[29] Father Sacleux (MS. notes).
[30] W. E. Taylor, *English-Giryama Vocabulary.*

said to be seen occasionally. It is malignant and, as it is of no
great stature, when it meets anyone, is jealous lest it should be
despised for its insignificant size. It accordingly asks, 'Where
did you first catch sight of me?' If the person is so unlucky
as to answer, 'Just here!' he is sure to die shortly; if he is
aware of the danger, and says, 'Oh, over yonder!' he will be
left unharmed, and it may be that some good will happen to
him." [31]

In Gabon at the other side of the continent, Dr. R. H.
Nassau speaks of the *Si-nkinda* (sing. *Nkinda*) as never having
had a corporeal existence. Nearly all are ill disposed. They
come into the villages, attracted by curiosity or desirous of
warming themselves near the kitchen fires. At times they
are mysterious messengers, bringing news from distant countries, announcing an epidemic, the arrival of a ship on the
coast, or the passing of a white man. [32] I must say that many
a time on my arrival at a village I have heard one or other
of the sorcerers affirm that he knew of my visit in advance, and
he would tell me the places where I had slept the preceding
nights, what I had eaten, what I had done.

These sorts of spirits are fond of busying themselves with
mortals, often going so far as to take possession of their
bodies. Still another class of demons more thoroughly
wicked, called *My-odi* in Benga, show their activity by
violent possessions.

Others are rather capricious, prankish, mischievous, who
like to make fun of men and play tricks on them; but they
can be disarmed by employing the proper means.

It is with these different evil spirits, both human and extra-
human, that the sorcerers of black magic have relations. We
shall return to them. Although evil is regarded as a sort of
diffused power that can be controlled to a certain extent, yet
there does not seem to be, in the mind of the Blacks, a supreme
power of evil at strife with the supreme power of good. Such
a systematic dualism that some have thought to find in Africa,

[31] Taylor, *op. cit.*, p. 81, art. "Religion."
[32] Nassau, *op. cit.*, p. 69.

does not exist there. It is a product of preconceived ideas that can not stand the simple and sincere observation of facts. The prince of evil or the chief of hell is lacking in the vocabulary of the Bantus and of the Africans in general: these mention only particular names whose owners act without any hierarchical arrangement. Wherever a special term does appear, as *Shetani* or *Satana,* it is foreign, of recent introduction and due to Mussulman or Christian infiltration.

At most, we might assimilate the notion of a great chief of the spirits to that other idea, known in certain places, of a spirit-master of the earth, the guardian of hidden treasures, presiding over terrestrial phenomena, and corresponding to the Great Spirit, master of the heavens.

But such generalizations do not enter into the mentality of the Blacks. Just as they have distinct names to designate the same being at different stages of its growth or in its different states, just as they often lack a generic noun to indicate a class as, for instance, the species "monkey," so also they propose a different spirit name for each kind of influence that they attribute to the same spirit sources.

Thus we have in Congo and in a great part of Africa those kinds of genii with their names and attributes, their ordinary following, and their ceremonies. Some preside over the elements, some over rivers, lakes, forests, crops, journeys, lawsuits, diseases, in fact, over everything. These spirits, calling to mind the *genii* and *dii* of the Latins, have their images and figures and special symbols; that is what, properly speaking, constitutes *fetichism*. We will speak of it in connection with the question of worship.

Before going further but without going into a deep discussion, we may remark how much these simple, naïve, primitive, and popular notions, which are also reasonable to a certain extent, differ from the complicated, learned, abstract, systematic, and often ridiculous theories that have been advanced as the religion of our savage peoples: naturism, totemism, manism, animism, fetichism, etc.

No doubt, we can use any one of these expressions to designate their beliefs and their form of worship; the important thing is to know what one intends to include therein.

So far as the Bantus are concerned, we have seen how to explain many strange facts gathered here and there by ethnologists, and confused and arbitrarily grouped by them to support preconceived systems.

We see that the personification of the elements, stars, stones, trees, or animals, is a pure misunderstanding, too often made and accepted, but not by our Blacks.

We see that the fear of ghosts which, according to Herbert Spencer, must have been the initial basis of the fear of God, forms only a simple element in the totality of the native ideas; we see that it depends entirely on the belief in the existence and survival of the human soul, and that it is impossible to find therein any proof that this fear has been or is the initial reason of all religion.

We see likewise that the "deification" of the dead, although it existed in Greek and Latin polytheism, is unknown among our primitives.

Moreover, to give all these theories a serious foundation, it would be necessary to show that the beliefs set forth relative to the manes and spirits, hold the field alone and do not coexist among the savages along with other points of view. If, in fact, all their present notions stopped there, it would still not be proved that they never had any others and that hence these are their initial notions. There would simply be undeniable probability that this was the case.

Let us continue our examination.

IV. God

"Everything is full of gods." The developments we have outlined relative to the souls of things and animate beings, to the manes, spirits, and the genii, show that this saying of the Greeks can also be applied to the black world. Everything is full of gods; but where is God himself?

God? In the black world he is nowhere to be found, we are often told by the most opposite parties.

When you have lived with our primitives a long time, when you have come to be accepted as one of them, entering into their life and mentality, and acquainted with their language, practices, and beliefs, you reach the conclusion that, behind what is called their naturism, animism, or fetichism, everywhere there rises up, real and living, though often more or less veiled, the notion of a higher God, above men, manes, spirits, and all the forces of nature. Other beliefs are variable like the ceremonies attached to them; but this one is universal and fundamental.

Everywhere among the Negrillos and Bantus, as well as throughout Africa, God has a name. Herein we find the particularizing spirit of the race. As each family has its father and each clan has its ancestor, so each tribe or group of tribes of the same origin wishes to have *its* God. How do they do it? They have given a special name to the supreme Being, as if to localize him with them: hence the different names under which God is known on the black continent. This remark has a striking application at the Niger delta, where each village, so to speak, designates God by a different name.[33] But when you question the natives, you very quickly perceive that in their minds these different appellations refer to the same sovereign Being: the *M-ungu* of the Swahilis is the same as the *Nkulu-Nkulu* of the Zulus, the *Nagi* of the Massai, the *Waka* of the Gallas, the *Allah* of the Mussulmans. The Blacks are not polytheists. In similar manner they multiply the names of rivers: each group living near a river gives a different name to the same stream, as if each one wished, by a name in its own language, to associate it with itself and, so to speak, to naturalize it.

What name do the Bantus give to God? The study of this question, if it can be settled, will not fail to be interesting and singularly helpful in enlightening us.

We have already seen that our Blacks, in their profoundly logical language have had recourse to ideas and words relating

[33] A. G. Leonard, *The Lower Niger and Its Tribes.*

to the special nature of man, as *life, breathing, heart,* thin and mobile *shade,* to designate the incarnate *soul* and the disembodied soul.

To name the spirits of an extra-human nature, they have employed an element that is outside of us: the *breeze,* the *wind,* the moving *air.*

But to give God a name, they have made use of a third method. Instead of trying to represent the nature of this unrepresentable *Being,* they have designated him by an epithet, an expression of quality and an attribute which, in their opinion, eminently suits him, or by an emblem indicating his dwelling-place, his greatness, or his power.

Father Sacleux, whom I have already quoted more than once, has sent me some pertinent notes which, in the present state of Bantu philology, he alone was able to furnish, and which are very suggestive.

1. A first series of these expressions of quality intended to signify God, turns about the word *-amba* (to say, do, arrange, fashion). Vestiges of it are to be found everywhere; the most important derivative and the one best preserved in the ensemble in the linguistic family, is the word *m-ambo* (words, deeds, actions). From this verb *-amba,* prefixed by the element *Nya-* or *Nyi-* (the having, he who), the Bantus from Kamerun to the Herero country, with lines penetrating into the center of the continent, have derived these expressions, easy to follow in their derivations:

Ny-ambe (Luyi or Rotse, upper Zambezi).
Any-ambye (Mpongwe of Gabon and neighboring languages).[34]
Nz-ambi (Vili of Loango, etc.).
Nz-ame (Fan of the Gabon forest).

These expressions mean "he who speaks, he who does, the organizer, the creator."

[34] It has been said that in this word the initial letter indicates the plural. This is an error: *A* is not here a prefix; it is *Any.* Moreover, *Anyambye* is always employed in the singular: a plural form of this word is even impossible.

The same notion is found expressed by other words, such as
-*umba,* -*vanga,* -*panga,* -*tunga,* -*tonda,* -*ilola,* -*hlola,* all having
the identical signification of *to make* (for example, of pottery),
to give the form, to fashion, to arrange. Whence the following
names consecrated to the Divinity:

Mu-umba (Swahili and neighboring languages), literally "the
fashioning."
Mb-umba (Vili, of Loango).
Mb-umbi (Shuna, of Mashonaland).
Umb-umbi (Tebele, between the Limpopo and the Zambezi).
Mu-vangi (Duma, Upper Ogowe, Gabon).
O-wangi (Ndumu, Upper Ogowe).
Tci-vanga (Vili, of Loango).
Ka-runga (Herero, south of the Kunene).
Ka-lunga (Kwanyama and Ngangela, of Angola).
Ka-tonda (Ganda, north-west of the Victoria Nyanza).

2. A second series of names, employed exxclusively to designate God, marks his power, strength, greatness, ownership,
supreme mastership. Several of these are from the root -*eza*
(to do, to be able, to have authority and power) especially
employed in the central region, and by infiltration into the
valley of the Zambezi. We can follow this root in the following composites:

Mwiny'ezi (Swahili and allied languages), literally "he who
has power," "the Powerful."
L-eza (Tabwa, Bisa, Bemba, Tonga, Luba, etc., Zambezi
valley).
L-ezi (Nyandjya, Lake Nyassa).
R-edja (Kanyoka, Karanga).
R-edza (Nyungwe, Zambezi).
Ka-bedja (Guha, West Tanganyika).
Ma-weza (Kanyoka).

Here are others of the same meaning but with different roots:

Ne-ngolo and *Nkwa-ngolo* (Lower Congo), "the Having
power."
Mpungu-ngolo (*Ibid.*), "God" or "Spirit-power."
Nzamo-mpuo (Tege of Leopoldville), "Strong God."

Nya-mpamvu-zentze (Tete, Upper Zambezi), "the Having all power."

Nya-ma-Kore (Nywangwe of Tete), "the One from on high."

Mu-kulo Nzambi (Lunda, Angola), "the Great God."

Nkulu-Nkulu (Zulu and neighboring dialects), "the Great Great" (the Very High).

Mu-lofo (Luba, Upper Kassai), "the Master," "the Chief."

Mw-ene (Sagala, East African), same meaning.

3. A third series of names will perhaps be found still more interesting, for herein the language seeks to translate the essential nature of God; and it is at least curious to meet this attempt of poor savages to express the "ineffable" name that Biblical tradition has handed down to us. We have already seen that in many Bantu tribes the human soul derives its name from the root *-ima,* which means *to live:* it is the principle of life within us. But, if a soul lives in us and animates us, another Soul animates the universe. From the same root *-ima* we get these words:

M-tima, n-tima, m-rima, umu-tima. .Human soul
Mo-dimo, m-limu, umu-dzimu, mu-
    zimu, m-zimu ....Manes
Me-limo (pl.) ....Spirits (inferior gods)
Mo-limo (sing.) ....GOD

And if in some cases a confusion might arise between the use of *Mo-limo* (God) and that of *Mo-limo* (inferior spirit), as in Tebele, recourse may be had to the ordinary proceeding: the difference of the connectives and the difference of plural prefixes.

4. Let us mention a last series of names. They designate God by his supposed dwelling-place, or his likeness or identification with the light, the sky, or the sun.

It is proper, first of all, to connect with this series the widespread expression *M-ngu, Mu-ngu, Mu-ungu, Mu-lungu,* etc., that we may translate by "the One from on high, the One of the sky." It belongs especially to the tongues of eastern Africa (about forty) and extends from the extreme limit of the Bantu languages at the north (Swahili, Kamba, Ganda, etc.) to the south of the Mozambique on one side and, on the other, to the heart of the continent, with echoes to the west in Ovampo and Angola.

We can not here digress into purely philological details. Let it suffice for us to point out the same root in the words *U-wingu* (heaven) and *Mb-ingu* (heavens): *Mu-ingu* or *Mu-ngu* (the spirit of the heaven). We may add that this word in the singular admits by way of agreement only pronouns relating to living, rational persons. The plural, on the contrary, which regularly should be *Wa-ngu* or *Wa-lungu,* is *Mi-ungu* or *Mi-lungu,* literally "god beings," or "servants of gods" (without reason or movement of their own): so that the language, making an exception in this case for the formation of the plural, isolates the word *Mungu* (God) in a rank that belongs to it alone. Is not the fact worthy of mention?

In the same order of ideas, God, in Swahili and other neighboring languages, is also called *Mu-anga,* literally "the One of the light" or "the One of the bright heaven" (from *Mu-,* personal prefix, and *-anga,* "light of the heaven").

The sun has also been taken as an emblem of the Divinity in some Bantu languages; but, by curious processes, they have always carefully marked the difference between the orb of day and the great living Being who borrows his name from it, either distinguishing the two by their prefixes or marking their quality by the pronominal inflections which they give them or adding to the word "sun" another word from a neighboring language or a special epithet that relates only to God. This is evident proof that, although the language finds itself embarrassed to express what it wishes to say, the spirit of the primitive has not intended to confuse or assimilate either the ideas or the terms.

Let us take the root *-ua, -uwa, -uba* (sun). In Nyambu (south-west of the Victoria Nyanza) they will say:

I-zuwa (sun).
Ka-zova (God).

In Sukuma and neighboring dialects (south of the Nyanza):

Li-uwa (sun).
Di-kuwe (God).

Or else:

E-kumbi (sun).
Lu-kubi (God).

The Tchagas, who inhabit the Kilimanjaro, make use of the word *Rua* to designate the sun and God. But in a phrase they take care to distinguish the two by the connective: that of inanimate beings for the sun, that of animate, living, rational beings for God. "The sun goes away": *Rua li-enda;* "God goes away": *Rua i-enda.* And the better to avoid confusion, they have the habit of adding to the word *Rua* the expression *Murungu,* which can be applied only to the Divinity. In an identical manner the Blacks of Kikuyu and of Kamba (east African), while preserving their own terms *i-wa* and *li-wa* for "sun," have borrowed from the Massai, their great neighbors, the word *Ngai,* which applies to the sky, the sun, infinite space, and God.

These testimonies, which might easily be extended to all the Bantu languages and, we may add, to the African languages universally, should be enough to show the strange confusion made formerly in trying to represent these natives as having no religious notions. It was the thesis of Sir John Lubbock as well as of all those who followed him; a thesis that has since been adopted by those who see in Black religion only a childish animism or a crude fetichism, without any idea of God, of his nature, or of his attributes.

All that Réville [35] can grant us is that "of all non-civilized peoples, the Blacks of Africa most easily familiarize themselves with the idea of God ruling the entire universe" and that "we never greatly surprise the negro when we speak to him of one, sole, truly existing God." He goes so far as to find "some traces of a worship positively rendered to a supreme

[35] Réville, *Les religions des peuples non civilisés,* I, p. 54.

God. He is called Woka or Waka among the Gallas and their neighbors, the Imomattas (?), to the east of the Sudan." And he adds: "It is the sky that is here meant." [36]

The same confusion is to be observed among the best intentioned scholars. In his careful study on the *Religion of noncivilized peoples,* Abbé Bros, relying on the word of Réville, Tylor, Frazer, and others, points out as matter of worship among these populations, only various "objects," "objects that the savage believes to be animated" and which "are regarded as gods and invoked as such." After citing the "Morimo" and the "Unkulun-kulu" of the Kaffirs, he mentions the "Waka of the Gallas" which seems to mean the "fecundating and rainy sky." [37]

If the Gallas (who are not negroes and who would not admit this first misconception) could read these learned works, they would reply that Waka designates also the supreme Being, real and personal, as does the Allah of the Arabs, the Jehovah of the Jews, and the God of the Christians. In fact, they have a very precise idea of him, as we shall see later on. If the meaning of "sky" is attached to this word Waka—a fact of which I am ignorant—it is not the material, spread-out sky that we perceive, but the sky personified, best giving the idea of the power and majesty of the great Spirit who dwells there. To converse with them is sufficient evidence that this is so. Besides, when we ourselves say: "Heaven permitted it; please heaven; heaven has not wished it," seriously, do we mean to speak of the blue sky and the clouds? As with us, so with the Gallas and the negroes.

It is beyond question or doubt that the Negrillos and the Bantus as well as all the Blacks of Africa acknowledge and proclaim the existence of a Being superior to all, to whom a special name is given, who is distinguished from other spirits, from the manes, shades, and elements, and whom we can identify only with God.

It is but just to add that if this knowledge seems to be no-

[36] Réville, *op. cit.,* p. 54.
[37] Abbé Bros, *Religion des peuples non civilisés,* p. 103.

where absent, it is far from being equally precise and living among all the tribes and especially with all individuals: it is, in a way, a diffused knowledge characterized, however, at certain points and certain times by astonishing precision; elsewhere and in the ordinary course of life, it is irresolute and, as it were, left to itself. Some of the Blacks, when naming God, appear to confound him with the sky, the totality of the luminous vault, the light of day, and so forth. That is, perhaps, what has caused the misunderstandings we have just noted. But, after all, that is only an illusion: approaching their thought more closely and questioning them further on this point, you soon perceive that there is no identification and that, at the most, they have considered God as united to the sky and to the light, like the spirit of man united to his body.

However, comparing the extraordinary precision of the linguistic data of the Bantus with their actual ideas, we have an impression that this notion of the Divinity has undergone an evident retrogression with them and that it was much more precise, more significative, more affirmative in the designation of God and his attributes than the people themselves generally are at the present time.

This remark agrees with observations that can be made in India upon the same subject. There, before the reform of Buddha, Brahmanism was more affirmative regarding the Divinity; before Brahmanism, Vedism was still clearer.

It was the same in China before Confucius and Lao-Tseu.

After establishing this fact, it is now opportune to make some interesting remarks whose importance deserves emphasis.

1. Nowhere in Africa is it thought that God can be forcibly influenced, summoned, or localized by magical ceremonies, as is done with the manes, spirits, or genii. In other words, magic has no power over God.

2. Nowhere in Africa is God represented under any material form whatsoever nor is he supposed to dwell in an image, a cave, or a temple. God has no fetich. The very idea of presenting a material object as God would appear extravagant. "On one occasion," says Dennett, "the writer asked a native if

the Bavili made no images of Nzambi. 'Who would be such a fool?' the man promptly answered, and the writer said no more." [38]

The same reply would have been made anywhere in Africa to the same question.

Real idolatry, such as is sometimes imagined, consisting in the adoration of an image or statue that would represent the figure of God or that would be God himself, does not exist in the black country. What we do find there is a worship of images or fetiches where it is thought spirits or genii dwell or exercise their influence. These spirits, after the manner of the Latins, in our languages are improperly called "gods." But this confusion is not made by our Blacks.

3. Nowhere in Bantu Africa is God, properly speaking, blasphemed. [39] At times they find fault with him, they think him indifferent or severe, they call him bad, as on the occasion of a drought, a misfortune, a public calamity, or a death. But they have no idea of addressing God with words of contempt or insult. What can man do in the presence of God except be silent and wait?

One day at Bagamoyo I was present at the departure of a European, an agent at Zanzibar for a Hamburg house; he was going into the interior to look for ivory at Tabira. The caravan, composed of Nyamwezis, was ready to leave. The chief of the porters uttered an invocation: "May God be favorable to us!" "God," replied the European, who no doubt wished to pose in a swaggering way and to magnify himself in the eyes of his men, "we have no need of him. My God is my money and my gun."

The porters looked at him, put down their burdens, and began to withdraw. The European (who was of Jewish extraction) asked me to intercede. "No," these poor people replied.

---

[38] Dennett, *op. cit.*, p. 87.

[39] Here there is evidently no question of Blacks more or less Islamized or Christianized. As for blasphemy, we sometimes hear it on the lips of natives: but even then, it is an evidence of their faith. Thus the Mpongwes of Gabon sometimes say in anger and by way of insult to God: *Ungulungulu jele Anyambye*, literally, *The Almighty is not God*, or, *God is not almighty*.

"This white man is bad; did you not hear him insult God? With him, we would be sure to have misfortune." And they all left him.

God exists. But where is he? Who is he? What is his origin? What are his attributes?

To these difficult questions, our primitives certainly do not answer with the abundance and clearness of orthodox philosophers and theologians. To tell the truth, they do not even put these questions to themselves; they find them futile, they ignore them, and there they remain.

Where does God live?—"There, above; everywhere." And they point to the great expanse of the sky. "God is on high," say the Giryamas (eastern Africa), "the manes are here below." [40]
According to Dr. Krapf, the Wa-nika say:

"Everywhere that you go, God is there."
"Take care. When you merely quarrel, he hears you."
"Even if you enter a ditch to hide, God sees you." [41]

On the other hand, certain expressions or explanations would tend to make us believe that God is conceived as a sort of Being extended throughout the world and, so to speak, keeping himself in the background. But it is an idle, insoluble question for the natives, a question on which each one may think what he wishes.

We will not insist on the nature of God. The Bantus do not discuss the question and could not furnish us any precise answer, no more than do our most distinguished philosophers.

Accustomed as we Europeans are to consider God as a Spirit, as the Great Spirit, we quite naturally transfer this conception and expression into the religion of savage peoples. But in doing so, we equivocate and lead those who read our words into real error. This is what happened to Herbert Spencer,

[40] W. E. Taylor, op. cit.
[41] Krapf and Rebmann, Nika-English Dict.

Tylor, and all their school. Andrew Lang makes some very just remarks on this point.[42]

In reality, the Bantus do not conceive God as we would be inclined to suppose. Let us question them.

What is *Mulungu?*

First of all, Mulungu is not *mtu kama watu,* "a man like men," i.e., a being like another being. No. But this does not prevent him from often borrowing a number of anthropomorphic attributes. Yet he is not a man.

Nor is Mulungu a *Mtima,* a human soul living in the world and animating it. The world has something like a soul, but it is not Mulungu.

Nor is Mulungu a *Mzimu,* not even an ancient one and the first of the Mzimu. A mzimu is a disembodied soul that has passed through death. Mulungu was never man, he never dies.

Might Mulungu be a *Pepo?* No. A *pepo* is a *pepo,* and every *pepo* (spirit) has its name. To say of Mulungu that he is a *pepo* is to insult him, is "to talk like a simpleton."

Nor is Mulungu *Uwingu* (the sky) nor *Dyua* (the sun) nor *Anga* (the light) nor *Mwezi* (the moon). He is no doubt in them all, but he is something other than that.

What is he then?

We do not know. He is, he lives, he sees, he does whatever he wishes, he is unseizable, is beyond our reach, he is *Mulungu.* But as logic is not the strong point of our good Blacks, they will easily attribute to this great Mulungu our good and evil passions, our ideas, our preoccupations, jealousies, and deceptions. With perfect incoherence, even in the same narrative, after showing the sovereign power of God who created everything, they will speak of the difficulties he has encountered in a given circumstance, of his having forgotten something, of his fits of anger, and so forth. According to Dr. Callaway (cited by A. Lang), it is the same with the Zulus. Unkulunkulu, which seems to have designated God in the past,[43] has been gradually confused with the notion of the first man. But

[42] Andrew Lang, *The Making of Religion,* p. 160.

[43] This conviction comes especially from the comparison of this word with like terms employed in neighboring tribes and among them solely consecrated to distinguish the Supreme Being. See footnote 40, p. 122.

this first man, Unkulunkulu, is "he who has made the rain, the grain, the food." As this word came no longer to signify clearly the supreme Being, what did the natives do? They took another word that would not lend itself to confusion, and now "God" for them has become "Utilexo," an expression borrowed from a neighboring tribe.

Therein we find a confirmation of what we have already said: the different names used by the different tribes to designate God, do not at all imply different gods. The Bantus have not the least idea of Hindu, Greek, or Roman polytheism. What is true is that they are concerned about God only for themselves and, in a slight degree, for their family and tribe. Let everyone look after his own affairs!

Ethnologists naturally have less reserve than our primitives in this matter of finding the origin and evolution of the notion of God.

Many of those scholars flatly denied that the idea existed among the savages. This was the thesis of Sir John Lubbock, a position which has had to be universally abandoned in the face of facts and the impossibility of honestly contesting them.

Then they managed to avoid the question or treated it in such a way that, amidst the enormous mass of facts, destined to show belief in the personification of material things, in ghosts, spirits, totems, etc., the idea of God passed unperceived. This was the method of Spencer, Tylor, Tiele, Réville, and others, a method sharply criticized by Andrew Lang in his remarkable work *The Making of Religion,* which they have treated with as much silence as they could.

It is certainly striking that the most primitive tribes have a notion of God which is the more precise according as they are more uncivilized. Such are the Negrillos of Africa, the San, the Andamans, the Australians. Some way must be found to explain the origin of the idea of God; hence a vast quantity of theories, the mere exposition of which would furnish material for a large work.[44] Here we will simply say that, in general, God is represented to us as the final and neces-

[44] It is undertaken by Schmidt in *Anthropos,* 1908.

sary outcome of the animist idea, as the chief that must be found for the multitude of spirits; or as the transformation and deification of an ancestor's spirit; or as the personification of an element of nature, of the totemistic idea or the social force. These theorists have taken great pains to get around a very simple question which they seem unwilling to look squarely in the face.

In the mind of our Negrillos and Bantus, Mulungu (i.e., God) is certainly not the sky—dry or rainy—nor the light nor the sun nor the moon nor the wind nor the water nor the earth, and so on. He is in all of them, he acts in and by all these elements, he is sometimes assimilated to them, but his personality is distinctly separate from them: he is something else.

God is not in their minds the "power" (totemistic or otherwise) of nature or society, in the sense that our philosophers and sociologists mean it: this refined, critical idea is altogether foreign to our poor savages.

God is not conceived by them as the "Principle of Good" in opposition to a "Principle of Evil," whose effects would appear to our eyes and for which our mind would seek a cause: that, too, is an idea that is not in vogue in the black country.

God is not to them a deified chief. The Negrillos have no chief, they do not claim any special ancestor; but they have a very precise idea of God.

God is not to them a "spirit," neither the "spirit" of a dead man nor an independent "spirit": he is conceived as anterior to death, as having never died himself; and he it is precisely who commands life. He has nothing to do with the spirits, genii, or demons: these latter, among the Bantus, are not considered as intermediaries between man and the Divinity. We repeat that the Bantus are not polytheists and do not conceive God as the chief or king of the gods. He is outside of all that.

Among the Blacks, God does not come from an abstract union in one personality of the multitude of powers and qualities attributed to different spirits, nor from the necessity of giving a president to the assembly of inferior divinities, nor from any like conception. Once again we repeat, these ideas proceed from speculations to which the black world is a total stranger.

Whence, then, have our Bantus received the idea of God? To tell the truth, in this study we prefer to prove that this idea exists rather than indicate its origin. In fact, we do not know its origin. At most, we can furnish some directive data on the subject. The natives, for their own part, do not put the question to themselves. Evidently they have no idea of *ens a se* any more than they have of eternity or of distinct creation *ex nihilo*. As to the beginning of the world, the appearance of man, and similar problems, the legends vary in the different tribes; this may be a proof that these legends are not very ancient. But everywhere we find God presiding over the formation of the world, even when all that exists is supposed to be born of the marriage of the sky and the earth: that is the reason for many of the names given him, as *Katonda* [45] (the Creator), *Muumbi* [46] (he who forms), *Murindzi* (he who preserves), *Ahendaye* (he who does well). These expressions and many others found in most of the Bantu languages, by placing in evidence the idea of author, maker, preserver, show the profound impression which the argument of causality has made upon the primitive. Instinctively he, too, feels that the marvelous machinery of the world was not able to set itself up. Our own opinion is that therein is to be found the primary and veritable basis on which the Bantus rest the idea of God.

This notion naturally suggests that of master, proprietor, and sovereign of the universe: *Mwiny'ezi* (he who has the power). "Hence probably," says Taylor, "the native scruple about selling a piece of land; it is the trees only that are considered salable." [47] This is just what we have said above.

God, the Master of the world, is also the Father of men: *Reri yajio* (our Father) the Mpongwes of Gabon call him; and the Bengas, their neighbors, have an identical appellation in the expression *Paia Nzambi*.[48]

[45] Mgr. Livinhac, *Les Baganda, Introd. à la grammaire ganda.*
[46] Taylor, *op. cit.*
[47] *Ibid.*, p. 47, art. "God."
[48] Nassau, *op. cit.*

He, the author of life, is also the author of death in the sense that he takes the souls of men when he wishes and as he wishes with no one able to hinder or reproach him. That is why, in case of death, the Blacks take pains to find out whence the fatal issue came: if it is the deed of an avowed or hidden enemy, the relative must be avenged; if it is caused by a spirit, he will be disarmed by a sacrifice; but if it comes from God, there is nothing to be done. What can be done against God?

The Wa-nika say that we are God's hens and chickens in this world; and when someone dies, it means that a stranger has arrived in heaven and God has need of some poultry for the feast.[49] But evidently that is only one of their fictions.

Mu-lungu amula-ye, apate ku-kala mzima (May God be able to forget him, so that he may live!), the Giryamas repeat on learning of the birth of a child to one of their friends.

This same idea rules over the nomad existence of the little Negrillos. If one of them dies, it means that God has discovered their encampment. So, after hiding the corpse with great mystery in the hollow trunk of a tree or in a stream, they break camp and silently depart in the middle of the night.

It is God who sends the rain, warning men of its coming by the voice of the thunder; and it is he who keeps it back; it is he who makes the grass grow in the plains for the herds; it is he who makes the forest green, makes the fruits ripen and the crops prosper; it is he who feeds all—trees, beasts, and men. The entire world, in fine, is dependent on him.

As God is nowhere the object of any material representation, as the family and tribal cult is first of all addressed to the manes of their ancestors, as no magic art can reach God, who is inaccessible to man, and as ordinarily he wishes us only well, they are very little concerned about him except in words; hence travelers have passed through Africa, seeing scarcely a trace of him anywhere in the religion of the natives.

This is ably set forth and explained by Robert H. Nassau, who lived forty years in the black country and is a competent witness.

[49] Taylor, *op. cit.*

"I can readily see," he says, "how the reports of some travelers—even of those who had no prejudice against the Negro, the precepts of the Bible, or missionary work—could be made in apparent sincerity, when they state that native Africans have confessed of themselves that they had no idea of God's existence; also, their belief that some pygmy and other tribes were too destitute of intelligence to possess that idea—that it either must be given them *ab extra* by the possessors of a superior civilization, or must be developed by themselves as they rise in civilization.

"The difficulty about the testimony of these witnesses in this matter is that, being passers-by in time, they were unable by reason of lack of ability to converse fluently, or absence of a reliable interpreter, or of being out of touch with the native mode of thought or speech—to make their questions intelligible.

"On the heathen side, also, the obsequious natives, unaccustomed to analytic thought, will answer vaguely on the spur of the moment, and often as far as possible in the line of what they suppose will best please the questioner. All native statements must be discounted, must be sifted."

"I am aware," he continues, "that some missionaries are quoted as having said or written that the people among whom they were laboring 'had no idea of God.' Even Robert Moffat is reported to have held this opinion. If so, it must have been in the earlier days of his ministry, under his first shock at the depth of native degradation, before he had become fluent in the native language, and before he had found out all the secrets of that difficult problem, an African's native thought. Such an unqualified phrase could be uttered by a missionary in an hour of depression, in the presence of some great demonstration of heathen wickedness, and in an effort to describe how very far the heathen was from God. That the heathen had no *correct* idea of God is often true." [50]

"After more than forty years' residence among these tribes," says Nassau, "fluently using their language, conversant with their customs, dwelling intimately in their huts, associating with them in the varied relations of teacher, pastor, friend, master, fellow-traveler, and guest, and, in my special office as missionary, searching after their religious thought (and therefore being allowed a deeper entrance into the arcana of

[50] Nassau, *op. cit.*, p. 33.

their soul than would be accorded to a passing explorer), I am able unhesitatingly to say that among all the multitude of degraded ones with whom I have met, I have seen or heard of none whose religious thought was only a superstition.

"Under the slightly varying form of Anyambe, Anyambie, Njambi, Nzambi, Anzam, Nyam, or, in other parts, Ukuku, Suku, and so forth, they know of a being superior to themselves, of whom they themselves inform me that he is the *Maker* and *Father*. The divine and human relations of these two names at once give me ground on which to stand in beginning my address.

"If suddenly they should be asked the flat question, 'Do you know Anyambe?' they would probably tell any white visitor, trader, traveler, or even missionary, under a feeling of their general ignorance and the white man's superior knowledge, 'No! What do *we* know? You are white people and are spirits; you come from Njambi's town, and know all about him!' (This will help to explain what is probably true, that some natives have sometimes made the thoughtless admission that they 'know nothing about a God.')" [51]

It is interesting to cite the testimony of another witness, for Albert Réville was well acquainted with him and often quotes him, except when this competent witness speaks of the knowledge of God.

J. L. Wilson writes:

"The belief in one great Supreme Being is universal [in Africa]. Nor is this idea held imperfectly or obscurely developed in their minds. The impression is so deeply engraved upon their moral and mental nature that any system of atheism strikes them as too absurd and preposterous to require a denial. Everything which transpires in the natural world beyond the power of man or of spirits who are supposed to occupy a place somewhat higher than man, is at once and spontaneously ascribed to the agency of God. All the tribes in the country with which the writer has become acquainted (and they are not a few) have a name for God; and many of them have two or more, significant of his character as a Maker, Preserver, and Benefactor." [52]

[51] Nassau, p. 36.
[52] J. L. Wilson, *Western Africa*, p. 209.

Here we conclude this brief survey of the religious beliefs of our Bantu primitives, which form the basis of their morals, worship, and ceremonial organization.

As we have said, these beliefs relate to visible nature and to nature invisible. In visible nature reside the innate forces or souls of things, dominated by the hidden presence of the mysterious and sovereign Master. There are some gifted men whose look penetrates the things beyond. They will tell you that invisible nature is arranged on three different planes: that of the manes of their ancestors, with which they should remain in contact; that of the spirits, genii, or demons who enter into their life and are capable of good and evil—of evil rather than good—and over whom they happily still have control; lastly, that of God who, from the depth of the universal scheme, rules over all, and men are not able to do anything for him or against him. This is why the natives of the black continent, passing through life in the same mentality, at once careless, fearful, and resigned, trying to face the surprises of life day by day, thinking of the morrow only to hope for better fortune, might all sing this song, so full of unexpressed significance, which the Pahouins of the equatorial forest of Gabon put on the lips of Fam, the first man:

> Yeye! O la! yeye!
> God above, man below.
> Yeye! O la! yeye!
> God is God; man is man:
> Each one in his house, each one
> at home! [53]

[53] Trilles, *Contes et lègendes*, etc., p. 83.

CHAPTER V

MORALITY

I. WHAT IS MORALITY?

Definition. Divisions

Morality, according to its etymology, is the rule of conduct, i.e., the rule of our free actions in relation to our last end; according as they conform to it nor not, they are good or bad, meritorious or deserving of punishment.[1]

This definition can be accepted by all the schools. They will all likewise agree that morality is necessary for man and for society. Is it not humiliating for our human reason to have to state that ever since the philosophers began to discuss the question—and that was long ago—they have never been

---

[1] A. Vacant, *Dict. apologet. de la foi catholique* of J. B. Jauger (art. "Morale"). St. Thomas said the same: "The whole life of man should be directed to the highest and ultimate end of human nature." (Eth. lib. I, Lect. 2.)

able to agree on the nature and foundations of a thing so simple, so indispensable, and so universally well known as morality?

Since they are not in accord as to the "last end" of man, they can not agree on what is in conformity with it and what is not, what is good and what is bad, what constitutes our rights and what our duties, and on what indisputable principles rests that moral law which should govern our lives.

But among all the discussions that have been carried on during the ages, we can distinguish two great trends of opinion.

1. One of them connects morality with religion so closely that, according to A. Franck, "it is no more possible to conceive a religion without morality than a morality without religion." [2] In fact, all religious belief, however imperfect and crude, necessarily offers man either a model to follow or a master to satisfy, i.e., a rule superior to any which he might be able to found on his own interests and passions. A god who asks nothing is reduced to a vain abstraction. On the other hand, it is also quite evident that legislation resting only on itself, i.e., on the promises and threats it is able to devise, with no appeal to a higher and indisputable authority than can be imposed on the conscience, without invoking any right or principle of a superhuman order—such legislation would be an undertaking condemned from the start.

"Thus, whatever aspect of morality we consider," says Vacant, "finally it is in God we must seek its reason and foundation. If we consider this law as the expression of good and evil, its rule is the infinite intelligence; if we consider its obligatory character, we find its source in the divine will; if we seek to know how it is possible to enforce the sanction of the moral laws exacted by justice, it is only God who possesses the knowledge, equity, and power necessary to do justice to these legitimate claims. In God alone, therefore, does the moral law find its rule, its principle, and its crown." [3]

2. Those who belong to the other current of opinion, utilitarians, evolutionists, positivists, subjectivists, independents,

[2] A. Franck, *Dict. des sciences philosophiques*, art. "Morale."
[3] A. Vacant, *op. cit.*

agree, in spite of partial differences, in seeking the rule and basis of the moral law outside of God and religion.   To-day in France and other countries, where the schools are officially more and more avoiding religious instruction, there is particular concern not to let morality vanish into the air, and to find a new basis for it.   Might not science be that basis, not complete science embracing philosophy and theology, but the natural sciences, medicine, hygiene, political economy, etc.? Thus guided, morality would be the continuation of the efforts by which man, from prehistoric times to our own day, has sought to civilize himself, by "cooperation and "solidarity." Hence, as Payot concludes, "all our duties . . . can be summed up in a single affirmation: to love and respect life, to live our life of man, i.e., our conscious life, by giving it all the intensity, breadth, and depth that it can attain." [4]   For these, our official moralists, "the end of man" is, then, man himself.

II.   The Basis of Morality

We considered it useful briefly to point out this double tendency towards two extremes clearly opposed to each other. But we have here no reason to mingle in these disputes. We have a plan of our own.   To remain faithful to our plan and stay in the realm of facts, it will suffice for us to answer the following questions:

1.   Have the primitives a morality?
2.   If so, what relation has it to religion?
3.   What is that morality?

To the first of these questions, the school whose assertions we have just considered, replies as usual without any hesitation:

"Morality has no more been always innate in us than the religious sentiment.   If it has finally become so, it is only after long ages of heredity have implanted it in our soul.   Like language, religion, and other institutions, it varies from one race to another.   There is no universal morality, but only local

[4] Payot, *Cours de morale*, 1907.

and temporary. Pascal's remark that 'theft, incest, the murder of children and fathers, all have had their place among virtuous acts,' is absolutely true.

"We see this to be the case when we examine in detail the customs of ancient civilizations. We observe usages so contrary to ours, we encounter acts so strange, yet approved and recommended by the morality of the time, that, in order not to depart from philosophical impartiality, in order not to approve or blame but only to understand, we must place ourselves face to face with the human conscience and be persuaded that it also, like the intellect and all the other faculties, is subject to the law of evolution."

"We are here," continues Gustave le Bon, "in the presence of a grave problem which illustrious minds, under the sway of powerful prejudices, have often wished to solve contrary to science. Kant, Condorcet, Buckle, and others have pretended that the morality of all peoples is identical and remains invariable through the ages.

"We can scarcely understand how philosophers have been able to maintain such an assertion. Pascal saw more clearly when he said: 'Truth on this side of the Pyrenees, error on the other side.'

"Let us take an example. It is an almost general custom among savage peoples, a custom that must have been very widespread at the beginning of humanity, to kill one's parents in order to save them from the infirmities of old age and especially to end this drain on the food supply. Among all those who follow this custom, no idea of crime attaches to it; on the contrary, nearly everywhere it has the sanction of religion; the sacrifice is performed with great pomp and is terminated by a feast." [5]

"There is no universal morality!" This is an error and the various assertions we have just cited, expressing the ideas of a whole school, rest on a simple confusion that can be easily explained.

Considering only the populations with which we are at present concerned, populations which, we repeat, are regarded among the least advanced in the whole world, we will state a

[5] Gustave Le Bon, *Les premières civilisations*, p. 87.

primary fact. Their languages, although generally well provided with verbs and nouns, are very poor in adjectives, yet everywhere you find some to characterize what is good and what is bad, true and false, just and unjust. The distinction of good and evil, not merely of physical but moral good and evil, is a thing so elementary that you would greatly astonish the most savage of these people if you seem to deny it. They have a number of things that are licit, and a number that are forbidden.

Moreover, the individual responsibility of the adult free man of sound mind is the very basis among them of reward and punishment.

When we look for the fundamental and primary idea that inspires in the primitives respect for laws and customs, restrictions on the absolute use of nature's gifts, and, to use Reinach's expression, "scruples"—just as we discovered behind all their beliefs the invisible and distant presence of a sovereign Being, so here, behind their morality and sustaining it, we shall find an innate and instinctive sentiment of justice, joined to a certain impulse for good and aversion for evil.

It is this sentiment of justice that must have originally inspired the principle of the sacred interdict or taboo. In taking what nature freely abandoned to him, man believed that he *ought* to restrain his hand from what his hidden Master had, by some sign or other, declared that he wished to reserve for himself.

Again, men worship because justice also requires man to pay a form of worship to the manes of his ancestors, tutelary spirits, the genii, and God. Religion is a right that the invisible world has from us: hence we have the duty of satisfying that claim. That accounts for funeral ceremonies, feasts, dances, songs, sacrifices, all that constitutes religion.

It is justice, well or ill interpreted, that obliges children to respect and obey their parents, give them their earnings, defend them against aggression, have a care for their manes, avenge them even to such an extent that they must bequeath the obligation to their own children if they themselves are unable to perform this vengeance: blood for blood! life for life!

But if parents or the heads of the family, in their turn, wish to concern themselves about their children, it is as they choose, they owe them nothing or very little; they have "made" them, and then, too, they are their masters!

So, also, is it with a man's rights over his wife. He has paid for her; she belongs to him, she is his property. In some tribes at least he may sell her again, put her in pawn, give her up, rent her out, or lend her. But if someone else uses her without permission or indemnity, justice requires that the wrong be repaired. This reparation is generally by means of a fine.

With all the more reason can a master dispose of his slaves not only for his work but to free himself from a debt, to make an exchange, to offer a human sacrifice, to substitute them for himself at a judicial ordeal, etc. Are they not his property? He bought them, inherited them, or took them in war.

The rights of a father or of a master are also those of the chief or the king and especially are they attached to the supernatural world and its representatives, i.e., authority and power. So it happens that, in Africa, solely to show his dexterity and independence, we sometimes see a powerful chief strike the head of the first man he meets or sacrifice human hecatombs, as formerly was done in Uganda, Upper Ubanghi, or Dahomey, without provoking any murmur on the part of his subjects.

Justice makes the Blacks respect their vows and oaths and alliances sealed by fraternity of blood. Justice punishes the perjurer, the traitor, the false witness, the calumniator, the thief, the assassin, the malefactor, all those who have wronged another. Justice inspires those interminable African palavers, those adjustments of accounts that are never adjusted, those old matters that reappear after ten, twenty, fifty, or a hundred years. Justice is at the basis of those judicial trials or ordeals to which so often appeal is made in Africa, which everyone accepts and the accused themselves are often the first to invoke in order to declare their innocence. As in other countries, in the name of liberty, fraternity, and progress, good simple people are ruined, thrown into prison, pursued, hunted, or killed; so in Africa, in the belief that justice requires it, false sorcerers are poisoned, the piles of ebony are lighted under criminals who are such by name only, and thousands of innocent heads are cut off.

It is justice, alas! And it is morality!

This feeling is so natural and so general that, although the Black accepts without recrimination or rancor the punishment that he has deserved by some fault for which he feels guilty, he does not consent to be punished unjustly. The children as well as the men are very sensitive in these matters, especially if they are thus unfairly punished by a European who, as a superior man, ought always show his superiority by his sense of justice. Africans say that, if many whites, in the "peaceful penetration" of the black continent, have fallen victims of their daring, stricken down by the savages, most of them have been victims of injustice, their own or the injustice of some one of their party, or of some European who preceded them.

Now we have the key to the misunderstanding noted above. If the very principle of justice, with the definite notion of good and evil, is the basis of the moral life of the Blacks, and of the primitives in general, the practical application they make of it in detail is often deplorably erroneous. To take the example given us above, there are American savages that kill their aged parents. No doubt! But in acting thus, these devoted children intend to render a service to their elders, to deliver them from the miseries of this life and procure another life for them in which they will be more agile; at the same time they act on a social necessity, since in their constant hunting life they can not take these poor stiffened members along with them. In Africa many tribes likewise practice infanticide: here it is a question of children "ill" born, who can not live, they think, without causing disaster to their family, their village, and their tribe. They must be eliminated; as in our well-organized societies we eliminate individuals who are recognized as a public danger.

We conclude, therefore, that the attentive and comparative study of our primitives proves that philosophers like Kant, Condorcet, Buckle, and others who have maintained that the basis of morality is identical, universal, and innate in man, are right. Nor was Pascal wrong in his well-known aphorism: "Truth on this side of the Pyrenees, error on the other." Pascal spoke of the application of morality: of these, and these alone, can we say that they are "local and temporary."

III. RELIGION AND MORALITY

The same school continues:

"The factors of morality are extremely numerous; some reside in a realm of most delicate psychology and their action takes place in the most secret depths of the soul; they are unequally combined and they do not everywhere influence the other factors in an identical manner. Consequently the evolution of human morality is very difficult to follow and it is not yet possible, considering the imperfect state of our experimental sciences, to indicate more than its principal features.

"At the outset," they tell us, "we must almost entirely eliminate an influence that was formerly supposed to be preponderant in the question of morality, but which, in reality, is always found to occupy a very secondary place. It is the influence of religious beliefs. . . . For some centuries past, in the West, we have seen the ministers of different religions assume the function of moral directors and dictate to us, as the expression of the divine will, the most precise commandments of daily conduct. But this is an innovation of modern times which would astonish certain oriental peoples who believe the gods too much above us to be concerned about our conduct with one another.

"Morality, as we understand it to-day, freed itself very slowly from the instincts of primitive ferocity. While it was gradually improving on the earth, mystic dreamers longed to locate it in heaven and see it descend and be joined to the religious principle. But for the philosopher, morality will remain eternally distinct from religion. The gods are born, grow powerful, and die. Their imposing shadows flit about humanity and can vanish without morality being diminished. Morality is in ourselves and must remain in ourselves. It is the daughter of the necessities that govern us. It helps us to support them. As the fundamental element of our societies, it develops with them and at the same time as we ourselves. Only when heredity shall have solidly planted it in our hearts and given it the force of an instinct, will we be able to say that it is truly constituted. We are too near ancient barbarism for it to be so yet.

"The chief factors in the development of morality are these: utility, opinion, environment, the affective feelings, heredity. For the reasons given above, we do not mention religion among them." [6]

"The relation of morality to religion," says Tylor, "is one that belongs in its rudiments, or not at all, to rudimentary civilization. . . . Savage animism is almost devoid of that ethical element which to the educated modern mind is the very mainspring of practical religion. . . . But these ethical laws stand on their own ground of tradition and public opinion, comparatively independent of the animistic belief and rites which exist beside them." [7]

Other authors unconsciously echo these assertions when they write, without explanation, that the various spirits rarely set a good example in the religions of the savages, or that evil gods occupy an important place, or that the knowledge of God has no influence on the primitive's conduct of life.

We wish to say at once that this last statement (with the modification we will presently give it) seems to us rather just.

As to the "evil gods" who "often occupy an important place in the religion of savages," [8] we will merely reply that this word "gods" seems ill chosen, for it is applied to beings very different from one another and seems to suppose a hierarchy which, as a matter of fact, does not exist. Do these "evil gods" form part of religion or of magic, i.e., of religion or anti-religion? If the evil spirits in question are opposed and repudiated by religion, we have no right to consider them the directing spirits of religion. The confusion is evident.

It is incontestable—perhaps this is what they wish to say— that the religion of the primitives does not seek examples or lessons of virtue in the manes, guardian spirits, or genii. The very idea would seem strange to the primitives.

But it is no less incontestable that religion as such and in

[6] Le Bon, op. cit., pp. 91, 95.
[7] Tylor, Primitive Culture, II, p. 360. "Numerous facts in favor of this thesis may be found in Lubbock." (Abbé Bros, op. cit., p. 219.)
[8] Abbé Bros, op. cit., p. 114.

the name of invisible beings that it represents, imposes certain
precepts and prohibitions as a duty upon its adherents, with
a sanction that reaches the responsible individuals. This is
largely the morality of the primitive and that morality is so
dependent on religion as to be, so to speak, identified with it.

Father Lagrange, in his fine *Etude sur les religions sémitiques,* incidentally touches on this question. He writes:

"We must recognize that all those who practice religion believe themselves obliged to do it. Nowhere do they resolve to
observe it by a free choice and because it procures advantages
they could neglect. Religious men have always believed that
the relations they wished to sustain with the Divinity were
willed by Him, that He exercised a certain control over their
life and expected certain acts from them. All religion contains
an obligation, and a moral obligation, for the morality of an
act is indissolubly bound to the idea of obligation. Those who
deny that religion has moral obligations, no doubt wish to say
that this primitive morality is not always the same as ours, but
that matters little for us at present. Religion supposes a double
belief: the existence of higher powers on whom man depends
and who require certain acts of him, and also the possibility of
entering into relation with these powers. These relations themselves constitute religion." [9]

Far from the field where Father Lagrange so brilliantly con-
ducts his labors and combats, Reinach comes to our aid. The
pleasure of appealing to him is more rare than we could wish
it were. He says:

"Let philosophy preach as she will that morality is the creation of reason, the human heart believes by instinct that it
is nearer of kin to religion. That kinship has always existed
nor can it be said that time has loosened the tie: still, the inti-
macy has been modified, and here, as elsewhere, specialization
has come into play.

"Morality is the discipline of custom," he tells us. "The
word discipline implies restraint—an influence exerted on man
with a view to curbing, in a given interest, his liberty of action
toward his neighbor and himself. A restriction of this type

[9] Rev. M. J. Lagrange, *Etudes sur les religions sémitiques,* p. 7.

falls into the category of taboos, of which prohibitions with a permanent moral validity are only a particular case. Now it is a characteristic feature of ancient religious codes, the Mosaic law included, that no clear distinction is drawn between moral vetoes and others of a superstitious or ritualistic caste." [10]

These remarks are perfectly just. Without insisting further upon a point that appears to us sufficiently well established, we will try to reply to the third question, the most important one: what is the morality of the primitives?

IV. The Morality of the Bantus

The reply is difficult to shape because it is not easy to arrange the matter in precise and complete divisions.

If, in fact, "morality is the rule of our free actions in relation to our last end," everything will depend on the idea man has of that end. But this is a question the Black does not put to himself. Like a traveler who has unconsciously lost his directions, he keeps moving and, while he waits to cross the mysterious bridge of death, seems to have no other care than to draw from life whatever good it can furnish him and to avoid whatever can bring him harm.

From this present tense and practical point of view, the primitive directs his acts and fulfills what he believes to be his duty.

As he has no precise symbol of doctrine, he has no clearly established moral code: customs make up his practice, handed down from his ancestors, carefully preserved, undisputed, generally observed, and nearly always enforced by the fear of punishments.

However, when our analytic mind tries to penetrate this mass made up of all sorts, excellent, good, useless, ridiculous, bad, and atrocious, we can distinguish, as in every other human society, two kinds of law.

There is the natural law, already referred to in speaking of justice, which forms the basis and substratum of whatever is good, just, honest, and, so to speak, moral in our primitives,

[10] Reinach, *op. cit.*, 202.

and, by the fact that they are men, is for them what it is for all men. We will not say more of this at present.

And there is the positive law, ordering or forbidding certain acts. Its purpose is to regulate the rights and duties of man in relation to the invisible or supernatural world, to external, visible nature, to the tribe, to the family, and to himself. Let us try to follow the morality of the black man in these different spheres.

The first law or positive custom imposed on our primitives —Negrillos and Bantus—is the obligation of observing certain religious practices; this constitutes their worship in regard to the supernatural world that they feel surrounds them, penetrates them, and dominates them: the world of manes, tutelary spirits, and genii, and the world of God.

As we have already seen and as we shall see better in what follows, this cult is addressed especially to the manes of immediate relatives or to one's ancestors. It is obligatory in the sense that if any one should refuse to perform it he would be dishonored before his own people, any misfortunes that befell him would be attributed to his negligence or impiety and, in certain cases, the family or village would believe it their duty to institute ceremonies of reparation.

It is proportionately the same with duties and deference towards the tutelary spirits and the genii. But a greater liberty is left to each individual. Except in cases where the family or tribal interests are at stake, no one is obliged to wear such and such amulets, to participate in such and such acts of devotion, to honor such or such a fetich.

As to God, he remains, so to speak, beyond the world accessible to man. He is not absent; his presence, on the contrary, dominates everything and his name is often on the lips of the Black. But, save in certain circumstances, there is no definite, public worship in his honor. They do not blaspheme him, or at most they do so unwittingly. "What evil has God done?" was the question used as a form of salutation by a visitor in the old days approaching the aged King Denis, who gave the estuary of Gabon to France. And the old chief replied:

"Death." Then, you wished him long days. Mgr. Bessieux, the founder of the Catholic mission, shocked by these terms, had them changed. Thenceforth the royal salutation was: "What good has God done?" "Life!"

Although religion presents itself to the mind of the Black as an obligation, it is but just to add that neither god nor the guardian spirits nor the manes are considered as examples of moral perfection. "Be like unto God?" he would say, "What extravagance!" "As to the spirits and manes, have they not the same passions as we have ourselves? And in what way does our perfection concern them?"

The savage is not free in relation to the invisible world. Nor is he entirely so in regard to external nature, because in his thought it does not belong to him and, in order to live, he feels obliged to ask permission of its Master.

We must now refer to an institution that is at the basis of all primitive societies and is no other than the moral law based on religious faith. We speak of the sacred interdict or taboo.

The *taboo* is a Polynesian word of the Tongan dialect: [11] it is composed of the root *ta* (marked) and *bu,* an adverb of intensity. It signifies, then, *especially marked,*[12] and applies to all—persons, animals, places, words, acts, etc.—that has been designated by competent authority as *sacred* and *forbidden* under pain of stain or sin. All infractions will cause death, disease, or some other misfortune, unless the guilty one has been absolved on each occasion on time and has made satisfaction by an appropriate penance, ordinarily an offering or a sacrifice.

This Maori word was destined to have a great career: to-day it is current, with its special meaning, in all European languages. But it has its equivalent among the Greeks (ἄγος and ἄγιος), among the Latins (*sacer*), among the Malays

---

[11] In the Samoan Islands, the Marquises, the Sonde Islands, New Ireland, and others, they say *tapu*, in the Hawaiian Islands *kapu*, the letters *t* and *k*, *b* and *p* being interchangeable.

[12] Cf. Frazer, *Golden Bough;* L. Marillier, *Grande Encyclopédie* (taboo); Reinach, *op. cit.*

(*pamali*), among the different races of North America
(*wakan*), among the Mpongwes of Gabon (*Orunda*), among
the Fans (*Eki*), among the Bantus of the eastern coast (*mwiko,
mzio*). This list might be prolonged indefinitely, for the notion
is universal and everywhere corresponds to the same idea.
The Swahili *mw-iko,* for example, comes from the verb *eka* (to
place, to put aside, to reserve) but it is applied only to what is
reserved and not to be touched in consequence of a religious
interdict.[13]

The law of the *taboo* was pointed out long ago, notably by
the missionaries of Oceania, while those of North America
have spoken especially of the law of the *totem*. *Totem* and
taboo are to-day welcomed by a number of anthropologists who
contend that these laws are nothing less than the original
source of all religion, morality, and civilization!

"Look as far back as we will into the past," writes Solomon
Reinach, "man submits to an inner or subjective restraint as
well as to an outer or objective one. Not only does he experience
obstacles, he creates them for himself, in the shape of fears and
scruples. In the course of time these fears and scruples have
taken to themselves names—moral law, religious law, political
law. And precisely as these three laws exist to-day and still
exercise their restraining influence on human activity, so they
existed—confused and undivided as yet—among the earliest of
savage communities. Morality, religion, and politics, as we
conceive them, had not so much as dawned on the primitive
mind, but man submitted to and accepted a multitude of
restraints which, taken as a whole, constituted what is called
the system of taboos. The general formula of the taboo is: 'Do
not do this, do not touch that.' It is the English *don't,* as
applied to children. The taboo, whatever form it may take,
has always the one characteristic, that it sets a bound to human
activity. This path is taboo, do not walk there. This fruit is
taboo, do not eat it. This field is taboo on such a day, do not
work there. Thus, unlike civil, religious, or moral law, the law
of taboo never implies action, but always abstention: it is a
curb, not a whip."

[13] This recalls what Voltaire wrote of the *Poèmes sacrés* of J. B. Rousseau: "Sacrés ils sont, car personne n'y touche!"

Reinach continues:

"Man is preëminently a social animal; at every stage of civilization he pictures the external world as an integral part of the same community as himself, and by a natural generalization concludes that the spiritual principle, which he feels to be working within him, must be working also in the infinite phenomena without him. Before he rises to a definite and consistent idea of godhead, he feels himself surrounded by gods, fears them and strives to live at peace with them.

"The general cause of taboos, then, is the fear of danger. . . . Are we not to this day everlastingly tempted to confuse temporal sequence with causal connection? *Post hoc, ergo propter hoc*—B follows A, therefore A is the cause of B—the fallacy is daily committed by education and illiteracy alike.

"The savage, lacking the notion of cause and effect but endowed with a memory, was certain to assign a given misadventure to some immediately preceding event, though nine times out of ten the two would be unconnected. Thus, in primitive communities, there grew up a vast oral tradition of leading cases: such or such an act has such or such a fatal consequence—on such or such a day I fell and hurt myself *because,* when I went out in the morning, I saw a snake. If all these hasty generalizations had taken root in any one community, fear would have suspended all action, and the community would have perished. But here, as in all things, selection played a part. The fears experienced by the tribal magnates—old men, chiefs, and priests—were shared by the rank and file, and gave rise to various scruples all more or less widely diffused: the rest were forgotten. Thus the taboos came into being. . . . The taboos correspond to fears, and the fears, in their turn, to rash generalizations from isolated facts." [14]

Did humanity stop there? Happily no. According to Reinach, it is due to religion that humanity did not remain imprisoned in the countless meshes of these taboos.

"Religion, organized in hierarchical form, was the first emancipator of man; it formed into codes such of these prescriptions and prohibitions as were given credit by infinitely varied superstitions."

[14] Reinach, *op. cit.,* p. 36.

Finally, by a fatal evolution, humanity necessarily tends to recognize and must preserve the laws that have a social utility; it must also free itself from religious laws, letting these fall into disuse little by little. Thus does morality get reduced to a good civil code. "All the rest is literature," or, as Reinach says, "scruples and prejudices."

In these theories—and their simple statement ill conceals the practical import of what is called, in the language of the day, "integral laicisation"—there is something to take and much to leave.

Has this system of taboos, prohibitions, or interdicts really the importance here given it? Do we find therein the initial germ of all the morality which has spread so widely over the world?

The reply to this question depends largely on the explanation we give of the taboo, the reason for its existence, what we will call its philosophy. This answer is contained in the conception, as we have already described it, which the primitive forms of nature.

This fundamental conception, ever living and inspiring so many of primitive man's other thoughts, is that man in this world is not completely at home. He finds himself placed here without quite knowing how, why, or by whom; he walks in a domain that seems to him open and free, and meets many things he desires. But he did not make it, he is not the proprietor and it would be wrong for him to use it as though he were. May it not be that all that nature thus offers him is a sort of bait placed within reach of his hand the more to tempt him?

Who knows? Here, for example, is a tree covered with fruit. He tries one, finds it good, eats it, and encouraged by the experience, he takes others: it is a permitted fruit. The day after, he perceives another tree; made confident by the repast of the preceding day, he takes some; but this fruit has not the same taste and makes him wretchedly sick; it was evidently a forbidden fruit. He will remember and, to save his children from the same experience, perhaps the same misfortune in relation to the hidden Master of creation, he will interdict that tree for them: "My children, that fruit is a forbidden fruit for us; do not touch it!"

This feeling, vague though it may be, is always keen and persistent in the mind of the primitive. While traveling one day in eastern Africa along with a European explorer who wished to become initiated in the things and people of the country, I arrived in the evening at an encampment where they pointed out many wild boars to us. My companion soon killed one. As our porters, true savages from the distant interior, refused to eat any of it because this meat was interdicted (*mwiko*) for them, he devoured an enormous slice by way of protest: what excruciating indigestion during the night! As my unfortunate companion, groaning, pressing his stomach, and making lamentable efforts to free himself, had awakened our men, they found nothing better to do than organize a circle about him, singing:

It's the pig, it's the pig,
It's the pig that revolts!

Then came the solo:

O pig!
Come out if you wish.
But do no evil to our white man,
For he ate you by mistake!

Finally the pig came out and this novice learned the true meaning of taboo that night.

But let us return to philosophy. The Master of things, when he conceals himself from the eyes of men, is only the more to be feared; by unexpected manifestations he frequently reveals himself and checks our immoderate desire to put hands on everything. Whence, not to speak of the indigestion by which forbidden food protests and comes forth, there are poisonings, diseases, deaths, epidemics, accidents, floods, droughts, etc., etc. For if the machinery of the world has gotten out of order, it is because, consciously or inadvertently, we have thrown handfuls of sand into the works, i.e., forbidden acts. In other words, if the universe appears stretched out before man like a well-laden table, there are, nevertheless, certain precautions to take before sitting down at it, certain forms of politeness to be observed, certain restrictions to bear in mind.

For safety, then, it is necessary "to know." And who will know, if not the "seer," the man in relation with the invisible, the priest who is at the same time, in primitive societies, the leader, the patriarch, the head of the family, of the clan, or of the tribe?

He it is who has been enlightened by a dream, forewarned by some inner or external notice, instructed by some experience, perhaps a painful one; it is for him to tell his followers what is proper and what is not, what is forbidden, what must not be eaten, what must not be touched, what must not be looked at, what must not be pronounced, what must not be done.

Once the interdict has been thus solemnly pronounced by the religious authority in the name of the higher Power whose will must be respected, absolute obedience is imposed under pain of compromising the whole community. In our judgment, such is the initial principle of the law of the taboo.

This principle has a double function. On one hand it separates the *sacred* from the *profane* and provides a place apart for whatever, in our external and visible world, is related to the supernatural world by appointment, service, and special consecration. Sacred persons, objects, places, ceremonies, all these must be kept apart in the use men make of them and must not be confused with the rest, with what each one may touch at will: for they have all felt the influence of the invisible world, are attributed to it, have become its property, have been *consecrated* to it. No one may henceforth lay hands on them except those who in fact or by identical consecration belong to that same world. In this sense we may say that the taboo is at the basis of religious worship.

But, on the other hand, it is at the basis of law, consequently of morality, and hence of civilization—all placed under the protection of the religious authority which designates, sanctions, and *consecrates* whatever it touches. By its religious character, the taboo is imposed as absolute and indisputable, and it implies immediate and severe penalties in case of violation. Thus it is particularly well suited to primitive society and organizes, disciplines, elevates, and restrains the too ardent inclinations of that society.

This explains why the English school of W. Robertson Smith, echoed by Reinach in France, has justly placed religion along with the institution of the taboo at the base of morality, law, and human civilization. "Religion has been the nurse and educator of humanity." [15]

But it is an error to see in the taboo, along with the totem, the initial and generating principle of religion itself and, through religion, of morality. In fact, since the taboo, in order to be respected, must rest on an authority of the invisible world, which is God or some spirit, this conception of the supernatural must necessarily be anterior to the taboo.

We have the profane world, the world of all those things that can be used without preoccupation or ceremony; above is the supernatural world, accessible to us only by a sort of mystical ladder represented by religious ceremonies; between the two, the sacred or taboo world which clings to both and consequently supposes both. This seems to be the primitive conception. Faith has preceded law.

Moreover, if we can assign the respect due to the sovereign Master of the world, the fear of nature and of the spirits that animate it, as original and general causes of the taboo, this religious feeling must necessarily coexist with a moral sentiment. In fact, if I feel that I ought not to touch such or such a product because the invisible world seems to have reserved it for itself, this implies that I have at the same time a conscious conviction that it is unjust and evil to lay hands on what does not belong to me. To observe the interdict will, then, be good, to violate it will be evil, that is, a sin creating a stain and demerit that can be removed only by condonation or pardon.

We will make another statement, which our ardent evolutionists can not reject. Animals as well as men find them-

[15] Reinach, *op. cit.*

selves in the presence of the products of nature; they have felt the same evil consequences from the indiscriminate use of everything, they have noticed the same dangers and have consequently experienced the same fears. Yet they have imposed no taboos on themselves. Why? Simply because the idea has not visited them that certain products might be reserved by an invisible world, that hence it would be unjust to touch them, and that, in case of violation, the injustice, the fault, or the sin would call for punishment.

The conclusion is always the same: the principle of the law or interdict, which supposes the religious notion, supposes also the moral notion, supposes conscience.

Once the principle of the taboo was admitted, it was too fruitful not to be utilized by all those who could profit from it. At first an instrument of religious moralization, the interdict soon became a means of government, a prescription of hygiene, a medical regulation, a source of revenue, a pretext for the exercise of real tyranny, and a nest of unreasonable, unjust, and oppressive superstitions.

Therefore it frequently happens that the use of meat is forbidden to women and children: what is good and particularly desirable is reserved for the men, or for such and such a class of men. The members of the secret societies, for instance, enjoy numerous privileges that are absolutely forbidden to the profane.

Along the Ogowe River (in Gabon), before the Europeans had established freedom of navigation, the chieftains on its banks opened or closed the river *ad libitum* by imposing or removing the interdict. When the river was closed, it was impossible for any canoe to set out: the Ogowe was *orunda* and no native would have ventured on it for anything in the world. But the interdict could be raised: it was simply necessary to pay the price.

In certain tribes no one may see the chief eat. In Oudoé (Zanguebar) the country is ruled by three chiefs who deliberate together on what decisions to take, but no one of them may look at the other without putting his life in jeopardy:

so they meet in a hut with three separate compartments and thus govern their states.

But the really interesting taboos, interesting because they are moral and moralizing, are those which apply to the family, through the family to the tribe, and hence to society.

It is indeed a remarkable fact and quite in conformity with what we have already established, that numerous moral prescriptions—in the sense in which we understand the morality of the primitives—operate to draw all the members of the family close together, fathers, mothers, children, from the crib to the grave, for the evident purpose of organizing the family, maintaining it, strengthening it, purifying it, preserving therein its blood, traditions, spirit, unity, and alliances, warding off all sorts of dangers that might threaten it, and procuring for the family the protection or at least the neutrality of the ancestral manes which have left it to enter the world beyond.

The animal, confined by an instinct of conservation that does not permit it to abuse a moral liberty to which it is a total stranger, has no need of these laws in order to reproduce itself and perpetuate its species: its *amorality* never becomes *immorality*.

It is not so with man. Because he is free, able to use and to abuse, capable of good and evil, he does need to be guided, restrained, watched over, and, in case of need, punished. If left entirely to himself, without any check, without any religion, without any law, it would have required no other means for his destruction than his own inclinations. In all primitive societies that we have studied, we find the family is the essential organ of social life, the guarantee against the most ordinary causes of perversion and dispersion.

The infant Black, even before its birth, is protected by various taboos that affect its mother and even its father. From its conception until its weaning, these latter may have no sexual relations. In many places certain foods are forbidden them, they must not touch a corpse, they will not even be present at the obsequies of their relatives, they will not eat (terrible privation!) any animal that has burst open. The little creature whose life is still embryonic would suffer from that contact with death, and its parents are responsible before the family.

After the infant comes into the world, it is necessary to see at once whether it is "interdicted"; there are tribes where infants often are. They are "interdicted," for example, if they are twins, if they are deformed, if they have made their mother suffer, if they have teeth at their birth, if the teeth of the upper jaw appear before the others, and so forth. In such case their lot is quickly determined: an aged sorceress, filling the office of midwife, strangles the unfortunate little being under her arm by twisting its neck; then the body is enclosed in an earthen vessel and, thus shrouded, is thrown into the neighboring forest where, in the space of a single night, bands of voracious ants remove its every trace.[16]

If allowed to live, the infant recognized as "good" continues until the age of two years to form one body, so to speak, with its mother like the young of the opossum. Perched on her back, astride her hip, or enclosed in a bag made of antelope's skin, it eats, sleeps, smiles, cries, and thus undergoes the apprenticeship of life.

Finally it takes to the ground, first on all fours, soon after on two feet. It grows fast and little by little, with extraordinary precocity and good humor, goes to work. The parents have great love for their children although they appear to take very little care of them and to be only vaguely concerned about their moral education. On the other hand, they watch carefully to see that the taboos imposed on the children are not infringed, such as eating certain food. Those who show vicious tendencies are punished, at times severely.

Generally a name is not given to the child until he is old enough to answer it himself. This name is taken from circumstances or depends upon the whims of the mother, father, or some relative. Names of animals are frequent.

Age is not counted by years but by the size, which is often indicated with the hand, the palm held vertically for men and horizontally for animals.

[16] Not long ago this practice was still widespread in the Zigua country (Zanguebar).

The age of puberty comes. Until then the child had, we may say, counted for nothing, he lived as he liked and was neither man nor woman. Now the time has come for him to be ranked in one of these two categories of the human species and definitely attached to his family, clan, and tribe. He possesses the qualities needful for forming a new social nucleus by founding a new home. This is the object of the initiation.[17]

The initiation, to which both sexes are subjected, varies in its ceremonial from tribe to tribe. But it is to be found everywhere, at least in a state of partial survival, here of a simple nature, there more complicated, symbolic, and solemn.

Naturally there is a difference between the initiation of the boys and that of the girls. But in either case the initiation does not take place until there is a certain number of eligible young people of the same village or neighboring villages. When the day arrives, the boys between fifteen and eighteen or twenty years of age are assembled under the direction of a specialist. Dressed in special costume, they are subjected to various ordeals which they must manfully endure. It is a sort of retreat that they make, living, eating, sleeping apart, generally in a near-by forest. They devote themselves to various exercises, repeat certain songs and dances, are mysteriously instructed in what is permitted or forbidden, receive new taboos, and become acquainted with the traditions and interests of the tribe. This is also the occasion for renewing the alliance with the totem by symbolic ceremonies, a sacrifice and a communion. The whole initiation lasts several days, often several weeks or months. Their black skin is entirely or partly covered by a white paint made of a chalk mixture or flour; this is the color of the spirits.[18] The ornaments of their costume are often very complicated. Dances follow one another. Often a new name is given: it is a second birth. Then the candidates

---

[17] This family initiation is not to be confused with that which preceded entrance into a secret society, properly so called. Cf. E. de Jonghe, *Les sociétés secrètes au Bas-Congo*.

[18] The spirits are white. With this white paint the people often mix some ashes from their ancestors' bones which thus "sanctify" it and put the new members of the family into relation with the manes of their relatives.

receive the distinctive marks of the tribe, file their teeth according to special requirements, are tattooed according to rule, and are relieved of the various taboos of childhood. Generally the whole ceremony is terminated by a great feast, including a solemn procession, dinner, dances, and presents, not to speak of the drinking which must be provided with particular care.

Ordinarily it is in the course of this initiaton that the ceremony of circumcision takes place wherever the custom exists. Though this practice is actively kept up among many Bantu tribes, in many others it is not, either because it has never become known among them or because it has been abandoned after long wars or extensive journeys, or for some other reason.[19] The Negrillos do not practice it. In some places where the primitive sense of the ceremony has evidently been forgotten, children undergo it at an earlier age, about ten years old or seven, and even at two years of age, in order to make it easier and less painful. But by ordinary rule it coincides with the period of puberty and the initiation that accompanies it.

What is the reason for it?

"It is impossible to give the reason," says a colonial physician, making allusion to explanations often assigned, "other than religious necessity. There is nothing to indicate any anatomical point of view; from the point of view of the passions it has very little influence on the temperament; and from the hygienic point of view it is insufficient." [20]

Our own judgment is that circumcision is related to the institution of the taboo: ordinarily it is the removal of a prohibition. Before passing through this ceremony, a young man may not marry; he is not received by any woman, and has no right to marriage relations. If, nevertheless, this happens— and it does happen!—the child that is born of this forbidden

---

[19] This is what has happened among the Zulus and, according to the testimony of Junod, among the Ba-ronga in 1820. Other tribes are mentioned where this practice has been introduced or reintroduced. There is evidently no question of Mohammedan populations nor of Islamized populations, among whom circumcision is an obligatory religious rite.

[20] *Dépêche Coloniale*, Sept. 3, 1907.

union is considered "bad," and must disappear. It is the same with the girls who become mothers before passing through the initiation that concerns them. In some places this accident is regarded as a public misfortune and must be expiated by a great sacrifice offered to God.[21] Therein we have an interesting and typical illustration of our principle established above. The transmission of human life takes place in a mysterious realm where the action of the sovereign Master of creation is manifested or at least suspected, and where man can be admitted only with a sort of authorization from him, obtained by means of an appropriate ceremony. At the appointed time the interdict can be removed but, as in all like cases, the "permission to use" must be acquired by a sacrifice, with effusion of blood: hence the circumcision, whose moral purpose is evident, since the taboo or interdict which it removes rigorously forbids the sexual relations between children who have not arrived at the age of puberty.

We understand also that this institution, which is known throughout Africa, is likewise met with in Oceania and even in America, among the Polynesians, Australians, and many of the redskins. For it to become thus widespread, there must be some general reason for its existence. This general reason is no other than the sacred interdict carried out in the moral interest of the family and removed, when necessary, in the same interest.[22]

The girls undergo a similar ceremony, which changes according to the place. R. E. Dennett thus describes it as existing in Congo:

"A small hut or shed is built outside the town for the girl. The hair of her head is shaved off and her whole body is covered with takula, or powdered red wood mixed with water. Thus painted, the maiden retires with friends of hers who have already gone through the ceremony to the little hut. Here she is presented with a fowl, or if the family cannot afford this, an egg.

[21] This is the case in Loango. See Dennett, *op. cit.*, pp. 67-70.

[22] At one time it used to be held that the practice of circumcision originated with the Hebrews. In this, as in many other matters, they made the Bible say what it does not say.

The maiden rests here for six days while her companions watch and amuse and feed her during the day, serving her as if she were a princess, and at night singing and dancing to the music of the misunga (the great dried pod of the Baobab tree).

"In the meantime a nice shinbec or hut is built for her in town, wherein two beds are placed. Upon one of these, accompanied by two of her older friends, the maiden sleeps, while the other is placed at the disposal of her other and younger friends. Each day she twice submits to the painting process, and for four or five months is not permitted to work in any way.

"When the time comes for her to be handed over to her husband, one of his relations proceeds to this shinbec at the break of day, and pulls her bed out of the hut by one of its legs. If she is not yet engaged to be married, then it is her father who pulls the bed out into the open. Then all the women of the maiden's family, carrying umbrellas and clean clothes and ornaments for her, take her down to the salt water, and beat the paint off her with pliant twigs; then they proceed to the nearest fresh water stream and wash and dress. The maiden's legs are loaded with great brass rings, her arms with smaller ones, while her neck and waist are hung with all the family's coral, across her breast a colored handkerchief is hung, and the general color of the cloth or skirt hanging to her waist is red; an umbrella completes her outfit. Then a procession is formed, and all her friends, twirling their umbrellas, sing and march through the town or towns on their way home again. All along the route the young men in the towns come out and dance before her, presenting her with some small offering. Then she is taken to her husband, and dancing is kept up during the night." [23]

After the initiation is over, it is really a new life that begins for the young man and woman. They can now think of marriage and mingle in what concerns their sex, in family affairs, and in the affairs of the village and tribe. The young woman does not have to wait long for a purchaser. But the young man must often wait a long while before he is regularly married, obliged as he is to gather the necessary dowry for the "purchase" of his wife. This dowry is often relatively high and while he is seeking it, the available young women are monopolized by the older, richer, and more influential. That

[23] Dennett, *op. cit.*, p. 69.

is one of the great social inconveniences of polygamy, which practically amounts to injustice and tyranny and becomes a cause of immorality and depopulation.

The Blacks are aware of this evil consequence, but as the passions and interests of the seniors predominate, the practice continues.

As to the young people, since the initiation has removed the interdict, they are allowed whatever relations they wish, provided they do not have any children.

Marriage is also surrounded by different ceremonies and numerous prohibitions. In the first place it can not take place between relatives nor generally between persons of the same village. Among these people the prohibitions on marriage between relatives are far more extensive and more strictly kept than with us.[24]

Incestuous relations between brothers, sisters, and in general all relatives are also forbidden.

Conjugal relations during pregnancy and the period of nursing, during the hunting time, during war, and at certain other periods, are likewise forbidden.

Adultery is forbidden.

Although marriage is generally unstable, yet it exists by virtue of a real contract of purchase and sale. For the contract to be definitely concluded, however, the dowry must be completely paid. But as this full payment, in western Africa, is often delayed for years after the delivery of the woman, she is at times tempted to return to her family, her family is also tempted to recall her. This is the cause of incessant and interminable conferences from which arise vindictive lawsuits, adjustments, insults, blows, vengeance, bewitchings, bitterness, hatred, which greatly complicate the existence of this man of pure, free nature, whom Rousseau once proposed to us for our model.

There are also recognized causes for divorce, implying the return of the dowry: for example, on the woman's side, wickedness and incorrigible habitual laziness, suspicions of magic,

---

[24] It is useless to repeat what we have already said about exogamy and totemism.

often adultery; on the man's side, an insult to the mother-in-law.

The woman who returns to her family usually takes her children with her: *partus sequitur ventrem*.

Other prescriptions enforced in the name of religion and moral duty govern the family relations, the obligations of children, of the wife and mother, of the husband, the father, and the head of the house.

Death comes. According to age, sex, and condition, the funeral is carefully regulated and surrounded with countless prohibitions. In short, life, death, and survival after death, are full of prohibitions.

Other customs, of the same character, preside over the organization, life, and defense of the village and tribe, which are the extension of the family. These prescriptions are published on occasion of public works, a feast, mourning, a ceremony, a new installation, an emigration, a clearing, a great hunt, a public misfortune to be conjured, an epidemic to be dispelled, a crime to be expiated, an invasion, a war, or some such occasion. Their character is permanent or transitory according as they proceed from the ancestors and have been transmitted as customs, or have been enacted as temporary measures by the chiefs or by sorcerers or especially by the executive committees of the local secret societies.

In addition to faults, offenses, or crimes condemned by justice as inflicting a real injury on another, such as abusive language, insult, calumny, theft, violent attacks, poisoning, bewitching, homicide, which everywhere in the black country are regarded as forbidden and punishable; in addition to proscriptions and prohibitions enacted by civil and religious authorities relating to the family and society in general, is there any recognition of "sins," in which one commits evil only against himself?

Is it judged, for instance, a moral fault to be wanting in temperance, to be slothful, jealous, proud, to be a liar, to give way to anger, avarice, luxury?

This question is difficult to answer with precision. In fact, we can scarcely detect that the primitive cares either little or much for his moral perfection. He is what he is and remains so, although he avoids the discredit of faults that are too unpleasant or shocking, that would bring reproach, alienate him from his friends and their gatherings, that would create a difficult situation among his relatives. But, on the other hand, all these faults or habits are infamous, and individual conscience in the depth of these dense natures certainly does awake at times to condemn them.

Sometimes a lack of moral sense is met with that quite disconcerts us: it may be a calm and ferocious egoism, or deep conceit, perfect treachery, cool and deliberate cruelty, or a shameless want of pity for the weak, the sick, the useless, the abandoned.

And yet, withal, what good dispositions we find, what easy and ever ready hospitality, what fidelity to their word, what attachment, generosity, disinterestedness, endurance, courage! By their reserve and modesty these savages frequently give civilized man wonderful surprises. Vices against nature are everywhere rare and seem even to be unknown in many places. Public indecency is not allowed. While in some places abbreviated clothes are worn, this paradise costume is worn with such ease, simplicity, candor, reserve, and, we may even say, with so much dignity that no one thinks evil of it and the most modest eyes easily become accustomed to it. Truly might we apply the adage: *Honny soyt, qui mal y pense!*

By way of summary and complement to what has been said thus far, we are pleased to cite a curious picture of laws and prohibitions among the Bavili of Loango. It is taken from the work of R. E. Dennett[25] already referred to.

"The Bavili," says Dennett, "have a very distinct idea of the moral and natural law, and classify their sins into five distinct sections of the one great class of laws called Xina or things forbidden.

"The first section is called Xina Xivanga Nzambi, or that which is contrary to God the Creator."

[25] Dennett, *op. cit.*, pp. 50-52.

The second refers to the magic mirror—resembling photography—into which only the *Nganga Nzambi* (the "seeing of God") may look to discover therein the successor of the chief of Loango, made, they say, after the image of God.

"The third we find in the way the mothers correct their children when they talk foolishly of God."

The fourth prescribes the observance of each fourth day. On this day "the prince or father may have no connection with his wife, he may not go outside of his town, he may not hold a palaver. The doctor of Nganga Bilongo may not bleed his patient. The women may not work in the fields.

"The fifth comprises all those ceremonies and things forbidden concerning maternity. A woman must not sleep with her husband on the ground. A girl must not have connection with a man before she has passed through the 'paint house' (that is, before submitting to initiation). No dishonor to their parents must be thought of."

Another series of "sins":

1. To kill (a man of your own tribe).
2. To commit adultery.
3. To steal.
4. To bear false witness.

Another series:

To desire what does not belong to you: for example, at the market, where everything placed under the tree of the place is sacred, as this tree is intended to shelter the body of the deceased king before his removal to the grave.

Lastly comes the class of totemistic prohibitions concerning marriage between relatives. Infraction of these prohibitions is punished by God, who then holds back the rain at the time when it ought to come.

In all the above we find no question of slavery, suicide, and many other matters. In Africa, slavery is not regarded as something forbidden: it is the only form of domestic service known. As a master has all the rights of property over his slave, he may use him as his interest dictates. But useless cruelties would be regarded as evil, and in fact are rare.

Suicide is little known except, it seems, among some tribes of the interior near Tanganyika.

As for sorcery, i.e., practice of black magic and witchcraft, there is no need to speak. It is an unpardonable crime, everywhere punished by death under the most terrible and ignominious conditions.

The transgression of a prohibition or the perpetration of a fault or crime is reputed to be "sin" (*nsem* the Fans say), involving moral stain and punishment.

Children, idiots, and fools are not considered as personally responsible for their acts but the party injured may obtain a suitable indemnity from the relatives of such.

To wound or kill an adversary in legitimate self-defense is allowable, and to take whatever one finds on a plantation when one is hungry—provided it be done openly.

But one is responsible for every death occurring in his home unless he can prove that he had nothing to do with it, which is not always easy.

In the casuistry of the savage, free consent is not necessary to create a fault or at least a stain. Every violation of a taboo, for example, whether willed or not, is bad and punishable. More than that; there are some people who, without knowing it, are guilty of practicing witchcraft, of killing their neighbor, of plucking out the soul of some one while he is asleep, of being the unconscious cause of numerous calamities. Some have a sort of vampire within them which, during their sleep, wanders about, puts different persons to death, and finally kills them themselves. Thus in Gabon, on the death at the one time of several persons, the bodies are opened to look for this dread beast and . . . they often find it!

These sins are not all of the same nature. In Loango, for example, there are offenses against God and offenses against man. For the former, not only the guilty person, but the whole community is considered responsible and held to reparation. Such would be a case of incest, of marriage between near relatives, adultery with the wife of the king, moral disorders between young people who have not yet passed through the ceremonies of initiation.

For other offenses, the guilty person is responsible and, in his default, each member of his family is responsible, but free to turn against him.

But where the sin implies personal stain and a punishment inflicted by the powers invisible, is there no means of purifying one's self and freeing one's soul?

It is curious to note that these people have felt that necessity. To free themselves from remorse, to recover peace of mind, and to resume the path of life without reproach, those who are guilty have special ceremonies which they undergo and, if needs be, are compelled to undergo. There is none more astonishing than the remission of sins, obtained in Kikuyu (British East Africa) by confession, followed by absolution and penance. It is worthy of note that Kikuyu has remained until these last years absolutely closed to Europeans and so there is no question that this may be a Christian importation. The ceremony is called *Ko-tahikio* (literally, *to vomit,* sc. sin). It is described by J. Cayzac, C.S.Sp., missionary at Nairobi. Among the Wa-Kikuyu, the *megiro* (taboos) are countless and the transgression of the least of them constitutes a *sahu* or *sin.* If, for instance, a serpent crosses my path, if the wind fells one of my trees, if a hyena deposits its dung near my hut, I have a *sahu* on my conscience; and if I keep it there, death will strike me, or my children will have to suffer or my herd will perish.

One must go "vomit" his sin.

Confessor and penitent install themselves in the open air at some deserted corner of the village. They squat on the ground and the confession begins:

I accuse myself of a serpent that crossed my path.
I accuse myself of a frog that jumped into my fire.
I accuse myself of a pot that poured the soup on the ground.
And I especially accuse myself of having shaved my wife's head.

At each of the *sahu* which he thus spits out, the penitent expectorates.

"These are the sins of the Kikuyus," adds Father Cayzac, "or rather some of their sins, for they have hundreds of them, without counting the others, the real ones, which they must also confess at times. They are so persuaded of the evil influence of sin that they even believe a child may suffer for the faults of his parents: thus, two or three days after its birth, every little Kikuyu is the object of a ceremony designed to free it from all moral stains it may have. Should it later on fall sick, its father and mother will go and make their confession to obtain its cure.

"As a preliminary necessity the penitent must be accompanied by a fine sheep that he presents to the 'confessor,' as a visible sign of his interior repentance. As to this offering there is no compromise, but they are more accommodating on the question of the avowal of sins. When any one finds himself embarrassed in confessing such or such a fault, the confessor hands him a little stick: the penitent retires, tells his sin to the stick, which he then hands back to the sorcerer. The latter gladly accepts the avowal as though made to himself.

"The absolution follows. Turning his eyes successively to the four directions, the confessor pronounces the formula: 'God who art in front, remove his sins; God who art behind, God who art to the right, God who art to the left, remove his sins.' Then he says in these very words: 'I free thee from thy sins, all, those which thou knowest and those which thou knowest not.' After this, he leans over the penitent, makes a sign of taking the stains out of his heart, and throws them far, far away.

"When this is done, the good Kikuyu goes away, relieved of his faults . . . and of his sheep."

At the other extremity of Africa, a sort of confession exists among the Fans, at least those along the bank of the Como (estuary of the Gabon).

A Fan who is sick is invited by the feticher to avow his sins so as to obtain his cure. The confession takes place before the men of the village, in the midst of a scene especially prepared. The sins that are to be revealed are usually ritualistic faults, violations of things forbidden or sacred, taboo or "eki," sometimes even acts that are insignificant in themselves and that imply no idea of fault. However, grave faults and even crimes have been made known under such circumstances, although this is not generally the case.

"Tell thy sin," cries the feticher to the sick man. And as soon as the latter has uttered a new accusation, the feticher, in his capacity of penitentiary, cries: *Kan oshu nki!* literally "May thy fault fly abroad, toward the sea." And the others present repeat: *Kan oshu nki!* "May it fly abroad!"

The ceremony is complicated by purifications, aspersions, and the sacrifice of a hen or goat on which the feticher and the rest of the gathering make a meal at the expense of the sick man. If he does not get better, it is because his confession was not complete.[26]

Although this particular practice of confession is special to certain tribes, yet everywhere sin implies a judgment, a compensation or a penance to obtain remission. Everywhere sin has the character of an offense or wrong against God, the spirits, the manes, the chief, the father, the neighbor; as we have already asserted, in the mind of the primitive every injury requires reparation or payment that justice may be satisfied and that the two sides of the scale, momentarily disturbed, may resume their equilibrium.

Children are chastised; but adults when guilty, are condemned to pay a fine in money, articles of exchange, goats, sheep, or oxen, women or slaves, according to the case.

Imprisonment, as we practice it, is unknown. But there are various substitutes. One of the best known is the use of fetters consisting of a long bar of wood which holds the prisoner's feet. Scourging is done with thongs cut from the skin of the lamentin, rhinoceros, or hippopotamus. In some places mutilation is frequently resorted to: for example, for a thief they will cut off one ear, a finger, and often a hand.

If the fault committed is an offense against the invisible world, a sacrifice is rigorously necessary. And if the crime

[26] Note of Father Briault, C.S.Sp., missionary in Gabon.

is such as to provoke the anger of God or the manes of their ancestors against the country or the tribe, the country or the tribe must free itself by a public expiation.

The judge may be the sorcerer, the father of the family, the chief, or the council of the ancients: all depends on the nature of the infractions.

One penalty may be redeemed by another. A man condemned to death can free himself by offering a sum to be determined by discussion, or by giving up one or several of his slaves to be killed in his stead.

We have remarked that all the members of a family are liable for the deeds of the whole family. We must agree that this legislation is readily explained in a country where it is so easy for criminals to disappear and escape the reprisals of justice. The family is supposed to surrender the guilty member or the one who is to take his place; otherwise he will be taken by hook or crook even if it be necessary to wait weeks, months, or years.

"Blood for blood": the law is absolute and universal, except in case one can redeem himself.

If, despite every effort, the author of some injury remains unknown, all hope of reparation, that is of vengeance, is not lost: there is still another resource; to find a good sorcerer, "file a complaint against person unknown," and wait. They will then proceed to a magical "envoutement," [27] and justice will be done.

But in case of doubt, as frequently happens, recourse is had to a judicial test or ordeal [28] which, in spite of its character, is a sort of appeal to immanent justice for a judgment to supplement that of men.

This test is of two degrees: for ordinary cases, when a question between two litigants is to be decided, when a thief is to be found, or a confession extorted; and for cases of witchcraft, on the occasion of a death or serious illness, an epidemic, or a public misfortune. It varies according to the place. In some localities the accused is pricked on the arm with a red-hot

* [27] See page 230.
[28] Ordeal, Anglo-Saxon *ordaal*, German *urtheil*, "judgment."

spear: if it does not burn, it is a sign of his innocence; if he feels the burn, he is guilty. In other places they use boiling water into which the accused dips his hand. But the usual ordeal is to have him swallow a concoction made from the bark of a certain tree, powerfully poisonous, that is called *Nkasa* in Congo.

"Sometimes the stomach rejects the noxious compound," says Bentley, "and the man vomits, in which case he is declared innocent, and the witch doctor loses his fee—indeed, in some parts is heavily fined for the false charge. More often, if he has not avoided the risk by ascribing the death to some charm, or to some person recently dead, he makes sure of his case. His victim staggers and falls. With a wild yell the bystanders rush at him, beat him to death, burn or bury him alive, throw him over a precipice, or in some way finish the terrible work, exhibiting a savage ferocity equal to their deep sense of the enormity of the crime laid to his charge." [29]

Among other tribes, the Fans of Gabon for example, a death is avenged in a different way: the guilty person is seized or, lacking him, some member of his family, killed and eaten. Thereby justice is truly satisfied: blood for blood, man for man!

This is not all. The sanction of morality is equally assured by the action of that higher, invisible world from which nothing escapes.

If any one has a misfortune, an illness, or other trouble, his neighbors and those of his own household will consider it a just punishment for faults committed by him. He will attempt an expiation by making an offering or a sacrifice to the spirits or the manes.

A village may do the same, or even at times a whole tribe.

Lastly, there is the sanction passed on a man's lot by the other world. Vague, undefined, and obscure it is in some minds, but with others it is evident in the different destinies that await the disembodied souls. *Quisque suos patimur manes* ("We suffer in our manes; each one in his own"), said Virgil. That is also what our Blacks think. No soul passing into

[29] Rev. Bentley, *Dict. and Grammar of the Kongo Language* (Nganga).

the other life is at first completely happy. Little by little those who have in themselves a greater power of initiative, as the manes of chiefs, warriors, or "seers," finally achieve equality with the spirits and genii.

Souls of no account fall into a lethargy.

The evil soul sometimes has to wander in a cold dark forest; sometimes, hanging on the trunk of a tree, it will shiver at night and grow pale from suffering and anguish; and sometimes, say the Fans, it will be cast into the *Ototolan* and there will end by gradually burning until there is nothing left of it, like the torches made of bark and resin which, in the equatorial forest, are burned as a guide at night.

Now that we have replied at sufficient length to the questions which we proposed above, let us summarize what we have said.

1. Beyond any doubt, our Blacks have a morality whose basis is fundamentally just the same as that acknowledged by the conscience of the whole human species, whatever race, country, or period of its development be considered. The soul of the primitive is made like our soul: between the two types there is not the slightest essential difference. Only the applications of morality differ, "on this side of the Pyrenees and on the other," as on this side of the ocean and on the other. This variability can be understood. In the *interpretation* of the code of universal laws, can we really expect agreement among the twelve or fifteen hundred million judges at present in the world?

Morality, we are told, gathers together the conventions and prejudices created by the mind of man and slowly evolves in accord with the general progress of human groups during the course of the ages. Hence Africa is a magnificent field of observation for us: if the theory is correct, there will be manifest a gradation in morality from the most backward populations to the most advanced in civilization. In fact, the gradation does exist; but the ranks are strangely confused and even reversed. It is well recognized that our unfortunate little Negrillos, who have stopped at the very first rung on the ladder of progress, have a speculative and practical morality certainly superior to many African tribes relatively civilized. The most disgusting anthropophagites at present in the world are without doubt the Bondjos of Ubanghi: but the Bondjos are very well formed, intelligent people, lacking nothing, superior in everything to the tribes around them, except in morality.

Let me cite another experience. The Catholic missions that are to-day found scattered throughout the African interior, receive children and young men belonging to the various tribes of the black continent and teach them, among other things, the text and the practice of the decalogue. It is found that, on the whole, the sons of savages and cannibals soon form a boarding-school as elevated certainly in morality, if not more so, as many European colleges. This transformation takes place in a few months. What was necessary for its accomplishment? Certainly not the complete reversal of these natures and the creation of thoroughly new consciences. All that is required is the removal of some errors, the rectification of certain prejudices, and on the common basis of universal morality found in every "soul of good will," the construction of Christian morality, which is admirably adapted to that foundation. I justly conclude therefore that it is incorrect to maintain, for individuals as for nations, that morality can be purified only by the long work of centuries and the persistent action of heredity.

Do not raise the objection that these same children, when they are set down in a European environment, often become more deceitful, slothful, dishonest, and worthless than they were before. I admit it at once and even draw therefrom another argument for my thesis. Among their tribes these children had a pagan morality. At the mission they adopted Christian morality. In contact with Europeans, where they now become "boys" for every kind of service, they have adopted the independent morality which, without support or sanction of any kind (except the club and the prison), becomes a deplorably lax morality. But who is to blame?

Will you say that, despite all, this training is insufficient for young human plants brought up in hot-houses, that it is a forced, hasty, and more or less artificial moralization?

We have other examples.

About sixty years ago, entire populations of black slaves— i.e., the lowest element from the moral point of view—who had been taken from the African coast and transported to the Antilles of the Indian Sea, were freed and Christianized. Since then unfortunately, in the French colonies at least, they have had to suffer a great deal from political conditions which fomented wars of races, colors, and persons, and too often resulted in the crushing of the vanquished and the monopoly of all the lucrative positions by the victors. Yet, if we wish to be just and impartial, we will agree that the average morality of these people is not appreciably lower than the generality of European morality; the courts are not more encumbered with cases; murder, theft, rape, and other heinous crimes are not more frequent. It is true that family ties appear less sacred; but in those countries where habits are loose, are the Blacks the only ones to practice "free unions"? If the Americans of the United States protest, it is easy to answer: "If your Blacks are without morality, what have you done to moralize them?"

2. The taboo plays a curious and interesting part in the discipline imposed on man and in the organization of the first societies which are an extension of the family. But we would greatly exaggerate the importance of the taboo if we made it the whole of primitive morality. The taboo is no more morality than the totem is religion.

Both are explained by the mentality of the first men and the mentality of those who even to-day still resemble them in their spirit, still continue their traditions, and follow their customs.

But both necessarily presuppose religious beliefs on which to rest and a foundation of natural morality to support all the prohibitions and laws that have been given to men. In fact, the totem and the taboo are superstitions: the totem, a superstition and parasite of religion; the taboo, a superstition and parasite of morality.

3. What remains to be added on the subject of the pretended lack of connection between religion and morality in primitive civilizations? If you have grasped the developments of the preceding pages, you will doubtless have concluded that this question has been ill put and ill solved. We willingly grant that morality does not come from naturism nor from animism. "Visible nature is not moral," A. Réville said with some reason.[30]

"As to the spirits separate from nature," he adds, "spirits whose worship constitutes animism, projections of the human spirits that adore them and that imagine them quite like themselves, these capricious, fantastic, irascible, and plaguing spirits do not offer the least evidence for attaching a moral sentiment to their character or for any advantage to be derived from a religious union with them."[31]

That is true. But we forget an essential fact: the religion of the Blacks is neither completely animism nor completely naturism, in the sense ordinarily attached to these words. Whatever that religion may be, it imposes on its followers, practices and prohibitions not all of which are dangerous, ridiculous, or useless. It places a check, often efficacious, on the evil passions of man, regulates his life in a certain way, and constitutes a moral rule for him. In other words, experience proves that it is better for a society to have a rudimentary religion than none at all, to be fetichist than atheistic. That is the plain truth.

It is a truth now confirmed by an interesting social experiment carried on at present under our eyes along the African coasts where European settlements are founded at regular intervals. About these "colonies" where Whites, Blacks, and half-breeds fuse together, called there by diverse interests, and where the moralization of the native generally counts for nothing, the local beliefs, the customs, practices, and prohibitions of the ancestral religion are soon forgotten and disappear. Family bonds are relaxed. The Blacks become more and more dis-

[30] Réville, *Les religions des peuples non civilisés*, I, p. 119.
[31] *Ibid.*

organized. Soon all that remains of the ancient tribes that
were found there, are some individuals without cohesion, with
little that is interesting and little that is commendable about
them, who do not reproduce themselves. In Gabon, for instance, under our very eyes the Mpongwes, the Bengas, the
Galoas, the Enengas, the Nkomis, and the Bavili are thus
coming to an end: our "civilization" has killed them. If the
savages of the interior did not continually come to settle on
the coasts, the coasts would soon be uninhabited. Everywhere
is the same decimation.

Why?

One day I was treating wth an old chief of Bata (now in
Spanish Guinea) in regard to the establishment of a Catholic
mission on his lands.

"Yes," he said to me; "come, and hasten: for if you delay,
you will no longer find us! The Whites have come here. They
have brought commerce here. They have settled soldiers here.
They have called in strangers. They have brought their boats
full of merchandise. All that is well. But my children no
longer believe in anything, my daughters are scattered everywhere, the ancients are no longer listened to. The Whites have
taken our beliefs from us and have given us nothing in their
place. That is why we are going to die."

And the old chief added:

"Come among us, you, the missionaries. You will not give
us back the customs of our fathers; but you will teach us yours.
We will hear you; perhaps God wishes to make us still live!"

And it seemed to me that day that my old black chief reasoned better on a matter of colonial sociology than many of
our parliamentarians, and better than some of our governors.

CHAPTER VI

WORSHIP

I. WHAT IS WORSHIP?

As morality is the practice of belief, external worship is its expression. Wherever there is a religion, there is a worship, and wherever we find a worship, we may say that it presupposes a religion.

Religion, in fact, rests on the conviction that above men and nature there exist higher powers on whom we depend, towards whom we have duties to fulfill, and with whom we must be on favorable terms so as to avoid at least the physical evils that always threaten us and to obtain leave from them to pursue our destiny.

At the same time the conscience of man, while showing the criminality of certain acts and making him fear the punishments that he feels he has deserved, leads him to seek the means of calming the mysterious powers he has offended and whose reproaches he hears echoing in the depth of his soul.

173

In fact, if man has one or several masters in the dominating invisible world, he owes them a homage of respect, an acknowledgment of sovereignty, an avowal of his dependence. His duty and interest lead him to implore their help, to endeavor to calm their wrath and win back their favor when he has lost it; and in expressing these various dispositions, to employ visible, external means, prayers and ceremonies that seem to him best suited to attain these ends.

All this ensemble of means employed by man to enter into relation with the world invisible, constitutes what we call WORSHIP.

In this homage of worship, we may consider: the object to which it is addressed; the ministers who are charged with it; the external manifestations that it occasions.

The question of worship must not be mixed with that of magic. As the counterfeit of religion, magic also has a worship with its determined object, its secret practices, its witchcraft, and its organization. But to unite under the one title and to treat together two things entirely opposed, would be a source of confusion. We must say, nevertheless, that, in the state in which religious matters exist in the black country, it is often difficult to mark out a clear line of separation between religious and magical worship: let us try to do so, however.

II.   THE OBJECT OF RELIGIOUS WORSHIP

The object of religious worship among the Negrillos and Bantus is evidently none other than the object of their beliefs: nature, in so far as it is dominated by a mysterious and sovereign Master, the manes of the dead, the tutelary spirits, and God. We must return at this point to a number of questions already touched on, and even repeat ourselves to some extent.

A. Réville has defined the naturism of the African Blacks as "religion, insomuch as it has for its direct object, phenomena, bodies, or forces of nature regarded as animated and conscious." [1]

[1] Réville, *op. cit.*, I, p. 67.

And he thinks he recognizes this naturism in the particular veneration shown in certain places for the moon, in a sort of worship rendered to the cow (this latter related to the worship of the moon because the crescent recalls the pair of horns or because the pair of horns recalls the crescent), in the adoration of the sea along the coast of Guinea, and in the personification of the earth as the spouse of the sky. He also cites lakes, rivers, and their sources as the object of negro adoration, trees, especially if they are tall and thick in girth, certain animals unusually clever, strong, and mysterious, and a number of other objects that strike their imagination, which they "animalize." [2] Abbé Bros likewise says that, for non-civilized peoples, the sun, moon, stones, trees, and animals have a history. They are born, live, marry, and die, have adventures, become angry, and are pacified. Nothing human is a stranger to them.[3]

We have already remarked how this conception of the savage seems to us greatly exaggerated and purely conventional. The savage, like the civilized man, speaks, imagines, invents, poetizes, and, although he has never pursued a course of rhetoric, composes numerous figures of speech, metaphors, hyperboles, prosopopœias. He has his stories and fables that he likes to repeat and hear repeated just as we do. He has fables in which he introduces animals and plants, like Esop, Phædrus, and La Fontaine; but for him as for them it is a "manner of speaking." He has legends also in which we learn the sun is married to the moon and has numerous children, the stars; but we would go beyond the legitimate bounds of credulity in believing him so simple as to put faith in the reality of this household.

The savage! The primitive! He is you and I, almost. He is a man, often an intelligent man; it is quite wrong to make his acquaintance and to judge him by the fantastic representations made of him by those who have never seen him.

If these writers speak to us of phytolatry, litholatry, hydrolatry, pyrolatry, geolatry, astrolatry, and zoolatry, we will understand. In reality, our Blacks "adore" neither the stars

[2] *Ibid.*
[3] Bros, *op. cit.*, p. 64.

nor animals nor plants nor bodies of water nor stones. As we have often remarked, we have here a confusion and a misunderstanding, a thing that can be explained easily enough for travelers or even European residents. If the Black, in fact, pays worship to a tree or a stone, it is not to the tree or stone itself that this homage is addressed, but to the tree or stone influenced by some agent of the invisible world. Thus in all the villages of interior Gabon, of Loango, and of Congo, we see in the center of the public square a little tree at the foot of which the natives place offerings and pour out libations. The passing traveler who has read authors treating the matter *ex professo,* will write in his note-book: "Dendrolatry, the religion of the Blacks of such a village." Or else: "Naturism (see Réville)." But if this traveler had witnessed the foundation of the village, he would have seen the chief or the sorcerer plant this little tree as a sign that they were taking possession of the place, offer a sacrifice, sprinkle the roots with the blood of the victim, and mix some ashes from the bones of the ancestors with the earth that is to nourish the tree. This is why the tree is *sacred,* why they pay a sort of worship to it, why these people appear to be "dendrolaters" to those who see only the surface.

If in many places, near a spring, on an islet, a cliff, a promontory, in a cave, or on the summit of a mountain we observe certain acts of veneration, we may be sure something happened there which is no longer remembered, which struck the imagination of the ancients and gave rise to this veneration; at least, we may be sure these places have been designated as sacred by a seer. There, perchance, a man fell where his remains still rest, here an extraordinary phenomenon appeared, there the presence and action of a spirit was manifested. Hence the place is "sacred."

In many localities groves are selected to which all approach is forbidden because a cemetery is there, because it is the meeting-place of a secret society, or because a little temple is erected there in honor of some genii.

Among the Wa-nika the hyena is a respected and sacred animal. This is because the Wa-nika leave their dead on the surface of the ground; the bodies are eaten by hyenas which thus incorporate the spirits of the ancients.

We have previously spoken of a lake on the mountains of Boura in Taita, which, by its solitude, the calm of its waters, and a certain mysterious aspect, inspires a sort of religious fear. The natives think that the manes of their relatives dwell upon its shore. They build little cabins there and make offerings. This is why the lake is sacred, as are also the numberless ducks that abound there and all the living beings that it nourishes.

We do not mean to say that the Blacks do not recognize many things as sacred, many sacred plants and trees, many sacred animals, but such objects possess this quality either because they have been taken as totems, or because of a particular property they possess, or of a symbolic signification attributed to them, or of a taboo that consecrates them.

In other words, there is always a reason extrinsic to nature itself in the worship rendered to nature.

If the Blacks of Africa are not naturists in the ordinary sense of the term, are they not at least animists?

"There can be question of animism," says Réville, "only when the spirits adored [4] are considered independently of natural objects, living without necessary relation to them . . . wandering through space, ordinarily invisible, sometimes taking a body, but always free to quit it." [5]

Animists our Blacks are indeed, but in a certain way and in a special sense of the term. The worship paid the ancestral manes is one thing, that to the spirits is another. And how many kinds of manes are there, and how many kinds of spirits!

It is certain that the Blacks firmly believe in the survival of disembodied souls, in their activity, influence, and power, in their ability to establish themselves in such or such a material

---

[4] We have already remarked how improperly this word "adore" is often employed.

[5] Réville, *op. cit.*, p. 67.

body, and in our power of entering into such relation with them
as summoning them or driving them away, interesting them in
our affairs, or charging them with the execution of our
vengeance.

The same is true of the spirits, good and bad, of an extra-
human nature. The tutelary spirits have a right to our worship
and it is to our interest to make sure they receive it. Often
are we obliged to be on the watch against wicked spirits lying
in wait for us, or against disembodied souls that wish us ill.
There is, for instance, the danger of our becoming "possessed."

The art of winning over the influence of the manes and
spirits, of associating ourselves with them in occult under-
standings by a pact, of compelling them to answer our call, all
that is neither worship nor religion : it is magic.

In the broad sense that we have set forth, this animism is
often manifested and affirmed in a worship which has been
called fetichism, according to the President de Brosses.

What is a fetich? Let us again quote A. Réville:

"The *fetich* is a common object without any value in itself
but which the Black keeps, venerates, and adores because he
believes it is the dwelling-place of a spirit. It is needless to
ask what can be a fetich in the eyes of the negro; one might
better ask what can not be. A stone, a root, a vase, a feather,
a log, a shell, a colored cloth, an animal's tooth, a snake's skin,
a box, an old rusty sword, anything at all can be a fetich for
these grown-up children. In the list of such objects we sometimes find even products of European manufacture." [6]

But this name "fetich" is applied especially to those more
or less crude representations, generally in wood but sometimes
in clay, stone, or ivory, rarely in metal, consecrated to various
genii, which we meet with particularly in the regions of western
Africa. In the mind of the natives, these are not at all
portraits, such as would constitute idolatrous images properly
so called; they are figures emblematic of such and such spirits
who are called to exercise their influence in a well-determined
sense.

[6] Réville, *op. cit.*, p. 81.

We must distinguish from these fetichist statuettes the images which, among many of the tribes, are connected with the worship of their ancestors. These images surmount or enclose relics of the dead, skulls, bones, hair, finger-nails, and other human remains. They derive all their value from these relics.

A third class of fetiches that must not be confused with the others, includes those destined for the operations of black magic, those that give diseases, cause death, satisfy vengeances. To this class belong the fetiches that we find (in Loango and Congo) covered with nails. We will speak of them later.

Thus we have three categories: family fetiches that derive their power from the relics of ancestors and are employed to protect the family, the village, or the tribe; fetiches of the tutelary genii, incorporating spirits whose activity is eminently defensive and protective; and fetiches of bewitching spirits, i.e., avenging fetiches.

Naturally these statuettes, figures, or objects are active only in so far as is the spirit that resides in them: when "vacated," they are nothing more than any other image that can be sold, given away, or put aside. Such is the standing of all the fetiches found in our museums. To-day on the coast of Africa there are even makers of fetiches for exportation: they are sold to Europeans.

The fetich is different from the amulet and from the talisman inasmuch as it is held to be conscious and to derive its power from itself in consequence of the spirit inhabiting it.

The *amulet* or *grigri* [7] is a little object carried on the person, which by a secret power, mysterious, innate, and unconscious, is thought to preserve the wearer from misfortunes, diseases, accidents, witchcraft, or procure good luck in traveling, in war, in the hunt, in fishing, housekeeping, and the like. [8]

[7] Amulet, from the Latin *amuletum* (from *amoliri*, "to ward off") and perhaps from the Arab *hamala*, "to carry." The word *grigri* has been taken from the native language of the western coast of Africa.

[8] Réville, treating this subject, profits by the occasion to write: "A blessed medal which is thought to ward off accidents, diseases, or death, belongs to the class of amulets." (*Op. cit.*, I, p. 80.) An official specialist like Réville should know that the Catholic Church has never attributed to medals any power in themselves; in blessing these little objects, her purpose is simply to place at the service of her children the efficacity of her

The *talisman* [9] is rather an object marked with cabalistic signs, intended to exercise a certain action on things or events which changes their nature or their course. It is not worn constantly, like the amulet; often it is placed over the door, inside the house, in the fields, at the entrance to the village, on the road.

This ensemble of various figures, of the powers attributed to them, and of the practices connected with them, which constitutes fetichism, is commonly said to be the religion of the Blacks with whom we are at present concerned. But that is a hasty generalization not altogether corresponding with the reality. There is fetichism among the Blacks, but that is another thing: fetichism is not their whole worship, still less their whole religion.

At any rate, among our African tribes of the equatorial zone, there are very marked differences that we will point out at once.

Among those of the western coast from the Niger to Angola and from the coast almost to the great lakes, i.e., all the zone covered by the forest, we meet classical fetichism, with its diverse figures, statuettes, and material representations, often publicly exposed in real sanctuaries and still more often hidden in huts or concealed in out-of-the-way places.

On the eastern coast and to the south of the vast country occupied by the Bantus, these statue fetiches disappear or at least they are rare. Why? Must we see in that fact an ancient and prolonged influence of the Semitic element; or is this relative immateriality of worship inherent in the particular nature of these people; or, as Livingstone remarked, do the open countries lead men to a more spiritual religion while the great forest leads them to idolatry? The problem has not been solved, but the fact exists.

own prayers, to recall by these symbols the idea of God and the saints, and to inspire in those who piously wear them dispositions capable of drawing down divine grace upon them. The medal has value only as a memorial and symbol to lead men's spirit toward God.

[9] From the Arab *telsam*, "magical figure"; in Greek, τέλεσμα.

Here is another fact that will doubtless prove surprising. Among the Negrillos, although many groups live in the equatorial forest, we do not find a sanctuary nor a fetich-hut nor a statuette: barely a few amulets—generally three little pieces of wood fastened about the neck or wrist—and a few "specifics" kept in the encampment in bark boxes in order to preserve the people from certain diseases, to give them a successful hunt, to ward off any possible accidents, to make them invisible, and so forth. The forest is their temple, their wretched huts are only temporary shelters in their perpetual wanderings.

There is still another curious fact to note. These Negrillos firmly believe in the survival of souls and also practice a certain worship of the dead, but one much less characteristic than that found among the Bantus.

They also pretend to have no public or secret worship of spirits and all their homage seems to be gathered about him whom they consider Master of all things; who gave them (with necessary restrictions) the forest and the fruits that it produces and the animals it shelters, him who communicates life and sends death, who follows them in their encampments, who comes to visit them (sometimes killing one of their number), whom they try to escape by hiding far from the places that he has stricken. Yet at the return of the seasons, they feel obliged to pay homage to him by the sacrifice of certain fruits on a new fire.[10]

The Bantus, on the contrary, leave God in the background of their worship. They have more or less complicated practices to influence the tutelary spirits and the genii, to get rid of evil spirits or neutralize their actions; but their real cult is the family and tribal worship of the ancestral manes. For these reasons, we find, on the whole, the expression *manism* or *supernaturism* more appropriate to characterize their religion than any of the terms mentioned above—fetchism, animism, or naturism.

[10] Le Roy, *The Pygmies.*

III. The Priesthood

In all religions are certain functions, ceremonies, rites which are not and can not be performed indifferently by all. Between the world in which we live and the higher world with which religion connects us, there must be intermediaries: hence the *priesthood,* i.e., an order of men charged with exercising sacred functions and the care of sacred things.

Our primitive religions are no exception. But it is easy to understand that we must not expect them to have a defined and learned organization such as the religions of civilized nations. By way of compensation, perhaps we shall find among them the true answer to a question often asked and, like all religious questions, answered in a great variety of ways: whence comes the priesthood, whence the priest?

In the first place, these terms *priesthood* and *priest* contain an indication of the true answer. The *sacerdotal priest,* if we may so speak, is the *ancient* charged with *sacred* functions: in Greek, πρεσβύτερος; in Arabic, *scheik;* in Swahili and the neighboring languages, *mzee.*

In fact, the true sacred functions, those constituting the regular and ordinary worship, those forming, as it were, the basis of all others, relate, as we have seen, to the organization of the family; they are performed by the "ancient," the patriarch, the head of the house.

Among the Negrillos this is a general fact, so far as can be observed up to the present. It is the same with the Bantus and, we may add, throughout Africa. And here again we find confirmation in the testimony of Major A. G. Leonard, with this difference, that in the Niger Delta the head of the family uses greater care than elsewhere in preparing his eldest son to succeed him in his office.[11]

Worship is, then, above all a family affair, and the minister of worship is the head of the family. He is also best situated to conduct the necessary relations with the world beyond and

---

[11] Leonard, *op. cit.,* p. 394.

to give the manes the satisfaction they ask when, at the death of members of the family, they pass into the other life or to recall their memory when they return during the sleep of those who remain.

The head of the family knows what is to be done when a child is born in his house; when it is time to give him a name; when there is need to preserve him from the countless evil influences that might cross his path, to subject him to the needful initiations, to have him marry; when a misfortune is threatening; when a journey is to be commenced; when the success of the hunt must be assured; when there is need to protect the crops; and when death visits the house.

The head of the family naturally finds himself designated as the minister of religion or the necessary and ordinary intermediary between this visible world and that invisible one which dominates our human destiny.

He is also the physician of his house, treating his children when they are ill, and sometimes curing them. In Africa, as in all primitive societies, the functions of priest and physician are found thus combined. The same word which signifies priest and curer (*fumu*) in certain tribes, as among the Wa-rundi and the Wa-nyanwezi, means chief and ancient in many other languages.[12] As sickness is often due either to the evil influence of spirits or to the mysterious forces of nature, the duty of the priest-physician will be to combat these influences by their opposites, these forces by other contrary forces. He often succeeds; many of these specialists obtain results that can not be doubted, by means of simples which they know, of recipes and processes they employ. But it rarely happens that the real, operative remedy is not surrounded by ceremonies or practices that give it a certain religious or magical character. In Urundi the healer wears a broad band of cloth about his head and has the patient wear a similar one. Each time this physician administers his remedies or goes to look for them in the woods, he must put on this band. In other places the

[12] Van der Burgt (*Dict. franc. kirundi,* art. "Prêtre") derives *fumu* from *Ku-fumura,* "to administer remedies, to perform sacred functions."

physician wears a horn fastened above his forehead by means of the same band as a distinctive sign.

Elsewhere the paraphernalia is much more complicated: the physician is covered with special ornaments; he wears amulets that keep injurious influences in awe; he carries the paws of wild animals, bones, skins, and horns filled with specifics; he brandishes the tail of a hippopotamus or some other powerful beast: and all this apparatus inspires fear and confidence in the beholder.

Wherever the Negrillos are found, they are celebrated for the art of curing, and many rival chiefs keep one of them near in this capacity. "As the Whites know all the things of the sea," a "scholar" of the African world said one day, "so the A-koa know all the hidden things of the earth and woods." These doctors' formulas or recipes are numerous, and each one has his own. Generally they make use of plants, little pieces of wood, leaves, or bark—in powder, infusions, lotions, dissolved ashes, applications, inhalations, ingestions, etc.

They also understand cupping, incisions, the sweat bath, and the treatment of pain by means of a heated stick or a red-hot iron. Several of these practices, notably the sweat bath, serve also to purify the patient from certain stains as, for instance, those contracted in funeral ceremonies.

It is but just that there should be a fee, sometimes a rather high one; but it is consoling to know that if the patient dies, the physician gives it back and receives nothing.[13]

Under exceptional circumstances the head of the family, as priest-physician, may acquire a reputation that raises him above the ordinary. He will be celebrated, for instance, in the art of interpreting dreams, in predicting the future, and the event will show that he is right. He will see at a distance, and witnesses will confirm what he says. He will cure desperate cases. He will summon the rain, and the rain will come. In short, in some exceptional situation his prestige will increase and his authority will be strengthened. If to this *savoir-faire* he adds some ambition, he will under favoring circumstances become a high chief.

[13] Van der Burgt, art. "Guérir."

In several African tribes these two functions are combined in the same man: the functions of political chief and of religious chief. At times a veritable organization maintains itself for a considerable time: but among the Blacks it can not endure indefinitely. Nothing endures in that country; and as nature covers everything with her invincible vegetation, so time levels the institutions that seemed most strongly established.

Although the political chief always has a certain religious character, ordinarily the public functions of worship are reserved to special dignitaries who occupy in relation to the people the place which the head of the family occupies in his own house. As there is family worship, there is also public worship. The latter is addressed to the manes of the ancestral founders of the tribe. It takes place at stated periods and also on the occasion of certain anniversaries, when an epidemic threatens, when there is lack of rain, when a public misfortune has fallen on the country, and when a war is about to begin.

As might be supposed, all the chiefs do not have the same religious aptitude nor the same tastes. Some are completely indifferent. But we also find that religious matters by their nature, dispositions, and interest, without speaking of other circumstances, tend to become a professional career. Often in a dream the religious dignitaries receive the revelation of their vocation. At other times they are selected and trained in special schools by a relative or a noted sorcerer. A mysterious illness, a possession, or some other personal event may serve to single them out and set them before the people. In this way arise the "seers," "diviners," "healers," "charmers," "rainmakers." And thus we imperceptibly reach a religious category that is no longer family or tribal worship.

It is to these specialists that one has recourse in difficult cases, when there is need to interpret a dream, to build or consecrate either a sanctuary or a fetich, to secure charms, amulets, or remedies, to exorcise a "possessed" person, to preside over the initiations of youth, to offer sacrifices, to summon the rain, to enact new prohibitions or remove certain others, to baffle the snares of sorcerers and their witchcraft, and to combat the black magic.

Here we touch upon a third category that must not be confused with the other two. Whereas the heads of the families or tribes are always respected in their religious capacity, and the diviners, healers, exorcists, and other specialists of that sort enjoy an authority and confidence proportioned to their success, there is no one more dreaded, hated, and generally more criminal than the conjurers or "sorcerers" properly so called.

The word by which they are designated in each tribe must never be lightly pronounced. It constitutes the gravest accusation that can be made against any one. When we treat of magic, we will return to the rôle of these persons on the border of religion who occupy so considerable a place in Africa and elsewhere.

In the list of the agencies of worship, mention must be made of the closed or secret societies which have so great an influence on the religious and social life of these people. They seem to be found in every part of Africa.

The chief aims of these institutions, which naturally vary according to the district, appear to be to maintain the customs of the tribe, to issue unquestioned orders in the name of a religious or magical authority, to make the women obey and work, as also the slaves, the children, and all the profane, to allow the dignitaries of these societies, who are also the political and religious chiefs, to meet in secret committee, adopt decisions that must be known to no one outside, free themselves from those who embarrass them, and to acquire whatever advantages they wish.

What renders these associations formidable is that the penalties imposed may be terrible; whoever is condemned to death by them will not escape. He will disappear in some manner and no one will ever know who struck him down. These executions are frequent and explain why the secret societies in Africa often exercise a dreadful tyranny.

Let it suffice for us to mention them here. As, in variable proportion, they are related as much to magic and political life as to religion, we shall have occasion to describe them later on.

All these agencies of the African religions are generally assimilated in the accounts of travelers and confused under the same name of "sorcerers" or "fetichers." It is easy to see that this confusion of ideas is not just.

The head of the family in his capacity of religious chief performs a sacred ministry that may truly be called sacerdotal: he is an intermediary, a qualified intermediary, between the children for whom he is responsible on earth, and the invisible world on which they and he depend and toward which they are all advancing.

The same may be said of the village chief and the chief of the tribe, who is, after all, only the chief of an enlarged family, whether he "officiates" himself or whether the national rites, as ordinarily happens, are performed by a special minister, qualified for the purpose and acting in the capacity of intercessor and intermediary.

Nor is it altogether the case of a specialist who can be called physician, healer, diviner, seer, exorcist, charmer, magician, rain-maker. Religion is mixed with science and superstition in variable proportions difficult to establish. Moreover, the practitioner who does not fill all these functions at the same time, is not an ordinary and regular minister of worship. He acts on request and gives his consultations, with a recompense or fee, either in favor of particular persons or for families, villages, or other groups. This is not, strictly speaking, a function, but a profession.

We must add, however, that often in the black world the two offices of religious minister, in the more exact sense of the term, and of practitioner of occult things are held by the same person. Some of these men have a great reputation and people come from afar to visit them.

Quite different are the "sorcerers" or "wizards" who by their secret practices and criminal relations with the bad spirits cause a great number of evils and become a veritable terror.

Though the native words that designate these different ministers of religion, of science, and of magic are different, they are often confounded with one another, which is to confound good with evil, day with night. This does not mean, nevertheless, that in fact the same individual is not at the same time religious minister in the family, diviner or physician renowned and esteemed by the public, and also a sorcerer of the lowest type at the service of those who, with great secrecy, come to ask him, in return for his fees, to kill such a relative, to carry out a revenge, to destroy an adversary, to strike a certain person with some misfortune, or a certain family, village, or country. The negro mentality easily accommodates itself to the same person playing all these rôles that seem so contrary.

Another question. Are these various sorcerers, fetichers, diviners, exorcists, healers, whatever name may be given them and whatever specialty may distinguish them, really sincere, convinced?

I think so. Strange as it may seem, they are "convinced" even when they know beyond doubt that some of their operations are only pure phantasmagoria. In a certain ceremony of *Ukuku* and *Yasi,* for example, the initiated are perfectly well aware that the spirit which comes out of the woods is a man, and a man whom they know. Yet they are not indifferent towards him: far from it!

Nevertheless that does not prevent them from amusing themselves and laughing at times like true skeptics at all these practices and all these practitioners—except the witchcraft. But this occasional skepticism alternates with a real faith in the rites as well as in the operator when the moment has come to proceed to the ceremony. This is because the mind of the Black is easily subject to suggestion and passes with strange facility from one conviction to another without completely abandoning the one for the other. Their mentalities are full of devices. Do not let us suppose either that their credulity after all has nothing to rest on. These healers do effect cures; these "seers" do discover hidden objects; these exorcists do free persons possessed; and when a sorcerer engages to rid you of an enemy, you can be sure—if you have paid the price —that your enemy will disappear. In other words, there are results, which make the sorcerers themselves believe in their art.

The manner of transmitting the religious ministry properly so called accentuates the family rôle in the religion of the Blacks. During the life of the head of the family, the eldest son is trained and gradually initiated in the functions which he will perform later on. There are often special ceremonies for that initiation, with the transfer of symbolic objects, unctions, ritualistic words, and chants.

In the country of the Niger this eldest son is the ordinary celebrant. In the religious ceremonies it is he who breaks the kola-nut and distributes it, as well as the palm-wine, to the members present. He it is also who offers sacrifice, cuts the necks of the victims, spreads their blood over certain emblems or even over the persons who are present, and he presides at his father's funeral ceremonies.[14]

The same is not always true of the occult sciences. A celebrated master will transmit his secrets to that one of his children who appears to possess special dispositions; at times, he receives disciples who come, with their fees, to be initiated at his school.

There are also men whom the spirits themselves designate as particularly consecrated to them: either because the soul of some ancestor has come to dwell in them, or some renowned master lives again in their person; or because, for some unknown reason, a spirit makes of this person "his man." The latter has only to betake himself to the school of some well-known sorcerer to be accepted.

In the same way the science of witchcraft is transmitted. It is scarcely necessary to remark that it is done with the greatest secrecy, and with initiations that belong to demonology.

14 Leonard, *op. cit.*, p. 345.

IV. The External Manifestations of Worship

The family character that we have noted in belief, morality, and the organization of worship, is found in the external manifestations of religion. The center of worship remains, so to speak, confined to the place occupied by the family, in its humble hut or its village.

In the open country of tropical Africa, the Blacks are content to build for the manes of their ancestors, either in the village or outside it, little huts under which they come to make their offerings. These huts, called "of the *mzimu*" (i.e., of the disembodied soul), are to be seen everywhere. In Uganda they assume more ample proportions: they are veritable sanctuaries, called *masabo,* in which a sort of altar or platform (*mwa-liro*) accommodates the bananas and the beer offered there; live goats are also brought.[15] In Urundi every village contains these minute huts (*ikigabiro,* from *kugabira,* "to give," "to make an offering"), consecrated to the manes who, the natives say, make frequent visits there.[16]

According to the idea of the Blacks, every family house has its real duplicate in the tomb, and the village has its in the cemetery. Thus tombs and cemeteries are sacred places. These little booths are built where the spirits of the dead are fond of coming to rest; small altars are erected to receive the offerings; there they come to make their ritualistic libations with prayers.

Naturally the funeral ceremonies vary in different tribes, but the idea is always the same. Among several tribes of the Congo the chief on his death has his house for a tomb: his body is left there until the roof falls in; then the village is abandoned. In other places the dead are interred in separate graves on the outskirts of the village; in still other localities there are real cemeteries, ordinarily little groves, where the dead are left and where no one ever enters except to pray and to make offerings.

Among the Ba-ronga, in each little clan governed by a chief

---

[15] Robert P. Ashe, *Life in Uganda.*
[16] Van der Burgt, *op. cit.,* art. "Mânes."

known as the king, we find a sacred object called *mhamba* for which they show a real worship.

"When the chief dies," we are told, "they cut his finger-nails and toe-nails, some hair from the top of his head and from his beard, and they mix all these elements of his body that are capable of being preserved, with the dung that comes from the oxen killed at his decease. Thus they obtain a sort of ball which is then wrapped in strips of leather. At the death of this chief's successor, they make a second ball which they add to the first one, and this goes on for centuries. This mysterious object is preserved in a hut built for the purpose behind the village of the guardian." [17]

In other parts of eastern Africa, the natives make earthen statuettes, put therein parts of the deceased, such as the nails, hair, skin, a little bone, and after the requisite ceremonies, these are exposed either in the little hut just mentioned or in the house or village or on the outskirts thereof, at the foot of a tree.

On the western coast, it is no longer merely a statuette with some elements taken from the dead, that is to be seen in the hut, on a little domestic altar. For example, among the Fans, a part of the skull itself is preserved, painted red and placed in a box made of bark on which there is a bust crudely cut in the wood.

In Loango and in most of the tribes of the great Gabon forest, real statues surmount the relics of the defunct, placed in niches at the back of the public house of the village. Before these statues a sort of altar is erected where offerings are made.

Elsewhere, and sometimes in these same tribes, another cult is observed for the fireside spirit, which is considered the special protector of the house and whose nature closely resembles the *penates* or *lares* of the Latins.

It is rare not to find hanging at the entrance of the hut or on the roof symbolic and protective talismans intended to bring life and plenty and to ward off all evils.

---

[17] *Bulletin de la Soc. de géog. neufchâteloise*, X, 1899, *Les Ba-ronga*, by Henri Junod, p. 399.

Among these people of the western coast, the village, which is the family enlarged, likewise has its fetich-protector. In the central place or near the hut of the chief, a tree or bush is planted, generally recognized by some special quality; at its foot different objects are placed: shells, the stone of various fruits, leopards' paws, antelopes' horns. Often there is a little hut in which they pour out palm-wine and make offerings from time to time.

In the community house where they gather to talk, the fire is never extinguished, and in many tribes of the great Gabon forest, you will see real chapels where statues are enthroned on the bones of the ancestors, before which a regular worship is conducted.

At the entrance to these villages or on the paths leading to them, you will also find, especially in time of war or epidemic, a sort of lofty trapeze from which hang different fetiches.

The tutelary spirits of extra-human origin likewise have their worship and their sanctuaries.

In east Africa, for example, little huts are built for them at the crossroads and spread out there are flour and other gifts. Travelers use various practices to win their favor. The same is true of hunters. A possessed person, after he is freed by exorcism, must construct one of these little huts for the spirit that has quit him. Various prominent places, such as promontories, cliffs, caves, lakes, mountain summits, are also consecrated to different genii.

In Urundi, besides the little huts intended for the manes (*ikigabiro*), there is a sacred enclosure called *ikitabo* (from *kutaba* "to offer, to sacrifice"). It consists of a round place marked off on the ground, from two to three yards in diameter. In the center a *ficus* is planted. There fine white grass is spread in the form of a bed. The national spirit is thus invited to come and rest. Sick people go there to sit on this bed or even sleep there in order to be cured. Often they bring the dying there and recite over them certain invocations intended to discover the threatening cause of death.[18]

[18] Van der Burgt, *op. cit.*, art. "Temple."

In many localities we find sacred groves in addition to those serving the purpose of cemeteries. At stated times the people meet there in great secret to perform certain ceremonies and offer sacrifices.

On the western coast, as we have frequently repeated, the worship finds material expression in strange statues. These fetich-statues must not be confused with one another; but it is very difficult to make a just and precise classification. We have one thing to add to what has already been said.

Certain tribes have desired living fetiches. Thus in the Lower Congo the good-luck fetich *Zumbi* consists sometimes of a bundle of charms, leaves, egg-shells, other shells, bones, animals' skulls, dust, serpents' heads, birds' beaks, sometimes a graven wooden image, sometimes a hen or other animal into which the spirit of the *Zumbi* has passed. This animal is never sold nor killed until, by reason of old age, it is necessary to transfer the charm elsewhere.

And the worship of God?

Nowhere in Africa do they make images of God: we have already remarked this above. However, it is not necessary to suppose there exists no material trace of the worship paid Him. To the south, in the Zulu country, are little heaps of stones piled up by travelers at certain steep and dangerous places. Each one, as he passes, adds a little stone, saying: *Tixo, ndincede!* (God help me!); or else: *Sipe amandla!* (Give us strength!). *Tixo* is, in Zulu, the name of God, a term supposed to be borrowed from the language of the Hottentots.[19]

At Zanguebar in the fields are little huts in which, they say, they offer God the first-fruits of the harvest. One might certainly collect various testimonials to show that the worship of the "Master of the sky and earth" is not totally foreign to the thought of the Blacks. Notably to Him they turn to obtain rain.

But what is true and what must be borne in mind is that nowhere do we find a material figure of Him; because no one pretends that he can enclose God's influence in a fetich or in

[19] Krapf, *Kaffir-English Dict.*

any amulet whatsoever; because no hut or temple is thought
to contain him; because, when they pay worship to Him, this
worship takes place in the open air, beneath the great sky
which He fills.

Further on we shall see the nature of the prayers they
address to Him and the sacrifices they offer Him.

But for the worship as for the belief, God remains in the
background, above and far away. Nearer and more often
entering into the life of the Black, are the spirits, genii, and
demons; and still nearer, even in the family, are the manes.
These are the invisible beings that he has especially to fear;
they are consequently the ones he must honor and appease.

The Negrillo does concern himself about God. It is fundamentally the same feeling that leads him to do so. Whereas he
fears neither spirits nor ghosts nor the manes, he does fear
God, and has a great dread of Him, and this is why he offers
sacrifices to Him, why he flees from Him.

In our black world fixed days must not be looked for when
all the people have a holiday periodically for the celebration
of their worship. So far as I know there are never any ceremonies to be performed on the same day in all the villages
or all the different groups of the tribe. It is at the residence
of the principal chief or sovereign, considered as the father
of all his subjects—a father who has all rights—that what we
might call the social worship takes place; it may be to honor,
implore, or pacify the manes of the ancestral founders of the
tribe; or to perform some extraordinary ceremony, for example,
a sacrifice on the occasion of a great chief's funeral; or to
ward off by prayers and public ceremonies some evils that
threaten all the people, an epidemic, a drought, a war.

Outside of that, each village throughout the whole country
occupied by the tribe proceeds on its own account, and likewise
each house of the village.

In other words, for the external manifestations of worship
as in other matters there is, properly speaking, nothing cen-
tralized, organized, disciplined. But with singular persistence,
beliefs, customs, and religious ceremonies are handed down

through generations and we are often astonished to find them still so much alive.

For the days consecrated to worship, the family is the master of ceremonies: not at determined periods, but on the occasion of a birth, an initiation, a marriage, a death, or other event touching the family circle or its head, or when there is some matter affecting a whole region, a group of villages, or a tribe, they pray, make their offerings, carry on their sacrifices, and perform ritualistic ceremonies.

The summons is given, according to the case, by the father of the family, the sorcerer, or the chief. Generally everybody responds.

In some tribes we do find a practice of abstaining from work, hunting, fishing, traveling, and other such undertakings, on certain days recurring periodically. It seems that these days are taboo. But the practice is not general.

To express his relation to the supernatural world that dominates him, we shall find in the primitive's religion all the feelings that vivify the most elevated religions: submission, veneration, adoration, expressed by the lowered and prostrate position of the body; grief (which assumes special marks in case of mourning—white paint covering the whole body or merely the forehead, torn clothes, fasting, etc.); joy (indicated by certain ornaments of the body and of the costume, by dances and songs); purity or purification (obtained or symbolized by various means among which we must point out the use of lustral water); the desire of imitation, which creates an additional affinity between man and the object of his worship; that sort of aspiration in man for a visible and tangible God, which results in fetichism and idolatry.

This "need that man feels of projecting and expressing his impressions, feelings, and convictions" [20] creates the *symbol*, that is to say "the act or the thing which by analogy represents either the object of belief or the various shades of religious feeling." [21] The ensemble of symbols grouped about a re-

[20] Réville, *Prolégomènes à l'hist. des. religions*, p. 168.
[21] *Ibid. Symbol*, from the Greek σύμβολον, an object having a conven-

ligious idea or religious act is a *rite,* and the rites organized
into a recognized ceremonial constitute the *liturgy.* All this
we find, with perfect distinctness, in the various expressions of
the religious life of our Blacks.

They have prayer. If a Christian has been able to define
prayer as *the breathing of the soul in God,* this higher notion
may be applied with truth to the prayer usage of our primitives.
With them prayer is essentially a request. Not only do they
pray for favors that are in no way spiritual—to keep away a
present or dreaded evil—but also to satisfy their revenge, to
seize the goods of another without being caught, or to kill an
enemy. There are prayers that issue spontaneously from the
inspiration of the moment, according to the circumstances and
the favors asked; and there are prayers consecrated by usage,
formulas that the ministers of worship must recite on certain
occasions. The prayer often expresses itself in a sort of wish.

Thus one of the Wa-nika, when told of the birth of a friend's
child, says: *Mulungu amulaye* (May God forget the child, may
it live). *Mulungu ni amulaye bai, apate kukala muzima*
(Well, God forget him, that he may become strong and well).[22]

Ordinarily prayer appears under the form of a request,
imprecation, or conjuration, according to circumstances. It
is spoken or sung, and is addressed to the manes, the spirits,
and even to God. It is God they invoke to guard the life of
the child, to have good crops, to obtain rain.

In the course of the ceremonies, offerings, and sacrifices,
there are always prayers indicating the purpose thereof. These
prayers are generally cabalistic utterances, obscure words or
phrases, allusions difficult for the European mind to grasp,
archaisms that come from distant ages whose meaning has been
lost but which have been faithfully preserved and are considered the more efficacious the less they are understood.

By way of example, here are some formulas of prayer and
conjuration gathered among the Wa-pokomo, who inhabit the
right bank of the Tana (eastern Africa). The *Mganga* (priest)

tional significance and serving as a rallying sign; *rite* from the Latin *ritus,*
group of ceremonies; *liturgy,* from the Greek λειτουργία, "public service."
    [22] Taylor, *Giryama Vocabulary,* p. 81.

begins, when the sacrifice has been offered, and the people answer in chorus.[23]

> O God, we ask Thee!
> O manes, we ask you!
> O ancestors, we ask you!
> God, grant us peace!
> Grant us tranquillity! And may the blessing come!
> He who bewitches our village, may he die!
> He who utters an evil spell against us, may he die!
> He who says this village is rich, these men are numerous, he who speaks thus is a jealous one, may he die!
> We also ask for some fish, may the fish come!
> We ask for some *ngoo* (fish), may the *ngoo* come!
> We ask for some *pfezi* (another fish), may the *pfezi* come!
> Thus eating, let us eat in peace!
> This woman is ill. O God, give her peace (health), to her, and to her village, and to her children, and to her man; may she get up, fly to work, take care of the kitchen; may happiness return, may it come from the other bank, may it come from the other bank! [24]

The following prayers we take from Dr. Krapf's Nika-English Dictionary.

For a sick person.

Thou God! And the Master! I say to Thee: Free this person from his sickness. We implore Thee, God, to relieve this person and cure him!

When going to cultivate a new piece of ground.

O Thou, God, I beg of Thee! I am going to cultivate this field. Very well, it is in order to have things to eat, that I may have life and health. Come, manes! I till this field that the grain may spring up abundantly and that I may harvest it when it is ripe.

Then he spits on his hoe and says:

May my hoe dig deep into the wet ground.

[23] Extract from a *Song of the Pokomos*, F. Wurtz in *Zeitschrift für afrikanische Sprachen*, Vol. I, p. 324.

[24] The whole life of the Wa-pokomo clings to their river (Tana). They fish in it and cultivate the fertile land along its shores.

When going on a journey.

Thou, God, who art on high! Behold, I am setting out on a journey. Thou, God, protect me. When I am trading, may I make profit! Have mercy on me, that I may return safe and sound!

For rain.

Thou, God, give us rain! We are in a wretched state, we are toiling hard; and we are Thy children. Give us clouds full of rain so that the people may have food, we beg Thee, O Thou, God, Thou, our Father! [25]

From these testimonials, among many others, the reader will judge whether the God thus addressed is not more living, more personal, and, in short, more real than that spoken of by A. Réville and his disciples.

The Bantus have hymns or religious chants with dances accompanied by the clapping of hands and stamping of feet, the beating of tam-tams, and the noise of various musical instruments. These dances ordinarily take place at night by the light of the moon or, if in the daytime, in large huts. The dancers always require special ornaments.

Like the formulas referred to above, the hymns, to which they attribute an operative power, must be very ancient. Their meaning even escapes us to-day and, moreover, when the Blacks use them, it is evident that they are little concerned with understanding them. In the extraordinary religious exaltation which they experience, they attend rather to following the rhythm and to preserving the melody. Most of these airs, in their simplicity and savage energy, repeated with earnest conviction, are extremely impressive and form a part of scenes that will never be forgotten by those who have witnessed them.

We do not know that there is need of returning to certain symbolic marks and practices, whose origin is more or less religious or magical. There are many of them, but the natives themselves are often ignorant of their meaning.

[25] Krapf, *op. cit.*, p. 284.

We have already seen that each tribe is distinguished by a special tattoo traced on his forehead, face, or some other part of the body; by filed, cut, or broken teeth; by malformations of the lips; by earrings, bracelets, necklaces, rings on their arms or legs, girdles, or an entire costume, not to speak of the hair, the form of the spear, the bow, and especially the shield. When a European arrives in Africa, he generally finds all the Blacks alike and thinks that it is impossible to distinguish them. The native not only distinguishes them, but he can tell at once to what tribe and what family a stranger belongs. The Negrillos are still more acute; they recognize a man by his footprints along the little paths of the forest. In Loango there are tribes that mark on their sticks, clothes, dwellings, and also on their ritualistic necklaces and girdles, signs which we must admit are real hieroglyphic writing.[26]

Certain colors have likewise something sacred about them. Rarely is a ceremony performed without the celebrant and the others present being painted. Throughout western Africa they employ a paint made of red wood mixed in palm oil, for their sacrifices. With this they also paint a new-born child, its mother, the sick who are about to be treated, as also the skulls of the dead, which are cut off and kept for domestic worship.

White is the color of the manes. It is used in funeral ceremonies, in the dances at the initiation of youth, and in all circumstances where the spirits of the dead are directly concerned. This paint is made of white chalk or, lacking that, of tapioca flour, with which are often mixed the powdered bones of the dead. Naturally the stronger, richer, more intelligent and powerful the dead man has been, the more eagerly his "powder" is sought after. In Gabon, minute precautions had to be taken to prevent the remains of the first bishop, Monsignor Bessieux, from being disinterred during the night and employed by the natives for this purpose, which the holy man had not foreseen. This custom of composing a specific from the bones of the dead is known all through Bantu Africa. Recently an explorer returned to Paris after a trip through the Gabon forest, which is occupied by the Fans. Among the impressions of his jour-

[26] Dennett, *op. cit.*, p. 71.

ney, he recounted to a reporter that one day he had arrived in a village at the very moment when the women were about to be eaten: "Already," he said, "they were covered with flour as we prepare a cutlet for the frying-pan." The journalist gravely reported the incident in the columns of his great daily. But the women whom this gentleman thought were all ready to be fried, were simply returning from a funeral and the flour was their mourning costume.

Special attention should be given to a form of blessing that is quite widespread. In Gabon it is called *iboto*. When parents bid good-by to their child, when a chief parts from his guest, or when any one receives a valuable present, he takes the head or the hand of the child, the guest, or the giver, saying: *iboto* (blessing)! At the same time his lips emit a rapid breath along with a little saliva.

"In Loango," says R. E. Dennett, "a sale becomes definite after the transaction has been accomplished in the presence of witnesses and the seller has 'blessed it.' He lifts his hands to his arm-pits, and then throws them out towards the buyer, and breathes or blows over the thing sold. This is called Ku vana mula, to give the breath, and is equivalent to saying, 'God bless thee.' " [27]

In central Africa between the Tanganyika and the Bangweolo, the Wa-bemba have a similar confidence in the blessing of the father, mother, or chief. The Wa-bemba when setting out on a journey, in the most solemn circumstances of life, or in sickness, never fail to ask it. The ancient spits a little saliva on them, then rubs them with his hand, saying: "May God cure you! May he protect you during your journey! May he give you to eat! May he bring you back in good health!" [28]

The Massai, who do not belong to the Bantu family, make great use of this blessing.

Lastly, all our populations practice aspersions and purifications with lustral water, in which they mix certain herbs prepared with ritualistic formulas.

[27] Dennett, p. 48.
[28] Dupont, *Gramm. bemba.*

An offering for a religious purpose is very common. It is connected with the sacrifice and the sacrifice recalls the communion.

Here we come to what Reinach calls "the crucial point of all cult, the central bond between man and deity." And he adds:

"In this respect it is comparable to prayer; but whereas the latter is a spiritual appeal, the former entails the employment of a material substance forfeited or destroyed in the sacrificial act." [29]

In fact, sacrifice is as universal as religion. In Africa we find it everywhere, notably among those tribes dealt with in this volume. Like prayer and the offering, it is addressed to the manes, the spirits, and to God Himself.

We might develop this subject endlessly but we must be satisfied with citing a few examples.

In the regions of Gabon, Congo, and Angola, as well as in the center, south, north, and on the eastern coast, on the highways, the river banks, or the lake shores, there are places recognized as being consecrated by a supernatural influence. Here a celebrated man died or met with some unusual incident. There some inexplicable event happened which was attributed to the action of a spirit; in another place it would seem that they wished, under that special point of the sky, to render a sort of homage to the sovereign Being who from on high presides over man's existence and who can at any moment take it from him. In these chosen places, every passer-by, stray traveler, caravan porter, or canoe paddler, throws a stone, a twig, a leaf; at length the piles become rather high. Mounds are met with along all the highways of the interior. In Gabon their homage is directed in this way toward *Ombwiri,* the genius of the earth, and is intended to protect them against the bad tricks he might play on them during the journey. On the caravan routes, the Wanyanwezi (eastern Africa) have recourse to the same practice in honor of the *Mzimu* (spirit of the dead). And we read in Declé that the Blacks of Tanganyika, at the pilgrimage which they make to the mountain of Fwambo-

---

[29] Reinach, *op. cit.,* p. 26.

Liamba at certain periods of the year, place on a sort of little stone altar some sticks to which are fastened pieces of calico, flowers, or glass beads as a homage to *Leza,* which is the name of God.

At harvest time nearly everywhere offerings are made of ears of sorgum, maize, or rice in homage to God or to the tutelary spirits of the fields.

"When we were constructing the chapel of Mandera (Zanzibar)," says Father Sacleux, "one day in the fields I found Kingarou, the chief, under a shed, occupied in watching over his ripening maize. He asked me how the construction of our chapel was progressing. I had often explained its use, inviting our neighbors to come there for instruction. Then, as I had perhaps insisted too much on their ignorance of the things of God, he added: 'We are not so ignorant as that. You others, you Whites, make everything big: you have spacious houses with separate rooms intended for different purposes, you build immense temples where there is room for everyone at the same time. With us, who are poor Blacks, things are done on a small scale; but we also build houses for God: come, let me show you one of them.' And he led me to the entrance of the field before a little shed, consisting of a tiny roof of straw resting on four sticks. He explained to me that it was there they offered God the first-fruits of the harvest, adding that they were careful not to taste anything whatsoever without having first made this offering."

In Zanguebar, and we might say in all Africa, sacrifices are offered on the graves by the families of the deceased. A little flour and water is spread on the ground. In some places, it is palm-wine or beer with some pulp of maize or sorghum: thus they offer to the disembodied souls the two fundamental elements, liquid and solid, of daily food. Under other circumstances some cocks, or even goats, sheep, or oxen are killed so that their blood falls on the grave. While this offering is being made, the dead are invited by name to come and partake of the repast and to carry it to their friends who are also designated by name.

In Giryama, at the head of the grave they set a piece of

carved wood for men; for women it is plain and small. In the one case, they fasten pieces of linen to the wood, in the other, a miniature of the national petticoat. If some of the Giryama become indifferent or not very religious, their friends recall them to their duty. The diseases that may spring up, a journey to be undertaken, a marriage, the birth of a child, the death of a member of the family, are all so many occasions for the practice of sacrifice.

In Giryama, when it is time to sow seed, they first grind a few grains, and, early in the morning, spread the flour before the door of the person who is to sow, reciting a prayer in honor of the *Koma,* or the spirits of the dead. At the harvest, the same ceremony takes place before the granary. When the *pombe* (beer made from sorghum) is brewed, they pour a little liquid at the village gate, at the foot of the consecrated trees, and on the graves, praying that those who will drink may go quietly to sleep after becoming conscientiously intoxicated, without stirring up a quarrel or beating their wives. When they instal a forge, on the anvil they secretly offer a sacrifice of incense.[30]

At Nyassa, the head of the family or the chief of the village is always sure to erect near his habitation or in the near-by woods a little hut for prayers and sacrifices. It is again flour that is poured out in little heaps or sorghum beer; but other offerings are also made without counting the animal sacrifice on the more solemn occasions.

These offerings are poured into a pot that is sunk into the ground up to the rim. The chief, who performs the functions of priest, alone in the consecrated hut, offers prayer while the people respond, singing and clapping their hands in time to the music. They pray to have rain, to succeed in the elephant hunt, to have peace, or to triumph in war.

Or again, as Mr. Scott testifies in his *Cyclopædic Dictionary of the Mang'anja Language,*

"The chief of the village goes out with his younger brethren (i.e., his people) and his wives, who bring 'nsima,' and fowls,

[30] W. F. Taylor, *Giryama Vocabulary,* p. 81.

and perhaps a goat to go to the thicket to the temple-hut there where there is a little house builded long ago; the people stay there and clean away the grass (from the sacred place— lambulira), and the chief answers, saying: 'God give us rain, and harden not thy heart against us,' and makes many prayers, while all those clap their hands 'wu! wu! wu!' and he prays again and again, they clap their hands; then they eat the 'nsima,' the whole of it, and the meat, some of which they place in the house; the children are all about with the portion of the 'nsima' in their hands (lapata!); and as the elder people, some of whom eat from the 'nsengwa' baskets, when they have eaten they put the baskets all together and they are carried away: other women sing the hymn and surround the thicket hedge, saying—'May there come sweeping rain,—sweeping down. The rain here has been restricted, Sweeping rain!' (And other prayers.) And the rain comes in truth, and the temple gatherers on their return come back with the rain pouring and garments and bodies dripping. Then the villagers say, 'You see it was true, God was angry with us.' " [31]

If any one sees his ancestors during sleep, it is a sign that they feel neglected and that they demand a propitiatory sacrifice, an *i-dini*.

When a man or a domestic animal is sick, if the doctor who is called conjectures that the ancestors are offended at not receiving their due, it is at once understood that a sacrifice is required.

If there has been a drought, the people go to the chief and say: "Why permit such a calamity? Why not have recourse to your ancestors? Will you let us die thus?" Another sacrifice.

In such a case the following program is carried out:

1. The kindlings are prepared, consisting of chips of special wood.

2. An animal is slaughtered in the middle of the cattle field in the evening. The blood is brought in a basket to the house of the person who dreamed of the ancestors or who is sick; it is placed in the hut, behind the door. While carrying it, they tip it so as to spill a few drops on the ground. All the bones

[31] David C. Scott, *A Cyclopædic Dict. of the Mang'anja Language.*

and flesh of the animal are brought into the same hut and placed on little branches.

3. The next day a fire is made on the spot where the animal was slaughtered. The flesh, except the portion reserved for the women, is brought from the hut and placed on little branches near the fire or hung from posts in the field. The women's portion is placed on the fire near the calves' field. The first part to be offered, the fat that covers the liver, is cast into the fire and entirely consumed. Then pieces of the meat may be roasted and eaten in the morning; but most of it is boiled, part of it on the fire in the middle of the field, part near the oxen's field, and part near the calves' field. All the meat thus boiled is taken from the fire in the evening and entirely eaten at the same time by the two parties, men and women. The day following, all the fat and bones, with whatever flesh and wood remains, are burned up in the fire in the middle of the cattle field. The blood, if it is not thrown on the fire, is poured around the palisade and inside of it.

The day on which the sacrifice is eaten, a man is stationed at the entrance to the oxen field and another at that of the calves' field; all who participate in the sacrifice must put something in the hands of one or other of these sentries, saying: *Kanagu!* (May he be at peace, may he be propitious), as we would say in Latin: *Prosit!*

A sacrifice almost the same is offered in the south of Kenia. These Blacks, who have fine herds of oxen, slay an ox, pour its blood around their pasture, and perform ritualistic aspersions.

When the fishermen of Gabon catch the first fish of the day, they open it carefully, cut out the entrails, and throw them into the sea: thus are the first-fruits of the catch offered to the spirit of the waters. Canoe parties, ascending the river in their long "pirogues," offer a sacrifice either at the beginning or in the course of their journey; they kill a hen so that the blood flows on the prow of the "pirogue" and falls into the river. To the north of Zanguebar, when they find honeycomb, they do not fail, before eating it, to throw some pieces to the four cardinal points of the compass. Throughout Africa, before taking any fermented drink, palm-wine, sorghum-beer, etc., they are particular to pour a little on the ground, as a libation or sacrifice.

The Negrillos have no harvests because they do no farming. Nor have they any cattle. But as they get their living from the forest, they offer the first-fruits of it in a very impressive manner by means of the sacrifice already described. On a new fire they burn the two first *nkoula* nuts of the year, which two young men have ritually gathered from the top of a tree and have carried in their mouths while descending head first. While these nuts are burning, the little men, dancing and singing around the new fire, pray God to continue to feed them. After this, they can eat the nuts of that tree and all other fruits that they find in the forest.

In Kilimanjaro, I witnessed an interesting sacrifice. The natives of Marangou, threatened with an invasion by those of Kibosho, killed a magnificent ram one evening and amidst different ceremonies, songs, and prayers, they divided the animal into four parts: one for God, the tutelary spirits, and the manes,—this part was entirely consumed by fire; one that they ate; one that they abandoned to the beasts of the earth; and one that they offered to the birds of the air. This was done, they told me, so that all that lives might join with them in a general alliance. They intended thus to associate themselves with all the spirits and all the mysterious and protective powers of their country in resisting their enemy. I confess that I found such an idea very elevated and impressive.

We will conclude—for we could go on indefinitely citing these facts—by an abridged description of what J. M. Van der Burgt of the White Fathers, calls the ceremony of the "great rite" among the Wa-rundi. Neighboring Negrillos have the same ceremony; in fact, they seem to have originated it. It takes place in all manner of circumstances: at the birth of twins, for a grave illness, for a marriage, etc. This "great rite" consists in the homage rendered to the sacred lance of Kiranga, one of the higher spirits of the Rundi triad (Inana, Rikiramba, and Riangombe). This spear is of the ordinary shape with half of one side white, the other black; it is thought to carry the spirit Kiranga on its point and is confided to the custody of a special "hierophant." When the ceremony is to take place, he appears with two assistants; he wears a sort of diadem made of tiger skin and the tail hangs down his back. The other participants arrange themselves in a semicircle around him, carrying in their hands little hollow gourds full of hard grains forming a rattle. This is the orchestra, which announces the beginning of the ceremony by the aid of these rattles with a particular measure. Then they intone a hymn which is sung to a singularly impressive melody with a note of deep conviction that produces an indescribable melancholy. During this chant of evocation, each one picks up a little straw to present as they bow before the sacred spear. They clap their hands and ask of the spirit that resides on the point of the spear the various favors they desire: "Make me rich, cure me, favor me, O thou, king of the Urundi"; or else: "To thee, my father, I offer my homage!" When everyone has formulated his requests, they go out from the hut all together, singing as they go. They then direct their steps towards the straw covered enclosure to be seen in every village, which is regarded as the resting place of the manes of their ancestors. Here they sit down and, after a period of silence and meditation, return to the hut. Then a woman, selected for the purpose, takes a sort of basket soaked in water and, holding it above the heads of the assembly, inverts it and strikes it with her hand in such a way that little drops of water sprinkle the silent spectators. During this ritualistic aspersion, everyone murmurs prayers and thanksgivings to the God who blesses them. This basket by its form represents the celestial firmament from which blessings descend on the people.

The symbolic aspersion concluded, they produce a large jug of beer from which each one drinks in turn without leaving his place. After that the assembly breaks up: the ceremony is over.[32]

However varied these different sacrifices may be, the offerings consist only of the products of the earth or domestic animals, cocks, goats, sheep, or oxen. At times the material of the sacrifice has a totemic character, for instance, the *nkula* nuts

[32] Cf. Van der Burgt, *op. cit.*, art. "Rite."

among the Negrillos, the cock among the Wa-rundi, etc. A mythological legend of the Fans relates that, at the origin of the tribe, the sacred and wonderful crocodile in which the spirit of their common ancestor was incarnated, was killed, immolated, sacrificed, and partaken of in communion by all the first Fans.[33]

But there are other sacrifices in which human victims are immolated in religious ceremonies, and eaten by those assisting. To-day these human sacrifices are limited to certain tribes. But we can say that, more or less, all the Bantu peoples are familiar with human sacrifice and anthropophagy, at least that they are carried on by their secret societies and by the great sorcerers who practice black magic and have meetings that are strictly private.

Among the Fans, when a man has been killed in open combat, or in ambush, or through the practice of supposed magic, the law requires his family to avenge him by seeking out his murderer and, in default of him, every member of his village or family. They will wait, if necessary, but they will never forget. So long as their vengeance is not satisfied, it seems as if the voice of the dead is perpetually heard in the conscience of those who represent him on earth: *Excoriare aliquis nostris ex ossibus ultor?*

A man who is caught under these circumstances is brought to the village of the deceased. He is made to sit down on the ground, in the public square, with feet and wrists tied. They start to dance and sing around him, shave his head, and upon this strange tonsure they place live coals. When night covers all with its darkness, the tam-tam is played furiously, and when the echo of the sinister chant is sent back by the forest, at a given signal, the head of the unfortunate man falls under the sword of the executioner and rolls on the ground; the body struggles in hideous convulsions, the blood gushes forth, and all at once the spectators leap upon the corpse and cut the flesh into thin strips which they cook and eat. The connoisseurs highly esteem the fingers, which they suck with great delight; but the heart is especially desirable as the seat of courage which is appropriated by eating that organ.

[33] Trilles, *Proverbes*, etc.

In French Congo we find anthropophagies still more hideous among those Bondjos of Ubanghi who have been surnamed the "hyenas of humanity."

That our African people have prayers, offertory, sacrifice, and communion is an undisputed fact. But to what ideas do these ceremonies correspond and what explanation can we give of them?

In order not to fall into false interpretations, first of all we must distinguish two kinds of sacrifice, perhaps three.

1. There is the sacrifice to the dead on the day of burial as also at determined anniversaries. Food, linen, or some other object is offered, recalling the material needs of man on earth. By a curious symbolism, the vases placed on the graves are always cracked or chipped, in a word, whatever is offered to the dead man must be "dead."

These sacrifices to the manes seem to be an expression of remembrance, a sign of the relations that one intends to preserve with his own kin, to bridge over the abyss between life and death, by continuing to maintain the common society, the common repasts, and the common meeting.

But to this feeling we must add another: that of guarding one's self by visible marks of attention against the disagreeable return of the ghost, with his appearances, extravagances, obsessions, and vengeances. Who knows all the unpleasantness he might cause us if he did not rest in peace? Experience and faith teach us that nothing appeases him like these offerings and sacrifices. Does the ghost consume them? Some say yes, others no; but this is only a detail. The important thing is that they be *consecrated* to him and that nobody touch them except perhaps the birds and the insects which, in his name or serving as a material envelope for him, come to partake of it. Even when the offerings remain intact, in many places they tell you that you see only the external form: the essence has disappeared.

2. Between these manes directly proceeding from the bodies of our fathers, whom we have known, who have brought us up, and the spirits of the past or those whose origin remains unexplained—the spirits of the wind, of the waters, of the woods—the transition is imperceptible. But as we get further away from

the idea of a human form in the same degree is the sacrifice transformed. There is no longer food in the symbolically broken vases. The offering becomes a homage, an acknowledgment of sovereignty, a sort of levy or tax paid to the spirit that we recognize as master. Thus, in the case of "possession" which is extremely common, they begin by asking the spirit, i.e., by addressing the sick woman (usually they are women) what it is that she wishes. If the specialist who is called has succeeded in his art, the spirit replies, gives his name, and specifies the sacrifices desired. Most of these obsessing spirits have a name and each of them must be appeased by particular ceremonies. So they call the appropriate exorcist and he begins his practices which are sometimes very long and complicated. But the capital point is always the sacrifice. At the appointed hour they slay the designated animal, collect the warm, steaming blood in a vase and give it to the possessed woman to drink. Those present participate in the ceremony by offering the spirit some grains of maize, rice, or sorghum. At least that is the way I have seen it carried out on the coast of Zanguebar.

The possessing spirit likes blood: he is in need of it and they give it to him. Both experience and faith (speaking from the native point of view) teach that this sacrifice succeeds, that is why they continue to offer it.

3. But the fundamental idea of a sacrifice is still more clearly marked when there is question of honoring living nature or the Master of the world under the name of a spirit or even of God. Then they are no longer concerned with the quantity or the quality of the offering, but with what it represents or symbolizes. Thus they offer the first-fruits of the crops, of their fishing, of the hunt, and sometimes of the herd and even of the family in the person of the first-born. They offer the first honeycomb which they find in the forest. Among the Massai the most significant sacrifice that can be made to divinity is a handful of grass gathered in the plain, offered to God or his representatives as a homage. The meaning is this: "It is you who have covered the earth with this grass, without which our herds and we ourselves could not live. You remain its master; behold it here." Thus, at certain chosen places, in passing they

throw a leaf, a stone, a few blades of grass. Evidently in doing this, it is not their intention to give any spirit something to eat, but they pay homage to him by acknowledging his dominion over the ground on which they walk or over the water on which they paddle their canoe.

These distinctions and remarks will help us solve the problem, never finally settled, of the origin and end of sacrifice. Many have thought that its *raison d'être* was to nourish the "god," to give him something to eat and drink, to take a meal with him and thus win his favor. This crude idea may possibly be that of some low savages; but even these would not acknowledge that as their whole thought. Moreover, this explanation does not harmonize with many of the cases we have cited; for example, the offering of a pebble or a handful of grass. In fact, it is abandoned to-day.

"The theory," says Reinach, "which considers sacrifice as a gift made to divinity—the divinity being regarded as an immortal and therefore trebly formidable man—can not hold good for the beginning of things, for it still dominates the superstition of to-day." [34]

Another theory affirms that the object of sacrifice is "to establish a communication between the supernatural world and the profane world by the mediation of a victim, i.e., some object destroyed in the course of the ceremony." [35]

"In view of this purpose, the victim becomes sacred: they regard as magically concentrated all the divine powers; these powers are multiplied by freeing them through the immolation; lastly, the priest, the assistants, and the faithful are made sharers in these divine forces by means of the flesh and blood of the victim with which the liberated energies remain in contact." [36]

This theory seems too complex and too elaborate to be primitive: it is a theory of European sociology. Moreover, sacrifice

[34] Reinach, *op. cit.*, p. 28.

[35] Hubert et Mauss, *Année sociologique*, 1897-1898 (Bros, *La religion des peuples non civilisés*, p. 177).

[36] Bros, *op. cit.*, p. 178.

appears by this theory to be a magical proceeding, as if it were not, above all, a religious act. We must look further.

An English scholar, F. W. Robertson Smith, formerly professor at Cambridge, considered sacrifice as a totemic rite. The totem animal had to be killed in order to be eaten and thus renew the sacred bond between the faithful and their god.

"The great discovery of Professor Robertson Smith," Reinach tells us, "has been to show that sacrifice by communion was older and more primitive than the sacrifice by gift; that it was, in fact, the oldest form of sacrifice; that traces of it are found among the Greeks and Romans as well as among the Hebrews; and lastly, that the communion as observed in Christian churches is only an evolution of this primitive sacrificial rite." [37]

There are indeed sacrifices of the totem or allied animal, and therein magic does enter; but these are not the only kind.

Totemism may be defined as the mysterious alliance with an animal or vegetable species in virtue of an ancient pact entered into by the chief of the tribe, or a personal pact concluded by the individual himself or by his father. Totemism is only a small part of the religion or rather magic of the primitive. It is impossible to find instances of it among all of them. It is a system that, thus generalized, can not really cover the totality of sacrifices.

At most, this explanation would only push the difficulty further back; for, if totemism is the origin of sacrifice, what is the origin and *raison d'être* of totemism itself?

Father Lagrange, examining this question in his *Etudes sur les religions sémitiques*,[38] approaches much nearer the probability and the truth of the matter when he says:

"We must look for a very simple concept, one that is, to a certain degree, common to all cases since we are here dealing with a universal institution. The idea of a divinity residing in things or governing things is this concept that we are seeking.

"Take animism, if you wish. In some natural object or near it, the savage perceives a spirit; the object, then, is not

[37] Reinach, *op. cit.*, I, p. 33.
[38] Lagrange, *Etudes*, etc., p. 249.

his, he can not use it without the spirit's consent. It is necessary in some way to induce the spirit to become disinterested in the object. The problem is not to consecrate the object to the spirit, but rather to remove from it all its consecrated character so that it will be available for profane use: because for the man who sees spirits everywhere, everything is more or less taboo. Perhaps the spirit will forgo his dominion if we freely offer him a part."

In reality there are several kinds of sacrifice. Each of them may have a different origin and a different explanation according to the spirit addressed and according to the purpose for which it is offered, not to mention the special and more or less elevated mentality of him who offers it.

Thus, the sacrifice of the totem animal rests upon a particular order of ideas. The totem animal is a member of the tribe, with which a man, representing himself and his descendants, has made an alliance in view of reciprocal services. Generally speaking, this pact has been sealed by the exchange of blood so that the animal and the man, the family of one and the family of the other, the tribe of one and the tribe of the other, are individuals, families, and tribes of the same blood. They are allies. From time to time it is well to renew this alliance by the sacrifice of a representative of the animal family: participation in this sacrifice is by communion. This is a new exchange, recalling the first alliance; it also reënforces the powers especially belonging to the totem, powers fortified perhaps by the presence or influence of the spirit of the ancestor in the animal or vegetable thus consecrated, sacrificed, and eaten.

But that is not the primary and general reason of the offering, the sacrifice, and the communion; these three things go together. We think we can look for the primary and general reason in that vague but actual concept of a primitive man whereby he considers himself as a stranger in this world. Finding himself in the presence of the products of nature and feeling obliged to use them in order to live, he fears to lay hands on them as everyone is always afraid to lay hands on the goods of another. It may be that his conscience (in its original feeling of justice) warns him also not to touch what does not be-

long to him, or perhaps the fear that he will be discovered by
the invisible owner, makes him circumspect and restrains him.
What is he to do? He will take what he needs, but he will first
offer a gesture of submission. By presenting at least the first-
fruits of everything and, at times, a symbolic part of what he
consumes, he will acknowledge the sovereign dominion of the
supernatural world. That invisible world may seem to him
to be a higher being who rules over all, or he may believe that
he has to do with particular spirits that guard one part of the
earth or of the waters, or he may think himself still in relation
with the manes of his relatives. At any rate, this levy is not,
properly speaking, a *gift* made to the spirit, but a sort of *tax*
due to a master who is clearly recognized. That it may be understood that the material forming this tax does not belong to
man, it is given, by special ceremonies, a sacred character. This
sacred character prohibits him and his fellows thenceforth from
laying hands on this material. If he stops at that, it is what
we usually call an *offering*.

But often his faith leads him to do more and better. To mark
his intention more clearly, he separates himself from the object offered, by making it unfit for the use of mortals and thereby, so to speak, transferring it to the invisible world for which
it is destined. This is the *sacrifice*.[39]

This object thus consecrated, offered, and sacrificed, is henceforth penetrated by a supernatural influence, if it be not indeed
now inhabited by the spirit to whom it was presented. This object will in its turn furnish the means of contracting or renewing a more intimate alliance with the invisible world if one in-
corporates himself with it, if one assimilates it with himself.
There you have the *communion*.[40]

Undoubtedly this is not all thus reasoned out in its entirety
by the primitives with whom we are dealing; but it exists, nevertheless, in the depth of their mentality.

Note this curious fact. The more savage man is, the Negrillo, for example, the more distinctly do we find it exemplified
by him.

[39] Sacrifice—*sacrum facere.*
[40] Communion—*cum unio, cum unire.*

If I myself set it forth as furnishing the basis of sacrifice, prayer, morality, and the prohibitions, it is because one day I found it expressed with surprising clearness by a village chief of the Wa-boni in the great forest of Sokok, on the eastern coast of Africa. I had the same experience among the A-koa or Negrillos of Gabon. It seems to me that this fundamental idea, which is so simple and which harmonizes with all these manifestations, should be regarded as the basis of the religious conceptions and practices of primitive man.

Later on we shall find it in the most civilized societies and the loftiest religions.

CHAPTER VII

MAGIC

I. RELIGION, MYTHOLOGY, AND MAGIC

Up to the present we have been trying to find out, from the Negrillo and the Bantu populations, the connection of man with the supernatural world by his belief, conduct, and ritualistic practices, making him recognize it, perform his duties to it, and ask its help. That is religion: its purpose is to connect man with the divinity.

But to succeed in discerning this triple character, dogmatic, moral, and liturgical, in what is rightly styled their religion, we have been constantly obliged to separate that religion from other elements that are more conspicuous, that form about religion a sort of parasitic garment under which it almost disappears, stifled and dishonored. These elements, very complex and frequently hard to disentangle, so intricately are they mixed with the strictly religious, we have already grouped under the names of mythology and magic.

"In this matter," writes Father Lagrange, "everything remained confused for us as long as we did not distinguish between religion and mythology." [1]

---

[1] Lagrange, *op. cit.*, p. 2.

Andrew Lang has stated that

"the rational factor (or what approves itself to us as the rational factor) is visible in religion; the irrational is found in myth. The Australian, the Bushman, the Solomon Islander, in hours of danger and necessity 'yearns after the gods,' and has present in his heart the idea of a father and a friend. This is the religious element. The same man, when he comes to speculate on causes or to indulge his fancy for fiction, will degrade this spiritual friend and father to the level of the beast, and will make him the hero of comic or repulsive adventures. This is the mythical or irrational element. Religion in its moral aspect, always traces back to a belief in a power that is benign and works for righteousness. Myth, even in Homer or the Rig Veda, perpetually falls back on the old stock of absurd and immoral divine adventures." [2]

Unfortunately the use of this word "mythology" is ambiguous. It is better to reserve it to designate the collection of myths and legends that relate the origin or the wonderful doings of the gods and of other beings or things. Thus considered, "the religious significance of these stories has been absurdly exaggerated." These are the words of W. Robertson Smith. [3]

"Strictly speaking," he says, "this mythology was no essential part of ancient religion; for it had no sacred sanction, and no binding force upon the worshipers. . . . Belief in a certain series of myths was neither obligatory as a part of true religion, nor was it supposed that by *believing,* a man acquired religious merit and conciliated the favor of the gods. What *was* obligatory or meritorious was the exact performance of certain acts prescribed by religious tradition." [4]

And Professor Jevons, in his turn, concludes that

"mythology is primitive science, primitive philosophy, an important constituent of primitive history, the source of primitive poetry, but it is *not* primitive religion."

[2] Lang, *Myth, Ritual, and Religion,* I, p. 328.
[3] See L. Jordan, *Comparative Religion,* p. 302.
[4] *Ibid.,* p. 303.

We will abide by these authoritative opinions and, confining mythology to this meaning, we shall have in the word "magic" a more precise, comprehensive, and exact term to signify what is related tô religion as false money is to genuine.

By magic we mean, as we have said above, "the art of making use of the forces of nature by certain occult observances that have a religious appearance, or of courting the influences of the invisible world. Hence it follows that magic is the perversion of science as well as of religion." This definition also shows us that magic is related both to nature and to the supernatural, thus possessing a double character.

II. Natural Magic

Natural magic, as one might suppose and as we have already given the reader to understand, is very widespread in the black country. Yet in this matter there are notable differences betwen the various tribes, villages, and individuals. It is everywhere practiced openly, has its specialists, ceremonies, and initiations. As religion is found mingled with it in most of its manifestations, we have had occasion to speak of it in previous chapters. Its practices enrobe religion with numerous superstitions, as in certain damp climates the moss covers aged trees.

The idea behind this natural magic is that there are about us and within our reach, certain products whose hidden, protective, or curative properties can satisfy all the needs of life and drive away all evils. The great thing is to find them.

The idea may be just and at any rate the motive is good. But the primitive's lack of a critical spirit, his credulity, his more or less animistic feeling, and an irresistible desire to satisfy his passions (which he shares with all humanity), have turned him into the false path of magic. Once started on that road, it is not easy for him to turn back. Here is the source of amulets, talismans, charms, philters, auguries, omens, the art of divination, not to speak of numerous sacred prohibitions or taboos.

The amulets and talismans are of an infinite variety: some there are against evil and some for good fortune. The form is as variable as the object. They are handed down in the family from father to son, from mother to daughter for long generations. Often little gazelles' horns are used as well as the big horns of antelopes or goats, into which, following learned formulas, they put dust, little sticks, thorns, ashes, bones, feathers, leopards' claws, snakes' skin, soot, etc., etc. Of these *gri-gri,* some make one invulnerable in war, some charm the fish, others draw down the rain, preserve children from certain diseases, drive away witchcraft, attract the game during the hunt, procure fecundity.

The idea seems to be that the power of many of these amulets is simply symbolized by the material objects employed: the real power with which they are endowed comes especially from their consecration, the formulas used, and the art with which they have been prepared.

Others are genuine remedies, usually taken from the vegetable kingdom, but gathered, prepared, and administered in great secrecy and according to changeable formulas suited to the effect desired.

Many means are available to "charm" the fish and to attract the game as also to make themselves invisible, invulnerable, etc.

The conjurers are greatly esteemed: they discover stolen or lost articles, denounce thieves and poisoners, render witchcraft powerless, foretell the future, deliver oracles.

Other specialists possess means of making the rain fall or of stopping it.

As might be supposed, the healers, charmers, conjurers, and other sorcerers do not always succeed; in these cases they have an explanation ready. But it is unquestionable that they do obtain results, some due to the real efficacy of their products or methods, others from their professional skill, and still others must be credited to the action of a happy chance.

All these things are nothing but corollaries from ideas originally just, the attempted conquest of natural forces, the effort of man struggling against the unknown and trying to subject to his own use the multiple influences by which he feels himself surrounded. As the critical spirit, knowledge, and experience develop in him, this domain of natural magic will diminish to the profit of science. Man will always try to preserve himself from lightning: but instead of carrying an antelope's horn hanging from his neck, he will place a lightning-rod on his house.

Progress in this knowledge, however, will in no way affect religion properly so called, whose sphere of action lies in another direction where experimental science can not follow. So, when the materialist Buchner wrote that "faith and science have two distinct domains; but their frontiers are constantly shifting to the profit of the latter," he was confusing his facts. Although this assertion is justified in regard to faith in magic and those external manifestations with a more or less religious aspect which are too often mistaken for religion, it is not at all true of genuine religious faith. This latter, far from being demolished by reason, takes it for its basis, and far from being annihilated by science, can only be illumined and strengthened thereby.[5]

As religion among the primitives has taken the family for its mainstay, so magic has not failed to follow it into that retreat which, it would seem, should have been closed against it; spreading from there, it extended to the village and the tribe and seized upon the government of these rudimentary societies.

Not to mention the countless prohibitions, superstitions, and magical prescriptions with which the primitive family is burdened, we must charge to magic the singular institution of totemism, or the pact of allegiance with the animal world. We have already spoken of it at length, and have no occasion to return to the subject.

Magic takes a hand, also, in the initiation of youth. This ceremony, considered in itself, has a *raison d'être* that can be usefully sanctioned by religion. But magic nearly always monopolizes, complicates, and deforms it.

It is especially in what we call to-day political and social action that magic, by very curious organizations, seems to have concentrated its efforts. Its visible and avowed purpose is to seize the government of the village and tribe. It does this by

[5] See Guibert, *Les croyances religieuses, et les sciences de la nature.*

means of closed or secret societies which, however, are not the same everywhere although everywhere they bear an appearance of undeniable relationship: now more lax and open, now more tightly closed, more mysterious, more active. By making the reader acquainted with the constitution of a few of them, we shall give a sufficiently accurate idea of all.

In Giryama (east Africa), for example, a secret society of the above kind, is perfectly well organized and forms the frame-work of a political constitution for the country, at the top of which a clever and rigorous selection installs only those who have received the complete initiation.

The whole initiation comprises three degrees: these are again divided, the first into three grades, the second into four, and the third into two, so that the ninth grade, called "the hyena" (*fisi*), is the highest. This last inner circle is composed only of men whom Taylor, from whom we borrow these details, calls "very select." And he adds:

"The members of the Hyena inspire great terror, as they are the depositories of the most potent spells and oracles. The Enye-tsi (Possessors of the Land) are the three elders that govern Giryama and judge the land. They are chosen in rotation from the last two classes." [6]

In Lower Congo the initiation of youth with the requisite ceremonies is known by the name of *nkimba,* which is the name of the fetich used for rallying the initiated or *Zi-nkimba.* But, besides that, there is the society of the *Ndembo,* whose object seems to be to recruit and train the sorcerers and dignitaries of the tribe. The initiation, lasting several weeks and sometimes months, takes place outside the villages, in the forest, and embraces several trials, the teaching of a particular language, ritualistic dances, the knowledge of remedies and magical formulas. At the end, when the initiated returns to his family, he bears a new name and is thought to be returning from the world of spirits: he begins a new life. [7]

[6] Taylor, *Giryama Vocabulary,* p. 45.
[7] E. de Jonghe, *Les sociétés secrètes au Bas-Congo.*

In the region of Sette Cama and elsewhere, the *Bwiti,* which is the great fetich of the country, has likewise its initiated. To enter the society, the candidate must first chew certain roots and drink a concoction from the bark of a tree known to botanists under the name of *Strychnos ikaja;* he is not long in falling asleep and losing all consciousness. Then a bind-weed is fastened around his neck. Three days later, when he begins to recover, the sorcerer bids him look into a piece of glass fastened to the belly of the *Bwiti.* There he will see certain figures of which he must give an account; if he does so correctly, he is received; if not, it is a sign that the fetich has not wished to show himself to him.

In Gabon, there are also many of these secret societies, some composed solely of men, as the *Yasi;* others including only women, as the *Ndjembe:* others are mixed. Initiation, trials, ceremonial reception, instruction, passwords, the whole thing is surrounded with an absolute secrecy, with solemn oaths and promises, under pain of death, to obey every order coming from the spirit under whose patronage the society is organized.

The initiated are divided into different grades, recalling in a strange manner our freemasonry which in civilized society— so they say—exercises a certain influence on our religious, political, and social affairs.

The high chief is generally a stranger to the village and known to nobody. The reception ceremonies like the others take place in the evening or during the night and are clothed in great mystery. At the call of the president, the Yasi comes out of the forest: he is a frightful being, all covered with leaves, wearing various ornaments, walking in a strange fashion, and talking in a sepulchral voice, giving orders and answering questions that are put to him. Naturally this mask is worn by a confrère, but that is one of the great secrets that nobody must know. As soon as the presence of the Yasi is perceived in the village, the cries of the initiated arise, the dances are begun, and all the uninitiated, beginning with the women and children, must withdraw.

When he reaches the hut reserved for him, the Yasi receives the candidates, usually young men, and proceeds to utter his oracles. Then they offer a sacrifice, followed by a repast; there are new dances, and the feast is ended.

The initiated bear a special tattoo on their arm; when taking an oath in the name of "Yasi," they place their hand on this tattoo: it is the great oath of the country.

The master or "venerable" is distinguished by a tuft of hair in the shape of a triangle.

No doubt, as a defense against the abuse of power to which they were exposed on the part of the men, the women have also organized their own secret societies, fully as mysterious as the others. Up to the present, no European can flatter himself with having ascertained what takes place therein. All that we know, outside of their abominably immoral initiations, is that often men are included in their membership and that many a poisoning is decided upon there.

When it is said that the religion of savage peoples has fostered no morality but, on the contrary, has been an inspiration of many evils, there is a confusion of terms easy to understand. It is magic, not religion, to which reference is made.

Magical morality, if one may use the term, is purely and often brutally utilitarian. That is good which is serviceable and pleasant. Everything is sacrificed to personal interest; in that contaminated atmosphere, egoism reigns supreme, as a tyrannical master. *Vae victis!* The vanquished are the weak, the slaves, the women, the children. This is the barbarous morality which too often conceals and stifles true morality in the black country.

Moreover, the native African, contrary to what we might suppose, is very ambitious, very eager to rise above his fellows, very anxious to become rich. That disposition, exploited by the slave-dealers, explains why the abominable slave traffic has gone on for such a long time. This fratricidal commerce has been able to exist only through the complicity of thoroughly depraved chiefs and courtiers, who are personally interested in having their compatriots seized and sold to foreigners.

So magical proceedings intended to procure success and wealth are especially numerous and highly appreciated. One of them, in Congo, which involves the murder of a near relative, a wife, a son, a daughter, is frequently employed.

III. SUPERNATURAL MAGIC

At the side of natural magic, there is another kind that pretends to derive its power from the beings of the invisible world, from disembodied souls, the manes of men and even of animals, or from independent spirits. In this matter, God dwells apart: magic does not reach him.

Like religion, this anti-religion has its forms of worship, its incantations, evocations, rites, fetiches, offerings, sacrifices, and ministers, its feasts and meeting-places. It is practiced along with natural magic and along with religion, parallel to them, mysterious, elusive, feared, execrated, hunted in its manifestations and representatives, yet indestructible. To apply the word "feticher" or "sorcerer" indiscriminately to all sorts of persons is incorrect and faulty. The natives themselves do not make this mistake.

All through Bantu Africa, the specialist in natural magic bears a name, *m-ganga, n-ganga, m-hanga, ganga, n-gan;* corresponding to it is another word meaning "remedy," and a verb from the same root whose meaning is to "treat, recommend, diagnose." According to the locality, this word *m-ganga* has several synonyms: they all testify to the high esteem which this position enjoys. In some places they give him the title equivalent to that of "chief," *m-fumu, mu-fumu,* etc., "the man with the spear" (he who has the spear of command). Elsewhere he is called "healer." Sometimes the office of "diviner" or "seer" is attested by special epithets.

As for the conjurer, he is the *m-logi, m-rogi, m-lozi, mo-lo, mo-loki, m-loo, e-loroi.* These words are all derived from a corresponding verb whose general meaning is "to charm, to bewitch." Another primitive verb, *-loa,* "to take to the bait," is similar to this one. Corresponding to the above nouns, each language has an abstract substantive "witchcraft," *ulogo, bu-logi, u-lozi,* etc.

This word "conjurer" has synonyms: *m-chawi,* literally "the wicked watcher," *m-wanga,* "the night-prowler," *mo-lemba,* "the poisoner." To address a native by one of these names is worse than an insult: it is a serious imprudence.

The sorcerers and sorceresses operate separately in casting their spells, but often they are organized into societies that are particularly secret about their meetings and councils. Nassau gives us the following account:

"These meetings are secret; preferably in a forest, or at least distant from the village. The hour is near midnight. An imitation of the hoot of an owl, which is their sacred bird, is their signal call. They profess to leave their corporeal body lying asleep in their huts, and claim that the part which joins in the meeting is the spirit body, whose movements are not hindered by walls or other physical objects and can pass with infinite rapidity through the air, or over the tree-tops. At their meetings they have visible, audible, and tangible communication with evil spirits. They partake of feasts, the article eaten is termed the 'heart-life' of some human being, who, in consequence of this loss of his 'heart,' will become sick and die, unless it be restored. The early cock-crowing is a warning for them to disperse; the advent of the morning star they fear, as it compels them to hasten back to their bodies. Should the sun rise upon them before they reach their corporeal 'home,' their plans would fail, and they themselves would sicken." [8]

While the sorcerer is thus going about under some form or other, a globe of fire, a night-bird or some other animal, if he is struck, if he is pierced with a pointed iron, if he is shot at, he finds himself beaten unmercifully in his hut, if in fact he ever wakes up: in striking his disembodied soul, you strike his body. Many facts and names are cited by the natives in support of these statements.

The mysterious power of the sorcerers comes from the pact which they have entered into with a spirit, by ritualistic and secret formulas, known only to the affiliated.

Often, to accomplish their evil designs and to carry out their vengeances, the sorcerers change themselves into animals and become an object of veritable terror to the country. Thus in

[8] Nassau, *Fetichism in West Africa,* p. 123.

Gabon the "man-tiger" is often referred to. In the evening
after sunset, he is to be seen prowling just outside the village on
lonely roads, or along the edge of the fields. If a child or
woman passes by, he jumps upon the poor victim and slays him.
At Bata twenty or thirty persons were known to have disappeared in this way within a few months. Elsewhere it is a man-
jackal, a man-alligator and so forth.

These are real murders and absolutely verified. How explain
them? Sometimes they are due to a real beast that has tasted
human flesh and has presently become a dreadful plague. Other
times it is a man who clothes himself in the skin of a leopard or
some other animal: the marks of its paws remain on the soil
and create the impression that a beast has passed. This man,
obeying a sort of diabolical impulse, seizes defenseless people
and kills them. The European police have been able to catch
some of these men-tigers and to execute them in various centers
of colonization along the African coast. At times, a series of
murders has remained unexplained.

Other sorcerers, under one form or another, are satisfied with
doing material damage. During my sojourn in Gabon, I was
called one day to Cap Esterias by an entire tribe whose tapioca
plantations were being ravaged by a mysterious band of wild
animals commanded by a sort of captain, also a wild beast. This
fanatic animal was insensible to bullets, avoided all traps, and
proved to be none other than an old sorceress who was pointed
out to me. Her victims wanted to cut her to pieces, and it was
not without difficulty that I saved her life.

Besides strange powers that are too often gratuitously attributed to them, the sorcerers have others that are only too
real. Whether they operate on their own account or at the request of some client, well authenticated poisonings occur which
one must never joke about. Sometimes they concoct charms
to inflict sickness or death, secreting them, for example, on
the path or under the doorstep of the person aimed at so that he
will trample them under foot; such charms or fetiches are generally evil only because of the bad intention attached to them.
But there are others, which rarely fail to reach their victim,
so that we shall not be surprised that the Blacks dread this kind

of sorcerers, seek them out, denounce them, and, true or false, execute them without pity.

Unfortunately, the judges in the black country are far from possessing the impartiality, prudence, perspicacity that justice requires. So as not to acquit any guilty person, they execute nearly all the accused: we may therefore say that, in certain parts of Africa, there is perhaps not a village in which some of these executions have not taken place. On the eastern coast, men or women accused of sorcery, when they have been judged and condemned, are generally burned on a fire of ebony outside the village at the crossroads. Passing along the caravan routes, you will often come upon little heaps of ashes, with debris of bones and some blackened brands. Near by, on a dead tree or one that has been stripped you will see some wretched rags hanging in the wind: black justice has passed that way.

What largely contributes to arouse the suspicion of the natives and considerably increase the number of the victims, is the mystery that surrounds sickness and death throughout the black country. As vengeance is a duty, whenever one loses a relative, especially a father or mother or the head of the family, after having assured them a worthy funeral, the first obligation is to look for the one who killed them. Recourse is had to a diviner or seer who discovers the truth by various means, according to the country. There are three possible causes of death: God, a spirit, an enemy. If death comes from God there is nothing to be done about it. We can not reach God to settle our claims and, besides, having given life He has the right to take it away. If death comes from a spirit, it must be that wittingly or unwittingly, the deceased has offended it, otherwise this spirit would have found no pleasure in killing him. In this case an offering or a sacrifice is necessary to appease it and commute his demands: that is what is actually done. But if it is discovered that death came at the hand of another man, that man must die. Otherwise justice would not be satisfied, and the spirit of the dead would not fail to disturb the indifferent family that should forget or neglect the pursuit of the murderer.

The natives on whom suspicion may fall, voluntarily offer to undergo the ordeal: vegetable poison, boiling water, hot iron, etc.; though some come out unharmed, many succumb. These are often the first to proclaim themselves guilty, asserting that they must have inflicted the death without knowing it.

In support of this belief, often the entrails of the corpse of the accused are opened and when they find anything strange there, even an anatomical part which they can not explain, it is deemed a proof that this man was really a sorcerer.

Another frequent manifestation of the world of spirits is "possession." The "possessing" spirit is sometimes of human origin but most often it is a malevolent and perverse being whose origin is little known and who feels for man only jealousy, bitterness, and hatred. In such a case the first thing to do is to call a specialist who will make the spirit speak and who will then know what exorcist to summon to deliver the sick person. The man of art arrives; he, too inquires of the spirit who he is, why he entered that body, what he requires, etc. After these preliminaries have been performed, they set about satisfying these demands. At times the spirit refuses to speak, and the sorcerer must supplement his silence. Generally, however, he speaks, and they obey him. Finally, after the tam-tam, ritualistic dances, and other ceremonies that are very long and complicated (they may last several days and nights), the sacrifice is offered as requested, the possessed one drinks the blood of the victim, those assisting join in this "communion," and the spirit goes away—sometimes. If he remains, they call in another sorcerer and everything must be begun over again.

What are these possessions?

Many of them are easily explained; they are cases that ordinary medicine would relieve, and the best exorcism as well as the least expensive, would be a strong purgative.

But there are other cases in which the most skeptical must acknowledge himself nonplussed. For example, the one possessed (they are most often women) disappears from her home during the night and on the next day is found high up in a big tree, tied to a branch by fine bind-weed. When the sacrifice is

offered and the bonds that hold her have fallen, she glides down
the length of the trunk like a serpent. For several minutes
she remains elevated above the ground and speaks fluently in
a language of which she theretofore did not know the first
word.

The natives recount many other similar cases which they
claim to have witnessed. It would be very interesting to check
up these and many other facts with all possible strictness; unfortunately it is all carefully hidden from the eyes of the European. If he succeeds in arriving on the scene at a ceremony of
this kind, they will either cut him to pieces rather than let him
be present, or they will promptly terminate the proceedings
and disperse.

We distinguish between protective fetiches and avenging
fetiches. Both may have their agents, either the manes or
independent spirits.

The fetich, Bwiti, for instance, which is very well known in
the region of Gabon and Loango and is the center of a secret
association, materially consists of a stick rudely carved in the
shape of a human figure. Pieces of glass form the eyes; a bit
of mirror takes the place of the navel; therein the sorcerer
will look for the truth. Beneath are a tiger skin, some little
bells, grass, strips of leather, etc. The bag from which this
sculptured stick emerges contains a skull filled with various
powders, corrupt matter from a corpse, and a bone from a snake.
The fetich is placed in a decorated niche in the interior of a little
hut that has no other opening than a door. A fire which, they
say, must never go out, is fed by three big logs renewed by the
sorcerer. A little path leads from this hut to a clearing in the
neighboring forest where the initiated assemble. As in all similar ceremonies, the mildest, simplest, and most approachable
Blacks are unrecognizable at this time; for whole nights they
will beat the tam-tam, sing, dance, and perform fantastic sara-
bands. To approach them at such a period is impossible.

Besides the fetich Bwiti, the fetich Mboyo also has its followers. As it occurs in the same part of Africa (Loango), let
us follow the consecration of an avenging fetich: it is said to be

directly influenced by a living soul forcibly snatched from a man who is known and designated. In this affair, we are no longer dealing with vain and laughable superstitions.

"When a party enters the woods with the Nganga (or the Doctor) attached to the service of the fetiches Zinkici Mbown, into which nails are driven for the purpose of cutting the 'Muamba' tree, with the intention of making a fetich, it is forbidden for anyone to call another by name. If he does so, that man will die, and his Kulu (soul) will enter into the tree and become a presiding spirit of the fetich when made; and the caller will of course have to answer with his life to the relations of the man whose life has been thus wantonly thrown away. So, generally speaking, a palaver is held, and it is there decided whose Kulu it is that is to enter into the Muamba tree and to preside over the fetich to be made. A boy of great spirit, or else, above all, a great and daring hunter is chosen. Then they go into the bush and call his name. The Nganga cuts down the tree and blood is said to gush forth. A fowl is killed and its blood is mingled with the blood they say comes from the tree. The named one then dies, certainly within ten days. His life has been sacrificed for what the Zinganga consider the welfare of the people. They say that the named one never fails to die—and they repudiate all idea of his being poisoned or that his death is hurried on in any material way by the Bganga, who, they say, may be miles away.

"People pass before these fetiches, calling on them to kill them if they do or have done such or such a thing. Others go to them and insist upon their killing so and so, who has done or is about to do some fearful injury. And they swear or make their demands, a nail is driven into the fetich and the palaver is settled so far as they are concerned. The Kulu of the man whose life was sacrificed upon the cutting of the tree sees to the rest." [9]

This is the classical proceeding of the "envoutement," known throughout Africa under one form or another.[10]

[9] Dennett, op. cit., p. 93.
[10] Envoûtement, from en, preposition, and voult (old French), "face" (from vultus).

Sacrifice, which seems to be everywhere the central rite of religion, is also the rite about which magic centers, or rather to which magic leads: in both cases sacrifice is the homage rendered by man either to the true divinity or to spirit or demon or man that usurps his place.

We have previously mentioned ritualistic murders and anthropophagy. One can exist without the other. As a matter of fact there are tribes which offer human sacrifices without practicing cannibalism. At the Niger delta, for example, until these latter years human victims used to be offered to the sacred crocodile. In the same region, known by the name of "Oil Banks," a girl was wont to be offered in annual sacrifice to the spirits of the water for the success of the hunt. In relating these facts, Nassau truthfully adds:

"Treaties with foreign civilized nations have now prohibited this sacrifice, but the maiden has not gained much in the change. Instead of one being sacrificed to a brute crocodile to please the spirit trade, hundreds are prostituted to please brutal, dissolute foreigners." [11]

Anthropophagy has closely followed human sacrifice. Primitively the object of this savage communion was the same as that of all communion sacrifices: to renew the alliance with the supernatural world, to participate in the new outpouring of a higher life, to appropriate mysterious and powerful influences by eating the material of the sacrifice consecrated to the divinity.

In many cases this is still the fundamental idea of this essential rite of all religion and all magic. But we also find the thought that, having subdued the victim in immolating it, they partly assimilate its courage and other qualities by eating its organs.

Another idea is clearly exhibited among the Fans. He whom they eat is their enemy or, what amounts to the same thing, the enemy of their family; it is he who has made a war on them, who has killed or has wished to kill one of their number. Consequently they accomplish this double result: avenge the dead

[11] Nassau, *op. cit.*, p. 93.

and humiliate the murderer. For, in the mind of these philosophers, there is no greater or more complete outrage to inflict
on an enemy than to reduce him to nothingness by passing him
piecemeal through the process of digestion.

When that is accomplished, the vengeance is complete!
Among the Bondjos of Ubanghi this seems to have reached the
last stage of brutality; anthropophagy openly and commonly
practiced until it has become habitual and almost without any
ceremonial. In fact, while the man destined for the butchery
is being greased by his owner, the clients come and finger the
parts that suit them best, one the breast, another a shoulder,
this one a thigh, and so forth. These sections are at once marked
with chalk. Then, when all his members have been parceled out,
the limbs of the poor wretch are broken and are soaked in water
to make them more tender; after that he is killed, cut up, divided, and eaten.

Father O. Allaire, who founded the mission of Lirango in
1889,[12] gives us valuable details as to the practice of Congo anthropophagy.

"Human sacrifices are always in use by the savage peoples
among whom we live," he says. "When I arrived at Liranga,
my neighbors of Nyambe, Butonu, Busuidi, and Irebu sometimes allowed themselves the luxury of two or three human
sacrifices a week. This ceremony is an occasion of public
rejoicing. All the villages round about take part. They sing,
dance, and pass around through the mad throng immense jugs
of palm-wine. The condemned person (or persons), firmly
secured, is permitted to witness the height of joy which his
death is to bring. At length they untie the victim, make him
sit on a log slightly raised from the ground, his arms hanging
beside his body, his hands fastened to the ground by means of
forked sticks whose extremities are securely fastened in the
soil; thus all movement is rendered impossible. Similar forked
sticks hold his legs stretched out in front while the bust is held
immovable by a kind of palisade which comes up to his shoul-
ders. About two yards behind the victim, whom all this

[12] Liranga is at the confluence of the Ubanghi and the Congo. Father
Allaire died there.

apparatus literally nails to the ground, a long solid pole is planted; by means of ropes the flexible extremity of this pole is brought down to the victim's head, making a spring that will stretch his neck. Suddenly the crowd is silent: the feticher has made his appearance. In his woolly hair more than two hundred feathers of different colors are arranged artistically to form an enormous headdress; two white circular marks surround the eyes which thereby acquire extraordinary brightness. His dress, though scant, is rich and quite modest for this land. On his forehead and cheeks are red lines that combine well with the black background of his skin. The bare arms and legs exhibit broad red and yellow stripes. He advances with short steps, swinging his feathery mane, holding in his nervous hand the terrible execution knife that must sever the head with a single blow; and he stops and greets the wretch whom he has to execute.

"Then, as though seized with madness, he goes through contortions that no pen could describe: he tosses himself about like one possessed, leaps, doubles up, advances so gently, so much like a reptile, that you can not perceive any movement of his feet. The crowd applauds. But silence is restored as soon as the fatal knife is raised. The sorcerer then begins a rhythmic chant: it is the chant of death. The people respond by repeating his words to the same air and clapping their hands in time to the melody. Thus singing and gesticulating, several times he approaches his victim who is a helpless witness of these preparations. With white chalk he marks a line around the victim's neck: it is there he will strike when the time arrives. Twice brandishing the knife, he touches the condemned man's neck with it. The chant is ended: with a leap, the feticher approaches the victim and again steps back; twice more his arm strikes the air by way of trial. Then the knife is lowered and a single stroke cuts off the head which the bent pole sends rolling far away. With a shout the crowd leaps on the body. All is over; soon the savages will joyfully return to their homes."

"I recently learned," writes Father Allaire, "of the death of a very influential woman chief named Komba-Keka, whom I knew quite well. Do you know how many slaves were slain to accompany her to the grave? Seventy.

"This is how they do it at Bonga, near Liranga. They bind

the victim, stretch him on the ground, and place a heavy piece of wood on his throat. The executioner, bracing himself by the aid of his spear, placed his two feet on the extremities of the log, and strangles the unfortunate mortal. . . . When the latter has ceased to breathe, they bury him and proceed to the next.

"When a chief wants to go hunting, he gathers his friends who are to accompany him and they drink and sing. But before starting out, as they must have some blood for the success of the expedition, they bring forth a little slave of ten or twelve years who has been tied in a corner the night before and without ceremony very prosaically cut off his head with a dull knife. Sometimes his blood is poured into the water of the river where they throw the body; then they confidently set out.

"Children up to the age of fifteen or sixteen years are the ordinary victims selected for all these horrors, for they are the weakest, and in Africa weakness is a crime." [13]

Let us pass from these horrors which exemplify the depth of degradation to which humanity can fall. But it is worthy of note that the tribes most given to anthropophagy, infanticide, poisoning, and all the plagues of magic, are not, from the point of view of material advancement, inferior to other tribes. On the contrary, because of their superior political organization, their social development, and their great skill in industry and commerce, they often dominate the others. Yet, just when they have reached this comparatively higher degree of civilization, we find them subject to these aberrations which complete their evolution by killing them all off: it is a process of tribal suicide.

It is scarcely necessary to dwell on other examples which show us that these strange and humiliating debaucheries are not the sole privilege of the primitives. Without speaking of what takes place in the shoals of our European society, we have lately seen numerous representatives of the most civilized races who were living in the African world for the work of colonization, astonish the lowest savages by the extremity of their moral perversity, by their useless cruelty, and by their shameless degeneracy. So true is it that man is everywhere the same and that, though neither angel nor beast according to the saying of Pas-

[13] Letters from Rev. Olivier Allaire, C.S.Sp., missionary in Ubanghi.

cal, he is nevertheless capable of mounting very high towards
the one and of descending very low towards the other.

The practical and social effect of this tyranny of magic on
the African population does not directly enter into our subject: we shall, therefore, be satisfied with a few words on this
point.

The first effect is the forgetfulness and corruption of religion
along with the degradation of morality. It is useless to insist
on this feature, for what we have just said sufficiently establishes the truth of the assertion.

The second is depopulation. In the black continent fetichism has slain more victims than wars, disease, or slavery. It is a
Moloch whose appetite is never sated. Human sacrifices at the
death of the great chiefs, as formerly in Uganda, the states of
Upper Congo, the valley of the Ubanghi, the Ashanti country,
and Dahomey, the accusations of sorcery, more or less ritualistic
poisonings, and judicial ordeals, have done to death thousands
of men, women, and children, and still continue doing so.

Has Islam, where it is established, stopped this plague? Islam in many places, as along the Upper Congo, in the environs
of the Tchad in Sudan, has brought devastation and ruin. It
has, besides, seized, killed, sold and distributed on all the caravan routes thousands and thousands of slaves. Wherever it has
penetrated without violence, entire populations have been affected with syphilis by contact with it.

But now comes European civilization to shed its light on be-
nighted Africa. This will perhaps end her misfortunes! Far
from it. European civilization, in the forms it so often takes,
disorganizes and dissolves the African family, introduces alco-
hol, spreads the gout, destroys the class distinctions of the
Blacks, increases everywhere dreadful diseases, such as the
sleeping sickness which was formerly confined to certain points
on the coast. No, alas! European civilization does not end
those trials which have fallen on the black world. But, everything considered, it has advantages, and we hope at least that
we can contribute to make it better and render it a means of
real progress for its African wards.

Along with depopulation, the tyranny of the secret societies
exercises a lamentable influence on the African population. No
class of natives, no sex escapes. That tyranny strikingly develops a tendency to dissimulation, suspicion, accusations, and
oppression to which the nature of the Black is generally already
too much inclined. These secret societies are undoubtedly to
be classed among Africa's plagues. Where in the world, we venture to ask, are they an influence for good?

These groups of institutions, usages, excesses, and abuses of
every kind have spread over these people like an atmosphere of
general mistrust, arresting all progress.

"There is no place in the world," says Wilson, "where men
feel more insecurity. A man must be careful whose company
he keeps, what path he walks, whose house he enters, on what
stool he seats himself, where he sleeps. He knows not at what
moment he may place his foot or lay his hands upon some
invisible engine of mischief, or by what means the seeds of
death may be implanted in his constitution." [14]

Nassau adds that in consequence of this lack of confidence,
the natural affection and duties of our most cherished human
relations are perverted. The women are afraid of their husbands, the husbands of their wives; the children have no assurance as to the intentions of their parents, nor the parents as to
those of their children; the village chief doubts his people; and
the entire community, which ought to live, eat, and work together, lives, eats, and works in secret, constant, and reciprocal
mistrust. This general suspicion, founded on reasons only too
well justified, is the principal cause of the scattering of African society into tiny villages, the dispersion of all this poor
world, the cause of its weakness in the presence of invaders and
slave-traders, of its powerlessness to rise, of its halt in the march
of civilization.

Moreover, this distress generates a strange jealousy that
strengthens still more the tyranny from which these primitive
societies suffer. No one can rise, become rich, do anything new
that distinguishes him from the common rank and file without

[14] Wilson, *Western Africa*, in Nassau, *op. cit.*, p. 269.

arousing envy and its consequences. A somewhat better constructed house, a better planted field, clothes more carefully made, attract attention for they indicate an ambitious man; the only means by which this man of progress may maintain himself is to make himself feared. Only the fear of his fetiches will keep the curious on their guard: otherwise he is a lost man.

Thus an equality in misery and barbarity has been maintained in Africa during the ages.

CHAPTER VIII

COMPARISON OF THE RELIGIONS OF THE PRIMITIVES

I. On Primitive Ground

With the manifestations of magic excepted, the religion of the Bantus and those tribes associated with their life has been that described in the foregoing pages.

We must repeat that their beliefs, morality, worship, and religious organization do not form a coherent, homogeneous, and scientific system such as we generally associate with the word "religion," as, for instance, that of Buddhism and Islam. All the elements appear mingled together, confused, and more or less dissimilar. But they are there and perceptible to the attentive eye, especially if we are willing to take into consideration the manner in which the Blacks understand life and civilization. We have no right to ask of them what they can not give.

However imperfect this religion may be and however imperfect the exposition we have been able to give of it, nevertheless both form a sufficient basis for the study we have undertaken.

We will now attempt briefly to compare the religions of the relatively primitive peoples that are actually living on the surface of the globe. Besides the special interest which this method has for us, it has the great advantage of placing us precisely on the ground chosen by the science that is devoting itself to studying the origin of religions: these primitives are that "limestone bank" of which we have spoken, flourishing in a country of floods and representing ancient ground on which we ourselves have built.

II. The Human Races

The human races have not yet been classified in a manner that is finally acceptable. As it would be so foreign to our study to bring forward an independent classification and offer our reasons for it, we will be satisfied to follow Quatrefages and seek the protection of the great authority attached to his works. He divides the human species into three fundamental types, under the conventional names that have been given them.

The White type, embracing the Aryans and Semites;

The Yellow type, including Asiatics and American Indians;

The Black type, composed of African negroes and the Malays of Oceanica.[1]

This division is the most popular and simple and perhaps not the least just.

According to the opinion of Quatrefages, Asia was the seat of the formation of these three fundamental types and most of the principal secondary types. This opinion has not been weakened by the studies undertaken since the death of that worthy scholar. We may be permitted to adopt it at least provisionally. "Asia," he says, "has remained the great fatherland of the Yellow race and has, so to speak, distributed to the other parts of the world the races sprung therefrom."[2]

[1] Quatrefages, *Introd. à l'étude des races humaines*, p. 335. Cf. Deniker, *Races et peuples de la terre;* Dr. Weule, *Globus.*

[2] Quatrefages, *op. cit.*, p. 335.

The negro type, for example, probably acquired its racial characteristics primitively in southern Asia. Its various representatives emigrated from there, some westward towards Africa, the others eastward towards India, Indo-China, and that part of Oceanica which to-day bears the name of Melanasia.

Thus several ethnic layers must have been deposited in Africa over the San and the Negrillos, mingling with them in various proportions. We can recognize among them the following general divisions: to the south, the Bantus, who have been the special subject of this study; on the equatorial side, the Nigritians, who form considerable tribes and have at times even constituted veritable states, such as the Achantis, the Dahomeyans, and various peoples in the valleys of the Tchad, the Niger, and the Senegal. They are all, in general, larger, stronger and blacker than the Bantus.

At the same time, through Oceanica spread the Australian negroes, the Papuans, the Melanesians of New Britain, New Hebrides, New Caledonia, the Fiji Islands, etc.

Asia itself preserved some more or less pure examples of this population: such, for example, are the Veddahs of Ceylon.

Upon this black population, at a date impossible to determine, there must have been deposited a new element: the element called Hamitic, whose skin is brown rather than black, and whose type, while neither that of the Yellow nor of the White, is, however, not that of the Negro.[3] By a movement similar to that which we have just mentioned, this population spread as follows:

In Africa, where, as the Massais, Oromos, Peuls, and ancient Egyptians, it occupies the northern parts, left more or less free to it by the Blacks who had penetrated into the continent;

In Oceanica, where the Polynesians show extraordinary affinities of type, manners, traditions, and even language with these Africans just mentioned[4];

---

[3] *'Ham*, from the root *'Hâmman*, "warm," related to *'Hûm*, "black." Ham, ancestor of the dark people, but not of the negroes, as a widespread prejudice considers (according to F. Lenormant, *Les origines de l'histoire d'après la Bible*).

[4] Wiçwa Mitra, *Les Chamites*.

In Asia, where it has left numerous evidences, notably in India.

While the Blacks and Browns were spreading especially toward the continents and islands of the south, the yellow race was multiplying and covering an immense continuous area that to-day extends from the eastern coasts of Asia all the way to Europe and even America; including besides the civilized populations of Indo-China, China, Thibet, and Mongolia, others, such as the Samoyedes, Kamchadales, Innuits, or Esquimos, which might be considered as races that remain in the primitive state.

The Whites likewise formed themselves into different powerful branches. One of them has left vestiges of itself in Asia, among the most primitive populations, as the Ainus of Japan and the Todas of India; another was driven back to the extreme north with the Finns and the Laplanders; another furnished the Semitic element, so important in ethnographic studies; and another is represented by the great Ayran family which to-day rules the destinies of the world.

As for America, it seems to have been peopled, for the most part, by emigrants more or less closely joined to the yellow stock; but in that vast continent, which extends from one pole to the other, we may say that the three fundamental types have contributed in unequal proportions to form the tribes which the European found there.[5] This mixed population is to be seen established at various points on the earth, notably at Madagascar and in all that part of the Far East to which has been given the name of Malaysia.

To conclude this rapid review of man's dispersion over the earth, let us repeat that science is far from having determined the classification of the races. What we have just been saying is not said to show a preference that would be necessary to found a theory. For the present, let us continue our search for the living black, yellow, and white populations, pure or mixed,

[5] Quatrefages, *op. cit.*, p. 550.

which most closely approach what is said to be the primitive condition of humanity. Our object will be to point out their religious beliefs, to compare them, and finally to succeed, if we can, in preparing a sort of symbol or *Credo* which may be said to be that of the first ancestors of mankind.

This study might occupy entire volumes. The information furnished by travelers, the studies undertaken on the spot, and the various works relating to anthropology have increased to unlimited proportions. Thanks to this abundance of documentary evidence, we can make the following statements:

1. All the peoples known up to the present—we may well say all peoples—have or have had a religion, in the broad sense in which we continue to use this word;

2. Among all these peoples, the foundation of religion is substantially the same;

3. Going down the scale from the highest ancient civilizations, like those of Egyptian, Chaldean, Assyrian, Phœnician, Indian, Cimmerian, Chinese, Mexican, and Peruvian antiquities, to the lowest social forms, we find religions that are less systematized, less complicated, less poetic, less rich in theogonies, mythologies, organizations, and other details. In other words, in the degree that these populations have a general primitive aspect, the more simple are the religious data, the more elementary and less complicated.

The rapid glance that we shall give the chief primitive populations of the world to supplement our study of the Bantus, will confirm the conclusions that we shall finally be led to make.

Let us now return to Africa.

Lower than the Hamites, Bantus, and even Hottentots, we find unfortunate little men who have taken the name of *San* (in the singular *Sab*), at the southern extremity of the continent, driven out from every locality and wandering in scattered groups through the desert lands of Kalahari. Dutch colonists long since designated them under the name *Bosjesmannen* (in English *Bushmen*). We find them also scattered in more or less important settlements among the Khoikhoi or

Hottentots, standing somewhat higher on the ladder of human civilization, but resembling the San in many ethnic respects.[6]

San and Khoikhoi at present inhabit the south of Africa on both sides of the Orange River. Towards the north, we find in the Negrillos, already spoken of, a population in many respects quite similar. Indeed they are found from the Orange where we left the San, all the way to Counene, in Angola, around the great lakes of central Africa, in the immense equatorial forest that extends from Gabon to the farthest tributaries of the Congo, then from Cameroun and the Niger to the Kenia and the valley of the Djouba. Not far away is Ethiopia and the Nile valley where the ancient writers of Greece, with Herodotus and Homer, formerly pointed them out.[7]

We find a similar race in the Negritos in the part of the world that faces eastern Africa, towards the lands washed by the Indian Ocean.[8] The Negritos are represented in relatively pure groups in the Philippines, by the Aëtas (from the Malay Hitan, "Black"); in the peninsula of Malacca by the Sakai and Semang; and in the Andaman Islands by the Minkopies.[9] But Quatrefages said, and has not been contradicted, that traces of them may be seen at a great number of other points in the Oceanic islands. "For, without speaking of more or less pure small groups that still exist, this race forms the common foundation of entire populations; it has left traces of itself in the midst of victorious races, from New Guinea to the Persian Gulf, and from the Malay Archipelago to Japan,"[10] not to mention India, Ceylon, Baluchistan, and Suziane.

Thus converging from the depths of Africa and the depths of Oceanica,—and perhaps we might also discover evidence

[6] Deniker, Les races et les peuples de la terre.
[7] See Le Roy, The Pygmies.
[8] Negrito, "little negro," name given by the Spaniards of the Philippines.
[9] Deniker, op. cit., p. 556. It is worthy of remark, by the way, that this word minkopi is unknown to the natives. It is of European formation and seems to come from the words Kemi kopi, "remain here," no doubt understood as an answer to the question: Who are you? These mistakes are very common. (Quatrefages, Les Pygmées, p. 99).
[10] Quatrefages, op. cit., p. 351.

of their passage on the European continent [11]—we find ourselves tending to a common center where the ancient and definite dispersion probably took place.

Over that immense area this interesting race presents inevitable differences due to a number of causes: the remote date of
their separation, the regions occupied, the action of environment, and above all the intermarriage in varying proportions
with neighboring tribes. Yet the Negrillo and the Negrito type
everywhere possesses surprisingly permanent characteristics:
smallness of stature, dark color of the skin, woolly appearance
of the hair, large size of the head, a vagabond existence, the disposition to pass unperceived, temporary and wretched habita-
tions, disdain for all culture and improvement, a wilful and conscious care to take no sustenance of life except the free products of the earth, a conviction which they have concerning themselves and which the neighboring populations have of them that
they were the first comers on the land which they occupy, the
aborigines, the "men."

If now we try to take note of their beliefs and religious
practices, another surprise confronts us: these resemble one another almost everywhere, as much as do their other ethnic characteristics, perhaps even more so.

Everywhere among the San, the Negrillos, and the Negritos,
the family is so established that, with the rare exception of
some important settlements, the head of the family is everything: father, chief, and priest. The family is monogamous.

A universal and very remarkable characteristic of their
religion is that nowhere does it seem to require temples, enclosures, huts, like the miniature huts pointed out among the
Bantus. Nor do they make fetiches: here and there they wear
simple amulets, ordinarily consisting of little pieces of wood;
these are rather considered as remedies in their thought.

They are able to prepare amulets against all the evils and for
all the needs of life, they know the best recipes for catching
game, they can make themselves invisible. What do they not
know? They are the ones who first learned, thanks to super-

[11] Skeletons of real pygmies have been found in the ancient tombs of
Schweizernbold, in Switzerland.

natural revelations, they say, to extract iron and to work it. Better than any others, they can find water, fruits, fish, game, and while others die of hunger, they are able to feed themselves abundantly.

The San, as also the Negrillos and the Negritos, have no worship of the stars; but we find something like it among the Khoikhoi. We are told that these latter sacrifice beasts to the moon and offer it flesh and milk; offerings that are accompanied by dances, prostrations, and songs in which they greet its return. They ask it for favorable weather, pasture for their flocks, and plenty of milk. Peter Kolbe,[12] an old missionary, informed us that the moon was regarded as a lower god, a visible image of the invisible God.

Like all the tribes of the south, the Hottentots also pay a sort of homage to the Pleiades, whose return coincides with the rainy season, impatiently longed for by the farming and pastoral population.

For the Minkopis, the sun, moon, and stars form a family that lives near the abode of Puluga (God), but never enters it.

The idea which the primitives have of the external world—a strange realm into which it is dangerous to penetrate without due precaution—is one that appeals to the senses, especially among this little race. So the San, Negrillos, and Negritos have numerous prohibitions or taboos: they are especially particular not to make use of the earth, of what nature keeps concealed from the eyes of men, without first asking permission by special rites, offerings, and sacrifices. The San, when they discover water under ground, will not use it until a sacrifice has been offered as a necessary preliminary. The same rule prompts the Negrillos to offer the first fruits of the *Nkula* nut.

The Minkopis of the Andaman Islands give the name *Tomo* to the first man created by Puluga. His direct descendants are called *Tomola*. At their death they are transformed into different kinds (Dr. Man counts eighteen) of mamiferae, birds, reptiles, and crustaceans, besides several of the fishes. Naturally, all these animals are forbidden.

[12] Quatrefages, *Les Pygmées*, p. 278.

The Pygmies treat as self-evident the distinction between soul and body and take great care that the mortal remains of their brethren shall receive proper funerals. The double purpose seems to be to conceal them from all observation and to hinder their manes from following them as ghosts. Belief in the survival of man's spirit is shown, among them, by numerous facts: it is for this reason the San place a spear beside their dead so that they may be able to hunt and to defend themselves.[13] According to Arbousset, who sojourned a long time among them, one of their proverbs says: "Death is only a sleep."

The same is true of the Hottentots, their neighbors, whom Sir John Lubbock, on the word of La Vaillant, once represented as being without religion. Livingstone said of them: "However degraded these populations may be, there is no need of teaching them the existence of God nor of speaking to them about the future life. These two truths are universally admitted in Africa. All the phenomena which the natives can not explain by ordinary causes are attributed to the divinity. If you speak to them of a dead person: *He has gone to God,* they answer." [14]

"They have a domestic, individual worship. In the morning, at the first light of dawn, they quit their huts and go to kneel behind a bush. There, with face turned toward the east, they address their prayer to Tsui-goa, the "Father of fathers." [15]

In each family, the manes of their ancestors are considered as a sort of lares to whom they pray and make offerings. Hahn reports that he met a troop of Namaqua beyond the frontiers of Kalihari led by a great woman of the country, whom he recognized, and asked where she was going. "I am going," she answered, "to my father's grave to pray and weep, for the drought and the Bushmen have ruined us. He will hear my voice and he will give success to my husband who is hunting ostriches, so that we may have means of catching some goats and cows that our children may live." "But," the traveler replied, "your father is dead; how will he be able to hear you?"

---

[13] Quatrefages, p. 294.
[14] Livingstone, in Quatrefages, *op. cit.,* p. 292.
[15] Quatrefages, *op. cit.,* p. 307.

"Yes," the Hottentot answered, "he is dead; but he merely sleeps. We, the Khoikhoi, when we are in trouble, always go to pray on the graves of our grandparents and our ancestors; it is an old custom among us." [16]

The Negrillos of equatorial Africa also believe in another life. They bury their dead standing up, in a ditch in the bed of a stream, face turned toward the sky: "for," they say, "it is to the sky that man must finally ascend," [17] to the sky where he will find great hunting, and the free life which he lived on earth."

The Minkopis think that every man possesses in his body *a spirit* and *a soul* which separate from each other at death, but which will some day be again united. When a man dies, his spirit, after having haunted the environs of the grave and the encampment for several days, arrives, under a human form, at a mysterious locale where he resumes his earthly habits, hunting the spirits of beasts and birds that Puluga sends there: Puluga is the supreme God.[18]

The Aëtas have likewise a great veneration for their dead.

"For several years," says Gironnière, "they visit the graves and leave on them a little tobacco and betel. The bow and arrows belonging to the deceased are hung over his grave on the day of his burial, and every night, according to the belief of his comrades, he comes out to enjoy the hunt." [19]

San and Khoikhoi, Negrillos and Negritos, believe in genii whose influence is frequently felt in the course of the world and of man's life. Are these genii the spirits of their ancestors, more or less transformed, or are they other spirits of independent origin? We can not clearly determine. But, among the San, for example, an evil genius Goha, lives above us and is occupied with the heavenly phenomena, while a female genius, Ko, dwells on the earth. There are others, too, one in

[16] *Ibid.*, p. 333.
[17] Le Roy, *op. cit.*
[18] Quatrefages, *op. cit.*, p. 189.
[19] La Gironnière, *Vingt années aux Philippines.* (In Quatrefages, *op. cit.*, p. 234.)

particular, a mischievous genius, Guana or Guanab, feared likewise by the Khoikhoi; he lives in a black heaven and is the cause of all evil.[20]

The Minkopis also believe in the *chol,* who are descended from a common ancestor, *maiachal:* these are the executors of Pulugra's vengeances. Men sometimes perceive them under the form of birds with long tails.[21]

What is especially remarkable among the Pygmies is the notion of a higher Being, of God, a notion that seems clearer among them than among many other tribes superior to them in several other respects.

Dr. Hahn, who lived nine years among the Bushmen and Hottentots, has devoted a complete work to the knowledge of God among these people: *Tsuin Goam, The supreme Being of the Khoikhoi.* Since then his observations have been confirmed. The San say that in heaven there is a *kaang,* or chief, to whom they give the title of *Kue-Akenteng, the master of all things.* This kaang makes all beings live and makes them die; he gives or refuses the rain; he sends or withdraws the game. They pray to him in times of famine and while performing the dance of the *mokoma* for a whole night before setting out for war. "According to the expressions of the natives," says Arbousset, "we do not see him with our eyes, but we know him in our hearts." [22]

The Hottentots, too, believe in a supreme God *Gounia Tiquoia* (God of all the gods), who created the world as well as living beings, and governs all things.[23]

The God told of by Peter Kolbe is often assimilated to *Tsuigoa* (of Dr. Hahn), in whom the Hottentots see a kind Father, all-powerful, and all-wise. The feelings which this belief inspires in them closely resemble those felt by the strongest Christians in their convictions. Dr. Hahn does not say this in so many words; he does better: he proves it by examples.

[20] Quatrefages, *op. cit.,* p. 323.
[21] *Ibid.,* p. 186.
[22] *Ibid.,* p. 295.
[23] *Ibid.,* p. 301.

The interjection *Tsui-goatse* (Thou, O Tsui-Goa) corresponds to our "Great God!" Stricken by some misfortune which he judges undeserved, the Hottentot cries out: "O Tsui-goa, what have I done to be so severely punished?" If unjustly accused and unable to prove his innocence, he appeals to his god: "O Tsui-goa, thou alone knowest I am not guilty!" When exposed to any grievous danger, he counts on the help of Tsui-goa and, should he escape, he attributes his deliverance to him.[24]

We have said that the Hottentots possess neither temples nor images. However, we frequently find among them and among the San, certain consecrated places which they never pass without depositing some little offering, accompanied by invocations. After a while, little heaps accumulate on which they throw a piece of linen, or some flowers, a branch, a pebble, whatever will enlarge the modest monument. Sometimes they bring honey or mead. It is a homage to Heitsi-Eibib, the grandfather of the Nama-Koa. We have observed the same practice among the Bantus.

In all the encampments of the A-Koa and of the Beku in the great Gabon forest, I have found this belief in God perfectly clear and living. It is to God only that they annually make their curious and impressive sacrifice of the *Nkula* nut. One day I was admitted among the A-Jongo of the Fernan-Vaz, a population of half-breed Negrillos, who pretend to have preserved the primitive traditions of their race.

I said to one of them who had been freely talking with me for a considerable time: "You just pronounced the name of *Nzambi*: what is Nzambi?"

He replied: "*Nzambi* in our language, is *Anyambie* in the language of the Nkomis (that is to say, God)."

"Very well, I understand. But where does he live, what does he do, what do they say about him?"

"Nzambi? Nzambi lives up above, it is he who speaks by the thunder to tell men that the rain is going to fall. Have you not heard it? There are days and nights when the whole forest trembles with it. He is the Master of all, he has made

[24] *Ibid.*, p. 303.

everything, arranged everything, and in his sight we are very small."

"Is it he who makes men live?"

"Yes, and he it is who makes them die."

"But," I said, "when a man is dead and when he has been wicked, when he has stolen from others, when he has murdered, when he has poisoned, what is it that *Nzambi* does with him, tell me all that; afterwards I will tell you what we believe."

"Well, listen."

And my savage assumed an air of surprising sadness, speaking in a low voice so as not to be heard by I know not what near-by spirit:

"Listen. When one of us has died, his shade enters the earth and plunges very far down. Then it rises little by little, upward, upward, upward, all the way to God. If the man has been good, God says to him: 'Remain here, you will have big woods and you will lack nothing.' But if the man has been wicked, if he has stolen the wives of others, if he has killed, if he has poisoned, God casts this larva into the fire."

"Into the fire?" I said, very much surprised. "Where is this fire located?"

"On high," answered the savage.

"Very good," I remarked after a few moments of silence. "Who has taught you these things?"

"It is what we all say," he replied. "That is what our fathers thought, and we think the same. But you others, you Whites, you must know still more." [25]

These ideas of reward and punishment in the other life are quite remarkable, for I have found nothing so clear and precise among the Bantu tribes near by and in particular not among the Nkomis.

Although only a passing traveler in the great forest of Lturi (Congo), Major Powell Cotton has made some good observations on the Pygmies he met. During a terrible storm, he saw his guide (head tracker) invoke the aid of a Higher Power. One of his men likewise noticed a group of Pygmies preparing to change camp: they were celebrating a sort of ritualistic repast

[25] Le Roy, *op. cit.*

with offerings, to ask the Supreme Being to give them good luck on their new hunting grounds.[26]

Let us pass to the other side of the continent, to the forest of Sokoke which extends beyond Malindi (Zanguebar). One day I had gone astray; after I had met and sought to gain the confidence of a certain chief of Boni (a group of Negrillos), we were talking of religion.

"Listen," the old chief said to me, "since you wish to know everything. When I kill a buffalo, I take a little piece of it, the best, and put it on the fire: part of it remains there to burn, and I eat the other part with my children. If I find some honey, I do not take any of it until I have first thrown a little of it into the forest towards the sky. And when I have some palm-wine, I must first pour a little of it on the ground. Is that what you wish to know?"

"Yes; but do you say nothing while doing that?"

"Yes, indeed, I say, for instance, 'Waka, thou hast given me this buffalo, this honey, this wine. Here is thy part. Lend me still strength and life, and may no harm reach my children!'"

Waka is the Galla name of God. I knew it; but it was better to seem ignorant and give this surprising savage the chance to explain himself.

"Waka?" I said. "What is Waka?"

"You do not know Waka?" he replied. "He is the Master of everything, he whom the Swahili call Mu-ungu. He has given us these lands, these forests, these rivers, all that you see: by them we live. But he is severe; he wishes his part, and we give it to him."

"Have you seen him?"

"Seen Waka? Who could ever see Waka? But he sees us very well. Sometimes he descends into our encampment and makes one of us die. Then we bury very deep in the ground him whose life he has taken; and those who remain go very far away: for it is dangerous to remain under the eye of God." [27]

---

[26] *Review of Reviews*, Nov., 1907, p. 495.
[27] Le Roy, *op. cit.*

E. H. Man,[28] who made a most serious study of the natives of the Andaman Islands, informs us that they have a lofty and profoundly spiritual conception of Puluga, although the childlike and crude mind of these savages appears in the expression of the ideas they form of him. Puluga lives in a large stone house in the sky, he eats and drinks, descends on the earth to replenish his provisions, which consist of certain fruits, roots, and grains which he reserves for himself and which it is forbidden to touch; he sleeps during the greater part of the dry season. But he it is who has given men all that is useful for their food. When any one offends him, he comes out of his house and sends the wind storms, the thunder, and the lightning.

We quote the following account of him from the work of E. H. Man.

"1. Though his appearance is like fire, yet he is (now-a-days) invisible.

"2. He was never born and is immortal.

"3. By him the world and all objects, animate and inanimate, were created, excepting only the powers of evil.

"4. He is regarded as omniscient, knowing even the thoughts of their hearts.

"5. He is angered by the commission of certain sins, while to those in pain or distress he is pitiful, and sometimes deigns to afford relief.

"6. He is the judge from whom each soul receives its sentence after death, and, to some extent, the hope of escape from the tortures of *jereg-lar-mugu* is said to affect their course of action in the present life." [29]

There is no worship of trees or rocks or stars, although some of their nocturnal dances appear to have a religious character. But they have sacrifice and prayers intended to appease Puluga: thus, on the occasion of a violent tempest, they burn leaves of *mimusopus indica* to calm his anger.

[28] E. H. Man, *The Andaman Islands*.
[29] Man, *op. cit.*, p. 89.

The Negritos of Malacca, to win God's favor, address invocations to him and burn benzoin, the odor of which is thought to please and delight him.

Until the account given of them by J. B. Logan, the Binua had been regarded as atheists. He relates that to his great surprise these people of the Malacca peninsula have what he calls a simple and, to a certain extent, rational theology. They believe in a god, Pirman, who created the world, maintains it, who is invisible, and lives above the sky. Below him wander the spirits, the most powerful of whom is *Jin Bumi,* the spirit of the earth, to whom sickness and death are due.

The moral characteristics of these little men are equally remarkable. The Andaman natives have a word "yubba" that Man translates by *sin, bad action,* which is applied to lying, stealing, violence, murder, and adultery. All these acts are regarded as provoking the anger of *Puluga,* the Creator. The family is respected. The crimes of rape, seduction, vices against nature, seem to be unknown, says Man. The feeling of modesty is universal and very evident.

Besides the faults and crimes reproved by the sense of justice, which we find everywhere in the primitive conscience, there are other acts that are injurious only according to religious ideas and are real sins in the strict acceptation of the terms. Such is, for instance, the throwing of beeswax into the fire. Engaged couples are subjected to a period of abstinence during which they can eat neither turtle nor pig nor fish nor honey. The violation of this prohibition is also a sin. We can say the same of the Negrillos and the San. In connection with the dealings which Stanley had with one of their encampments in the great equatorial forest, he pays homage to the character of their moral law and their sense of justice and modesty. They, too, have their prohibitions, the transgression of which constitutes a religious fault, that is to say a sin.

The ancient race of Negrillos and Negritos by itself could not serve as a sufficiently broad basis for a theory of the primitive religion of mankind. But it happens that all the other races, Black, Yellow, and White, which form the fundamental types of the human species, have religious notions strikingly similar to those of our little primitives, every time we meet them any place whatsoever on the earth in a state of more or less rudimentary civilization.

First of all, we find the family everywhere established, and religion everywhere serving to maintain, strengthen, and purify it by prohibitions or taboos, to develop and protect it by totemic pacts, to prolong it in the beyond by the worship of the manes, to preserve it from accidents, diseases, and the various other evils that threaten it, and to try to ward off from it all dangerous influences. The family is not the *raison d'être* of primitive religion, but we may say it is religion that organized the family and that the family, in turn, has preserved the chief elements of religion.

The family has been the center of belief; it has also been the center of worship, which spread from it to the encampment or village, to the clan and the tribe.

This family is monogamous among those populations that we consider the most ancient, the San, the Negrillos, and the Negritos, save for a few exceptions that are easily explained as due to contact with neighboring tribes.

Moreover, everywhere among the black populations polygamy prevails; but a disciplined and organized polygamy that does not destroy the family. Polyandry, which has spread very little, has prevailed in some small avaricious societies only for the purpose of keeping about the mother a common *matrimonium.*

And if there have really been countries where, as Reclus maintains, "all the women belonged to all the males of the tribe without distinction" and where "children had no other father than the whole of the warriors," [30] nowhere in the history or traditions or in the observations of savage peoples do we see that this promiscuity has been anything but a condition altogether exceptional and abnormal.

On the contrary, marriage is everywhere surrounded by certain regulations whose religious character is evident, whether these rites take place at the time of the marriage or before,

[30] Elisée Reclus, *Primitive Folk,* p. 157.

for instance, at the period of puberty and on the occasion of
the initiation of youth. With this idea is connected the practice of circumcision, known not only by many black populations
of Africa and the Polynesians of the Oceanic islands, but
even by many tribes of America. This practice must be due
to the idea that man can not enter a domain reserved by the
mysterious Master of life, without first proceeding to the removal of the prohibition by a sacrifice expressed by circumcision.
In fact, before the accomplishment of this rite, matrimonial
relations are strictly forbidden; by this regulation the home is
safer and more respected, the relations between neighbors more
guaranteed, and public morality better protected.

For this same purpose of moral protection, with which the
primitives are much more preoccupied than we think, another
prohibition, imposed on the relations between near of kin,
severely forbids incest.

Everywhere it is the rule for the young man to take a wife
from outside his own family.

In many countries, maternal descent regulates relationship
as well as inheritance. The reason is always the same: as far
as possible, to assure the purity of the race and to give the
power with its prerogatives, to the descendants who really have
flowing within them the blood of the family, i.e., of the mother.

Moreover, men from tribes considered inferior, are not always
allowed to take a wife from a superior tribe.

No doubt, in the long run mixtures of blood do take place.
But through the whole extent of the African continent, and
elsewhere too, the scattered members of the tribe thus maintain themselves in relative purity in the midst of other populations. They often adopt the language, but they keep their own
beliefs and customs, their own manner of constructing their
houses, their own weapons and dress, their distinctive marks on
the skin, the teeth, and hair.

The primitives feel the need of distinguishing between themselves, family by family, and tribe by tribe. To this the natural
desire to adorn themselves and to call attention to their bodily
advantages by their dress is soon added. So we have tattoos
which in certain countries, Polynesia for example, have attained

the height of an art.   Other tribes have real coats-of-arms traced
on their shields.

Still others, by adopting certain ethnical mutilations, have
succeeded in disfiguring themselves in the strangest ways, as
the Ba-yanzi of the Congo, and the Boto-cudos of Brazil.

We have spoken of totemism at considerable length.   This
institution, which is maintained among all the North American
Indians, is also connected with the instinctive religious desire
to preserve the family bond, to maintain its purity, and to
respect its blood, by extending its relations into another world,
by a pact with beings that are strangers to the human species,
by placing the family under the continual protection of invisible spirits acting through a totem.

Totemism has another effect.   The totem animal, plant, or
object, having a sacred character, naturally becomes *taboo* and
is associated with numerous prohibitions whose purpose is to
surround the family with a sort of protective palisade.

Although some of these prohibitions are puerile, ridiculous,
unsuitable, others are highly moral and socially necessary.
Such, for example, are certain prohibitions which naturally
create the sense of modesty found among the most debased tribes.

These various reflections apply to all black Africa.   Speaking
of the races in French Guinea, André Arcin writes in a recent
and remarkable work: "The black society is patriarchal."
Moreover, the family "includes not merely the father, mother,
and children, but all the descendants of the same ancestor.   That
is why the Blacks of the same village call one another brothers
although they have neither father nor mother in common." [31]

Thus the grouping of several families, in the strict sense
we give this word, forms the negro family, with a patriarch
at its head.   When this group is agnatic (related in the
paternal line), it exactly corresponds to the *gens Romana*.

The totem, known in Guinea under the Soso name of *ntene,*
the mythological ancestor of the clan, supplies them with an

[31] Arcin, *La Guinée française,* p. 244.

emblem and gives them a name, although to-day this primitive institution has lost part of its meaning.[32]

Further on Arcin adds:

"Private or family worship is at the very basis of the social organization. The father of the family, the patriarch or secondary chief is the priest. The honors, sacrifice, and offerings are addressed to the manes of the family ancestors, and more especially to the founder of that family or that member of a tribe from whom it is sprung." [33]

We find the same ideas and organizations in all the Negritian tribes of the Niger and Sudan valleys.

In Dahomey, the whole political constitution of former days rested on the relation of the king to his ancestors. This was carried to such a point that each time an unusual event occurred, the monarch had to send the news to the other world by sacrificing one or more messengers.

So all through Africa, they naturally pass from the family constituted in this way to the family surviving beyond. Everywhere, beside the influences of nature (influences sometimes localized in fetiches, as on the coast of Benin, along the Niger, in Dahomey, etc.), we find belief in the manes. Then come the spirits, some of which seem to be merely transformed souls, while others are of extra-human origin, and lastly, the supreme Being who becomes more and more distinct as we approach the regions of the north.

Among the Worbas, God is commonly called "Olorum," i.e., "the Master of the heavens." [34] But a great number of other divinities are also venerated—401 according to some, 600 according to others—divided into two classes, 200 of the "right" and 400 of the "left"; there are "Orishas" who preside over the atmosphere, fire, commerce, births, the sea, war, hunting, farming, etc.

Let us not forget the household gods, the *Egum,* represented by the spirits of the ancestors. The Yorubas inter their dead

[32] *Ibid.,* p. 246.
[33] *Ibid.,* p. 422.
[34] James Johnson, *Yoruba Heathenism.*

in their houses and believe that their spirits continue to be interested in the surviving part of their families. A place is left for them, generally indicated by colored designs on the walls or floor; but this does not hinder them from assigning another place of worship to *Esu,* an evil spirit whose image is often placed on the left of the entrance, in a family enclosure, while another place is marked out for *Esi,* in the public square.

The fetichers or *Babalawo* enjoy an important place among them in their relations with the dead, in the many sacrifices that are offered, and in the divination and the interpretation of omens.

The Yorubas have also a real system of religious morality, commanding respect for the gods, obedience to parents and other authorities, marital fidelity, the exercise of hospitality, forbidding murder, stealing, magic, adultery, suicide, etc. All is based on an immanent Providence who rewards what is good and punishes evil.[35]

In his work on the tribes of the lower Niger, Major Arthur Glynn Leonard furnishes similar details. Founding his study on numerous facts, he concludes by saying that the religion of the natives embraces the totality of nature, both material and immaterial; that their essential and primary belief is connected with the human or ancestral spirits who busy themselves not only with natural phenomena but continue to dwell in their homes; that this belief in the transmigration of spirits under material form has given birth to totemism, fetichism, idolatry, and sorcery; that the Spirits are of two kinds: some with a double power of good and evil, and others (which have never had any body) capable only of doing evil.[36]

The writer adds:

"In the first place, then, it is very evident that the natives believe in the pantheistic or god-supremacy principle, and that the Creator or supreme God and his existence is acknowledged by one and all of these people, irrespective of tribe or locality. . . .   Indeed, strange though it may appear to a

[35] Dennett, *op. cit.,* p. 267.
[36] Leonard, *The Lower Niger,* p. 475.

theologian or man of science, and although these natives believe in the spiritualism of nature and in witchcraft, and practice demonology, they believe as firmly as does, e.g., the Christian, that there is a Being who lives, it may be in the sky or it may be everywhere, that is the Father and the Master of all beings." [37]

Among the populations of the Hamitic family, who are especially given to the pastoral life, like the Massai, the Gallas, the Peuls, etc., the family organization is perhaps still more faithfully preserved than among the Negritians and Bantus. These pastoral people live in encampments and move with their flocks. The families gathered about their chief are divided only when they become too numerous to get a living together. Under these conditions the form of worship is generally and of necessity of a family nature.

These Massai form a people of high originality, magnificent in stature, an Apollo type, of pastoral and warlike habits. Until lately they were inaccessible not only to Europeans and Arabs, but also to the Bantu and Negritian population, on whose borders they have been camping for centuries past along with their herds of oxen. The Massai have neither temples nor images nor fetiches nor amulets. But they have the name of God, *En-Ngai,* perpetually on their lips.

What is God, in their mind? It is rather difficult to specify their idea of him with all the precision we could desire. *En-Ngai* is the sky, animated nature, the totality of the universe, strength of life spread out in all directions, the light—he is all; but much more justly, he is the immense Being whom we nowhere see, whom we can not grasp, whom we can not reach, but who, while everywhere, shows himself especially at certain places in the world: in the sky from which he sends the rain and withholds it, on the summit of *Kibo,* at Kilimanjaro where he likes to dwell, and in certain men in whom his intellect appears. When some of us missionaries on the eastern coast of Africa visited a Massai encampment for the first time, as soon as we were announced, the chief, who was the ancient

[37] *Ibid.,* p. 469.

and the priest of the place, advanced towards us with some of his children; then he gathered a few blades of grass and presented them to us, saying: "Receive this offering, for in you we see God who comes to visit us. It is He who has given us these plains: it is just that He should take possession of some of it to-day." No doubt, that was only a manner of speaking; but did not this fashion of receiving "the children of God" possess charm and grandeur?

The Massai women generally pray twice a day, morning and evening, as also in exceptional circumstances, for instance, while the warriors are fighting. The men and children pray very little except in time of drought and when some disease afflicts the cattle. Bloody sacrifices are common especially in time of war, disease, and mourning. They believe in the existence of the human soul, sufficiently independent from the human body to abandon it temporarily. When any one is asleep, he must not be suddenly awakened; he might be brought out of his sleep while his soul is absent, and that would be his death.

They do not fear the spirits, some of whom are in the air, rambling about us. When one of the cattle fixedly stares into space, surely it must be gazing at these spirits.

When a child, a woman, or an unmarried young man dies, his body is carried far from the encampment, his name is buried with him and must never more be mentioned by his family. The corpses of ordinary people are deposited in a wood with the bones of a young ox that has been sacrificed on the occasion and its flesh eaten at the funeral repast. The hyenas, soon drawn by the remains of the feast, devour the body and that is the last of it. But when the corpse is that of a seer, an ancient, a rich man, a great warrior, or a prominent chief, the funeral ceremony begins by the slaying of an ox or a sheep; with its fat they rub the dead body, which is then wrapped in the hide of an ox and interred in a sort of trench under a tree. Above it they put some stones to which each passerby adds a pebble. The souls of these great men live again in a serpent that is to be seen from time to time going to the *kraal* of his children to watch over them. So the Massai are careful not to kill the sacred serpent; and if a woman sees it in her tent, she hastens to pour some milk on the ground which it drinks and then goes away. Each clan has its sacred serpent.

Some great religious chiefs, as Mbatyan, go directly to the sky after their death.[38] With the Gallas or Oromo we reach clearer religious notions and a more defined organization. In Oromo language God is called "Waka." When the natives invoke him—as frequently happens—they add an expression of tender confidence: *Waka-yo,* "O good God," *Waka-yo-ko,* "O my good God." We must admit that if their voices are constantly raised to him to ask his help, at times their aim is to interest him in some bad act; but the Gallas never blaspheme, nor do the Massai. They pray a great deal in the form of litanies and chants, as also do the Massai; by way of response in these sacred chants, there are refrains, religious expressions and thoughts that are sometimes very impressive, lofty, and beautiful. One of their missionaries, Father Martial de Salviac, writes:

"We may say that the Gallas breathe the idea and the name of God so often that Waka, heaven, and the angels embellish all their conversations and speech." [39]

Beneath Waka and subject to his orders, the Oromo religion places the good spirits, "Aoulia," i.e., "the blessed."

They build no temples. Waka's temple is the studded vault of heaven; his altar is the surface of the earth; the victims to which he has a right are the first-fruits of the fields and of the herds. So the Oromo offering is his flour, milk, and honey, a small portion cast to the four winds: the blood of the victims is poured on the ground and a piece of meat put aside that a vulture will soon carry away toward the sky to present it, as the Arushi say, "to Waka and the souls of our dead."

The chief act of the Galla religion is the Wadadja or ceremony of alliance (from *Wada,* alliance). It is a family, regional, or national ceremony, according to the circumstances: it is a sacred repast, presided over by an officer called *rabsa.* Before beginning, a few drops of some beverage are poured on

[38] Hollis, *Massai, the Language and Folklore.*
[39] Martial de Salviac, *Les Gallas,* p. 130.

the ground and some bits of wood cast in four directions, in front of them, behind, to the right, and to the left. Then the person officiating stands up and intones a prayer to which all the others respond. Toward the end of the ceremony the children are brought in to receive the blessing, symbolized by a shower of fine saliva which the father, mother, and *rabsa* void on their heads while pronouncing happy wishes.[40]

In concluding his account of the native religions of Africa, Réville writes that

"religion like society has nowhere on this continent attained to anything complete, definite, and well constituted. The incoherence and undisciplined imagination of the negro, the lack of argumentative judgment and ignorant sterility of the Kaffir, the imbecility of the Hottentot and the Bushman have not permitted the religion of nature to expand into poetical and dramatic myths analogous to those of India or Greece."

All that is just. But he adds:

"Naturism, the worship of personified objects of nature, the sky, the sun, the moon, the mountains, streams of water, is general in the African country. Among all those peoples of whom we have spoken, the worship of one or more of these natural phenomena is fundamental."

Then he goes on:

"Animism, the worship of spirits separate from nature and without necessary connection with determined natural phenomena has assumed a preponderating and an absorbing place. Hence we have the fetichism of the negro, a fetichism which gradually rises to idolatry, to belief in sorcery wherein we here and there discern the rudiments of a regular priesthood, confidence in amulets, and lastly the worship of the dead or of dead spirits which are assimilated to the original spirits of nature and with them enter into the course of destiny."

All that Réville can grant, as we have seen above, is that

"the native of Africa is not hostile to the idea of a single all-powerful God. The head spirit of most of these crude religions

[40] Martial de Salviac, *Les Gallas*, pp. 138 sqq.

might readily become something like Yahweh or Allah. The Njongmo on the coast of Guinea, the Waka of the Gallas, the god-judge of the secret societies, the Ounkoulounkoulou of the Kaffirs, the Heitsi-Eibib of the Hottentots, would easily lend themselves to that transformation." [41]

While the distinguished founder of the chair of History of Religions at the Collège de France has been at considerable pains to investigate the beliefs and practices of the Blacks, has he, alas, been able to understand them at all?

His plea is that, having never lived among these populations, he has had to begin by creating their religious mentality for himself and then he has gone ahead constantly guided by that false light. It must be said that since 1883, the date of his studies, the African populations have become much better known. However, men like Livingstone and Wilson were not witnesses whose testimony he could afford to despise; and we ask ourselves why Réville always forgets to cite them when their testimony does not agree with his own theories. He has nothing, or almost nothing to say about the Nigritians and Hamites, who are, nevertheless, so interesting. Evidently the mind of this scholar has been led astray by his own preconceived system. By virtue of the dogma of religious evolution, which we do not dream of rejecting en masse, since we ourselves intend to invoke it—but which it is dangerous to apply blindly to everything—it was necessary that man, springing from the animal, should have been at first a naturist, then an animist, then a fetichist, then an idolator, and finally a theist. To find the knowledge of a living and personal God among the most primitive populations would upset the theory: so Réville, as well as many learned men of the same school, has been too blind to perceive the idea of God in Africa, even among the Gallas.

Criticizing one of his most illustrious predecessors, namely Herbert Spencer, who set forth the worship of the dead as the starting point for all history of religions,[42] Réville writes:

"The method employed by the English philosopher to demonstrate his theory consists in gleaning from the abundant

[41] Réville, *Religion des peuples non civilisés*, I, p. 188.
[42] Herbert Spencer, *Principles of Sociology*.

accounts of travelers and missionaries that he was able to read, details that are favorable and systematically neglecting the contrary data. This method may deceive the reader who is not familiar with the vast number of works, of varying competency and merit, that treat of the life, customs, and ideas of the uncivilized. But it is only a deceptive way of arguing that can be used by all sorts of contrary theses."

Réville is certainly right in this criticism of Spencer. But how justly it may be turned against himself!

After this glance at Africa, we must turn to the primitive populations of Oceanica, America, and even Asia and Europe. This review can be made very rapidly: everywhere, in fact, we will note the same basis for religious beliefs and practices although there are notable variations, many of which are plainly due to ethnic characteristics, to circumstances, and to environment.

The Australians, who have long been said to have no religion, surprisingly resemble our African primitives in their religious ideas. "They have an idea of an omnipotent Being, the Creator of heaven and earth, whom they call *Motogon.*" He is a very wise and powerful being, of blackish appearance. When he created the heaven, the earth, the water, the plants, the kangaroos, he breathed and said: "Heaven, earth, plants, trees, kangaroos, come forth." And they came forth.[43]

The Australians also have an idea of an evil spirit whom they call *Cienga.* He it is who stirs up the tempests, sends the heavy equinoctial rains, and makes little children die by withering their flesh. He lives in the center of the earth. But the savages render no worship either to Motogon or to Cienga.

They likewise believe in the survival of the soul, which is supposed to enter the body of a bird or some other animal.

Naturally they have a number of superstitious practices and often attribute death to the influence of sorcerers, who are able to kill at a distance. This power resides in a sort of stone which the sorcerer carries in his stomach; it is enough for him

---

[43] T. Bérengier, *La Nouvelle Nursie*, p. 182. See also Lang, *The Making of Religion.*

to hurl a piece of this stone at any one to destroy him. Strange to say, a rather similar belief exists in Africa among the Bantu tribes of the western coast. The relatives of a dead person are also obliged to avenge him.

The Australians, too, are always grouped by families, and each family is entirely independent.

As a sign of mourning, the women, as in Africa, utter great lamentations and paint their faces with white clay. The corpse is interred in a ditch which has first been purified by a fire lighted there; beside it the remains of the dead one's last meal are placed along with his broken weapons. Then near by they build a little hut and kindle a big fire on the grave, around which they sing of his mighty exploits. This fire is kept up for some months and it is a pious duty of all the relatives who pass by not to let it go out. Before the coming of colonists, the Australians made their burrying-ground the center of their settlements.[44]

The Malanesians, Papuans, Fijians, and New Caledonians evidently had the same religious beliefs, the same superstitions, and the same abominable practices, such as legal infanticide, human sacrifice, and anthropophagy.

In Oceanica, the idea of the *taboo* is universal, arising from the persuasion that what is sacred must be preserved from all human contact, under pain of sacrilege and misfortune. But it developed especially in Polynesia. From there the term entered European literature. Nowhere else is this institution so widespread, nowhere does it occupy such a predominant place in life. Once admit the principle that one can not take or touch anything made sacred by religion, and the political and religious chiefs do not fail to use it in the interest of their ambitions, their profit, and even their vengeance. They have even gone so far as to divide everything into two classes: what is permitted (*noa*) and what is forbidden (*taboo*).

Fortunately, in Oceanica as elsewhere, the prohibition can be removed. But certain rules, ceremonies, ablutions, and sacrifices are necessary.

[44] Bérengier, *op. cit.*, p. 267.

Let us repeat that there is need for some prohibitions and that the taboo in itself contains nothing that is not entirely legitimate. If it does not pass beyond bounds, it is nothing more than a moral law, often becoming civil law, based on a religious principle and bearing a religious sanction.

Another custom peculiarly widespread in Polynesia, more perfected and artistic than elsewhere, was that of tattooing. This operation was entrusted to a religious chief and ordinarily took place at the age of nubility, as in Africa, where the initiation ceremonies of youth are quite general. Originally it was the permanent mark intended to recall, by its image and the designs surrounding it, the alliance that had been made with the protective animal or totem (in Polynesian *tiki*). Thus there were hereditary tattooings, taking the place of coats-of-arms. We have already referred to these customs, as also to the practice of wearing certain articles of dress, of arranging the hair so as to resemble the allied animal, of fastening various ornaments or symbols to the ears, nose, lips, or filing the teeth, and so forth.

One of the strangest and most widespread mutilations current is to remove one joint of the little finger on the occasion of mourning. This practice was formerly well known in Oceanica, notably in the Fiji Islands.[45] At the funeral of a great chief, his wives used to dispute the honor of being thrown into his grave. Parents underwent the amputation of one finger joint and it is certain that at some burials the fingers complete fell beneath the dread hatchet. Not even children at the breast were spared.

This custom, too, is found in Africa among the San and sometimes among the Negrillos of the equatorial forest. It is a sacrifice. They intend to show that they accompany the dead into the other world by this surrender of a part of themselves. Or else, as is rather the case in Africa, they ask the author of life to be satisfied with what they cut off and not take all; by abandoning a part of their body to him, they redeem the rest.

As for the idea of God, it exists everywhere in Oceanica.

[45] Piolet, *Missions catholiques*, IV, Océanie, p 199.

Let us consider America next. From one end to the other of this vast continent, extending from the north to the south pole, European navigators, ever since the days of Christopher Columbus, have found tribes that differ in aspect, speech, manners, and civilization. So modern anthropologists agree in saying that the population of the two Americas, before the coming of Europeans, was made up of the three fundamental races, the yellow, the black, and the white, mingled in various proportions.

To-day side by side and often in the same school, are the American Indian and the descendant of the African negro. The difference between them is striking. Whereas the former is taciturn, reserved, proud, melancholy, and disdainful, the latter is expansive, vain, and jovial.

But from the religious point of view, we here find very nearly what we have found everywhere else: the idea of a great Spirit who rules the world; inferior spirits that are revealed in the cosmic phenomena, the stars, the streams and lakes, the forests, the animals, the plants, and that seem more clearly separated from the human form than in Africa; the souls of men surviving the destruction of the body, often punished or rewarded, often disappearing into the unknown, often coming back among the living and reincarnating themselves either in the child whose features are the image of a dead parent or in the totem animal, plant, or object.

We have observed traces of totemism in Africa and Oceanica and have seen survivals of this institution in Asia and Europe,[46] but America has been the scene of its greatest development, or at least has best preserved it highly developed.

Individual totems abound in North America. They generally spring from the dream which a young man has in the course of his initiation, for example, seeing such an animal or such an object. It is a sign that this is his totem, i.e., his ally. For

---

[46] In Homer, Virgil, and Ovid the heroes have different signs on their shields by which the warriors are distinguished and recognized. Alexander the Great reserved to himself the right to give soldiers whom he wished to honor certain marks to carry on their armor and standards. Plutarch (*Life of Marius*) remarks that the Teutons and Cimbri had figures of ferocious beasts or birds as emblems on their shields.

the ceremony of initiation of youth is also well known in America.

These same beliefs in a higher world, with an appropriate worship and morality, have been found among the primitive populations of northern Asia and Europe.

"But in this whole area," says Quatrefages, "among all the nations concerning whom our information is exact, by the side of secondary divinities, or rather spirits more or less deified, is found a supreme God, creator and preserver of the universe. It is the *Jumbel* of the Laplanders, the *Num* of the Samoyeds, the *Jumman* of the Votiaks, the *Yuma* of the Tcheremis, the *Artoyon, Schugotoygon,* or *Tangara* of the Jakouts. All these great divinities are evidently the *single and eternal* God, of whom Mangou spoke to Rubruquis, although he was surrounded by shamans, the chief of whom dwelt close by the great Khan. Far, then, from being incompatible with a very lofty and spiritual religious conception, Shamanism shows itself associated with this in the countries where it holds the greatest sway. There, as at many other points on the globe, coarse practices and absurd or childish superstitions have too frequently covered up and concealed from Europeans the superior notions existing among these savage populations. "The Jakouts declare that their *Tangara* is invisible; we know that the Votiaks, the Tcheremis, etc., celebrate special festivals in honor of their God, and address to him prayers, which present them to us in a most favorable light. . . . In fine, in the whole geographical area here in question, the religious beliefs appear to me to have a very great analogy with those of the ancient Chinese, who also believed in a *supreme sovereign of heaven* and in subordinate spirits." [47]

May we appeal to the testimony of the men whose remains have been found scattered here and there in quaternary soil? It would be interesting to hear from these real primitives after having listened to those of our own day.

Unfortunately we must renounce any hope of reconstructing the beliefs of the races whose existence is revealed to us by remains found in alluvium. They have left no more trace

[47] Quatrefages, *Les Pygmées*, p. 203.

thereof for the historian than do the Negrillos and Negritos of to-day; although these do actually have clearly defined religious ideas. This absence of material proof, therefore, attests only one thing: if these first men had any religious beliefs, fetichism had as yet no part in them.

But when remains of prehistoric man are found sufficiently well preserved in tombs, we note that to the dead, both adult and child, were left all that had been used by them in the way of ornaments. Near them at burial were placed objects that we may suppose to have been considered useful or agreeable for them in another life; they painted the bodies of adults red (tribe of Menton [48]) precisely as the west African tribes still do.

In many prehistoric remains in France and Belgium, numerous objects have been found which Broca himself has no hesitation in considering as amulets.

"The religious spirit of the men of the polished stone period has been doubted by no one. The belief in another life is evidenced among all the neolithic tribes by the remarkable care given to burial. Whatever be the nature of the tomb, we always find there mortuary offerings, which have become ethnographical treasures for us. Thence have been brought to light most of the utensils, vases, ornaments, and weapons which were to serve the dead in their new existence: our museums are enriched with them.

"In the neolithic tombs numerous amulets have been found; it is needless to reiterate the significance of this fact. But it is worthy of remark that idols and fetiches are almost as entirely lacking as in the graves of the preceding epoch." [49]

If the land of western Europe conceals, along with the dust of their bones, the secret of the religious beliefs of the first men who ventured there, we are able to gather more extensive and more precise data concerning a still remoter past in the Orient where the constant tradition of mankind has located the cradle of religion.

[48] *Ibid., Introd. à l'étude des races humaines*, p. 278.
[49] *Ibid.*, p. 281.

In the Italian peninsula we can go back to the eighth and even eleventh century before our era, in the case of the Etruscans and the first Latins. From astonishing remains in this region we observe that their civilization was also based on strict family organization, which was the center of worship and religion.

About the same epoch and on the same basis, the Pelasgic tribes gradually formed what was to become the brilliant Greek civilization, the spirit of which is still alive among us.

With Carthage, the market of Sidon, and Utica, the colony of Tyre, we are back to the twelfth century B. C.

Sidon, "the mother of the Phœnician cities," was a very active center of commercial, intellectual, and religious intercourse with the most ancient cities, kingdoms, and empires, such as Assyria, Chaldea, Elam—names that carry us back to more than 3000 years before Christ.

At a great distance, in the Far East, another type of civilization was at the same time developing with another race. If the appearance of the Chinese ruler Fu-Hi can not be maintained at the remote date sometimes assigned (3000 B. C.), at least seven or eight centuries later Yu or Ya-o appears as the first emperor of the Hia dynasty and the historic era of this great people begins. They also furnish an example—an altogether secular proof—of the power of cohesion and social conservation coming from the strong constitution of the family based on religion: for that is the whole secret of the long existence of the Chinese empire.

In India the Aryan language was formed between 2500 and 2000 years before the Christian era. The first Vedic songs of that period show us a complete organization of worship, with prayer and sacrifice as its center, the survival of the soul and future retribution as its sanction.

But we must turn towards Egypt for evidence of the greatest antiquity, the most ancient yet known. In fact it is at 5000 or 6000 B. C. that scholars place the vestiges of the first civilization of this astounding people who seem to have wished to represent only "what is eternal: the future life and the gods."[50]

[50] Le Bon, *op. cit.*, p. 11.

However far back the Egyptian monuments take us into the past, the peoples who built them, who were connected with the more or less mixed Barbary race, knew of other men who preceded them in the Nile valley, who belonged to the pure Hamitic family.

These latter must have driven out the Negroes or Nigritians. The Nigritians themselves had driven out the Bantus.

And the Bantus had perceived here and there mysterious little men, real savages and real primitives, wandering in nomad groups, without cities or villages, without farms, without herds, without industry, without any of those things that seem to us necessary for the constitution of a human society. These Pygmies come before us again to-day exactly in the same state, it seems, as that in which the Bantus found them, just the same as later the Egyptian artists represented them on the obelisks, the same as when their representatives, the captives of Pharaoh, passed before the great eternally smiling Sphinx of Memphis.

Older than the Sphinx, older than the Pyramids, older than all the texts preserved on papyrus, camels' bones, bronze, brick, or stone, are these African Pygmies of ours, whose testimony we have examined. More exactly than hieroglyphics could have done, they have told us their living thoughts.

A continent like Africa, accessible only by a narrow strip of land that connects it with Asia, could never have been peopled before the arrival of our little men, or how could these latter have penetrated there? Never would it have been possible for them to open a passage through all the populations of that immense land, in order to occupy the various places where we find them to-day. On the contrary, we can understand very well that they arrived alone, with the only domestic animal they still have, their pitiful little dog, and found no one had preceded them. So they established themselves and multiplied at whatever places were most favorable for their existence until the day when other populations surged in upon them; then some of them wandered off into little settlements in the forests of the equatorial regions, others were driven to the extremity of the continent, and others were absorbed by the various tribes wherein they have contributed to the formation of the present stock.

What has just been said of Africa, may be said of Asia and Oceanica. To-day it seems to be the common opinion of anthropologists that the first ethnic stratum of all these countries must have been formed by that little race which has left behind it numerous testimonials and whose chief characteristics are maintained to this very day in a certain number of living representatives.

Is it not a curious fact that, wherever we find them, they pretend to be, so far as man can be, the proprietors of the land where they roam? To them, they say, God gave the forests, the plains, the bodies of water, the fruits, the game. The others merely invade their domain; that is why they, the "men," have a strict right to gather from the agricultural products and the cattle of their farming neighbors whatever they need to support life. These levies in a way compensate for the wrong which the "strangers" commit in penetrating "their forests" and scattering "their game." This theory has been explained to me at great length and quite as precisely as I have just set it forth, in various encampments of Negrillos and in particular among the Boni of the Sokoke forest (near Malindi).

In southern Africa the San consider themselves the first occupants of the soil and their conception of life is not different from that of their cousins to the north.

In Gabon the Negrillos are of like mind, and the same may be said of the Negritos. We may add that all the African populations in whose midst these little men are scattered, who have dispersed them, pursued them and given them the name of Wa-twa, Ba-twa, Aba-twa, i.e., "the vagabonds" (from the verb -ta, "to chase, pursue"; passive -twa), unanimously acknowledge the Negrillos' priority of occupation.

In Gabon, when they go hunting in the forest, custom forbids them to pronounce the name of the Pygmies, A-koa; they must use a circumlocution and say, for instance, "the short men" or "the great race." It is also recommended, if they meet one of these little men and wish to preserve their good luck in the hunt, that they offer him a part of the beast that is slain: by this act of justice they render homage to the proprietor and acknowledge his rights.

But a question suggests itself. Why have these children of nature who have been thus wandering about for so many centuries, never progressed along the road upward that all other men have taken, with more or less consistency and success? Are they, like the animals, condemned to that psychical fixity of which Richet speaks? Are they incapable? Are they unsuited to progress?

Assuredly, the atavism of the ages, which to-day weighs upon them, does not dispose them favorably toward progress as we understand it. But they are what they are because they *wish* to be so. And they wish to be so for this double reason, as they have repeatedly told me: first, because God made them so, because it is their "manner" which they can not alter without destroying their race, just as the monkeys could not cease to climb the trees, the birds to fly in the air, the fish to live in the water. Then, they add, since they have no need of houses or farms or herds, since they have no wealth to arouse any one's jealousy, since they are free in the endless forests, living without labor and knowing all the secrets of things, they would enjoy the best lot possible to man if God did not visit their encampments from time to time and strike down some of their number.

In pointing out the religious beliefs and practices of this little race and of those peoples that are the most closely related to them by the sum total of their conceptions, we have gone as far back as the conditions which mankind offers us to-day render possible. Compared with our savages, the Latins, Greeks, Chaldeans, Aryans, Chinese, and even the Egyptians appear to us with a later and more elaborate civilization, with theogonies more complicated as they advance, with myths that seem to grow like the forests, with systems supported by reason, with more or less poetic inventions that give play to their imaginations, with sacerdotal organizations wisely hierarchical, with magical practices that upset, corrupt, and obliterate the religious data.

At the same time, there is nothing that throws more light on the religion of these first later civilizations than their comparison with the religions of the primitives of to-day. We find all features, in some fashion, in both of them; the one helps us to understand the other.

The Chinese of the remotest period, for instance, adored a supreme God to whom they gave the name *Chang-Ti* (*Chang,* "superior"; *Ti,* "master"). It is the *Mwiny'ezi* ("the having power") of the Bantus. Later on this all-powerful and all-great Being seems to be confounded with the heaven (*Tien*), of which he is the living, conscious soul. The same process took place in Africa. In many parts reluctance is felt to mention God by name, due to fear rather than respect; that is why they say: *"The One of the heaven, The One from on high, The One of the light* (*Mu-ungu, Mu-anga,* etc.), and also simply *the heaven,* with a prefix and a connective personifying it.

Maspero tells us with much insistence that in Egypt each "nome" or district had a god—and a god in three persons; the most ancient monuments mention his existence and call him *the god, the one god, the only god.* "But," he adds, "this god was never *god* simply. The only god is the only god Amon, the only god Phtah, the only god Osiris, i.e., a determined being having a personality, a name, and attributes. The conception of his unity is then geographical and political at least as much as it is religious: *Ra,* the only god at Heliopolis, is not the same as *Amon,* only god at Thebes."[51]

We have an exactly similar conception to-day in many parts of Africa, notably in the Niger delta. There also God appears as a triad that seems to be based on the constitution of the human family, an image of the heavenly family.[52] Although the supreme God, Creator, Author, Master, and Proprietor of all living things,[53] is *Tsi,* yet each district inhabited by a distinct clan gives him a special name: this is *its* God. In other words, for these peoples the name specializes the person. And it would seem to them that if they called God by the name which every one gives him, he would belong to them less. As the father of the family has a name, as the father of the tribe has one, it must be that the father of their fathers, who is God, has one that

[51] Maspero, *Histoire ancienne des peuples de l'Orient,* p. 27.
[52] Leonard, *op. cit.,* p. 416.
[53] *Ibid.*

ranks him, so to speak, among them and at their head. This is what Pierret very well understood when he took as the epigraph of his essay on Egyptian mythology these words: *Numina nomina.* The God of the primitive Egyptian religion was, then, the sole, infinite, eternal Being, "the only begetter in the heaven and on the earth who is not begotten, the father of the fathers, the mother of the mothers."[54]

The sun (*Ra*), which is the most brilliant creature of the Almighty, and, as it were, the living body of the *Divinity,* is often assimilated with him: this is also noticeable among many of the Nigritian tribes, among the Massai, some of the Bantus, the Hottentots, the Polynesians, etc. But, in their mind, God is not the sun, and the sun is not God; the special connectives that differentiate these words in the Bantu languages plainly show that; and the other tribes likewise assent to this distinction by attributing to God deeds and movements which evidently can not belong to the sun as, for instance according to the Massai, his dwelling place on the Kibo.

Before the formation of the kingdoms of Babylon and Nineveh, the Akkadians and the Sumerians who, in the judgment of most Assyriologists, preceded the Semitic populations on the banks of the Tigris and Euphrates, had a religion whose basis was a belief in innumerable spirits, good and bad, set over the phenomena of nature, the movements of the stars, the vegetation, the preservation of life, diseases, and death. The practice of magic was held in great esteem along with incantations, conjuring prayers, talismans, amulets, exorcisms, "envoutements," etc. The same things may be observed throughout the whole ancient world; and in the present world of the primitives, in Africa, Oceanica, and America, everywhere.

The Egyptian conception of the soul explains the ideas of several black populations on the same subject, scattered and confused but still perceptible. This soul appears to them as composed of several envelopes: an animal envelope that disappears with the body, an intellectual one that returns to the region of the spirits, a conscious one that must correspond to the life of the man. This disembodied soul is constantly

[54] Harlez (*Dict. apologet. de la foi cath.*, art. "Religions").

searching for a material support, and upon his family is laid the duty of furnishing him with it.

The Egyptian priests employed certain animals as symbols and frequently they put the head of the symbol animals on human bodies to serve as these symbols. To appeal still more strikingly to the people's imagination, certain animals were reputed to bear, concealed within them, the divinity, who, from this hiding place, watched over human beings.[55] Now this symbolism is very well known in black Africa. R. E. Dennett has recently discovered it accompanied by very curious details, in the region of Loango. There, as formerly in Egypt, fetich animals are consequently venerated entirely apart from any totemistic idea or function. There also in the initiation ceremonies, ritualistic dances, etc., the fetichers appear with a mask representing an animal's head (the symbol animal) and are thus supposed to be bearers of the spirit that is concealed in that animal which speaks by their tongue.

Similar comparisons might be made with the same success between the Chinese, Aryan, Mazdean, Greek, Roman, and other religions and the present beliefs of our African Blacks. Greece, for example, at the Pelasgic period, had no priesthood.

"The fathers of families and the chiefs of the people offered the sacrifices and prayers. Later on, these chiefs had priests attached to their person, whom they appointed to perform the ceremonies of worship. Only the places where oracles were given possessed sacerdotal bodies devoted to the study of the will of the gods and their expression. When temples and sanctuaries were erected, they naturally had their ministers. Greece had then two principal orders, the priests and the diviners.

"The Greek temples were generally built on the heights. Some were of great magnificence. For these sites they chose the shade of woods, a smiling valley, a lofty mountain, the bank of a stream, a location especially majestic, mysterious, or pleasant.

"The first idols were merely stones or rude images; but in the course of time they became works of art. Temples and altars had to be consecrated by offerings, prayers, ceremonies,

[55] Harlez, *loc. cit.*

and particularly by anointings with oil. Certain enclosures were also consecrated to the gods; and fields whose product went to the priests.

"The acts of worship consisted in sacrifices, prayers, and offerings, libations, and the burning of incense. Bloody sacrifices are said to have been introduced only at a later date." [56]

A great part of Africa has neither temples nor statues nor fetiches. This was true also of primitive Rome. The Latin adored his "gods" in the woods, in the fields, without making any image of them. He had several classes of gods; the "gods" of the heaven or "higher" gods, at whose head reigned the author of life, the master of the empyrean and of the sun, the *divum deus;* the earthly "gods," protective and avenging genii; the "gods" of man, consisting of disembodied souls and including the *lares* and the *penates,* connected with the protection of the family, the roads, the crossroads, and the district, the *manes* or benevolent spirits of the dead purified by funeral ceremonies, the *larves* and *lemures,* evil, angry spirits that appeared under the form of phantoms, specters, and ghosts. All that is Africa over again; it epitomizes the religious world of the Blacks.

But we must conclude.

At all times and places, we have seen that mankind is gathered into families and these families are bound together by a religion. At the basis of the ancient civilizations as also in the societies of primitive form that are to be found up to our own day in different parts of the world, the principal elements of that religion are identical. The differences pertain to the external and adventitious habiliments which each people, according to its genius, its particular nature, its degree of culture, the wealth, poetry, or severity of its imagination, the boldness of its spirit or the discipline of its organization, has been able to give to that common basis; the differences are due to the neglect into which it has let certain parts fall; to the predominance given to some elements over others, for instance, to magic over religion; to the alterations, voluntary or other-

[56] *Ibid.*

wise, undergone in the course of ages, migrations, and revolutions or social evolutions by the primitive portion of their beliefs and prescribed practices.

And this also explains a fact disconcerting at first glance but perfectly comprehensible to us now. We find the Romans and Greeks with a religion more elaborate but less pure than that of the Assyro-Chaldeans, the latter with beliefs less elevated than those of the Egyptians, the Egyptians with practices more multiplied and systems more complex but an ensemble less easy to penetrate than that of the Hamitic, Nigritian, or Bantu tribes. We find these last with religious data more complete but more diffuse than those of our humble little Pygmies whose poor imagination found nothing to enrich the dogmatic and moral foundation which they bore with them in their wandering life. Nevertheless it has maintained them through the long series of centuries past and gone.

To the eyes of an impartial observer, the human family appears as a religious and moral family in varying degrees, with a religion and a morality fundamentally universal. This separates it by an unbridgeable chasm from that other, the animal family wherein it has sought alliances but with which it is never confounded. Thus understood and maintained, the rôle of the family has been fundamental for religion. In fact, a religious doctrine can live only on condition that it take root in society or become socialized. It is the primitive family with its double power of conservation and expansion that has preserved the primitive religion; but religion in turn has rendered the same service to the family. Through beliefs, practices, and institutions without which the family must seemingly have disappeared, religion has preserved it and enabled it to expand.

No one, we think, has better understood or better set forth this rôle of the family in history than Fustel de Coulanges. We quote his testimony:

"If we transport ourselves in thought into the midst of those ancient generations of men," he writes in *La Cité antique*,[57]

[57] P. 40.

"we find in each house an altar, and about that altar the family gathered together. It meets together each morning at the fireside to offer up its first prayers, and again in the evening for the last prayers of the day. In the course of the day it comes together again around the same fireside for the dinner which it partakes of piously after prayer and libation. In all its religious acts, its members all sing hymns together which their fathers have bequeathed to them.

"Outside the house, near by, in the neighboring field, is a tomb. There several generations of ancestors rest in common; death has not separated them. In the second existence they are still grouped together and continue to form an indissoluble family. Between the living part and the deceased part of the family, there is only this distance of a few steps separating the house from the tomb. On certain days, determined for each one by his domestic religion, the living meet together near their ancestors. Thither they bring the funeral repast, and there pour out milk and wine, place cakes and fruit, or burn the flesh of a victim for them. In return for these offerings, they claim their protection; they call them their gods and ask them to make their field fertile, their home prosperous, and their hearts virtuous."

A little further on he continues:

"What unites the members of the ancient family is something more powerful than birth or sentiment or physical force; it is the religion of the fireside and of the ancestors. It makes the families form one body in this life and in the other. The ancient family is a religious association more than an association of nature. We do not pretend that religion has created the family, but assuredly religion has given the family its rules, and hence it happens that the ancient family has received a constitution very different from that which it would have had if only natural feelings had formed it."

Whether we study savage peoples or civilized nations, whether we pass from Africa to Asia, from Oceanica to America or Europe, whether we go from present times back as far as we can in the course of the ages, everywhere we find the pure elements of religion invaded, in variable but appreciable proportions, by beliefs and practices that are foreign and even opposed, that divert it from its purpose, that deform it, that compromise it. This is what we have designated as *natural magic* and *supernatural magic*.

Like those mysterious vampires of Germanic legend, magic under a thousand different forms emerges from nature and the supernatural to attach itself to all that religion is intended to sanctify: the family, society, morality, belief, prayer, and sacrifice.

This distinction, for the matter in hand, is of capital importance. Because of their failure to observe that distinction, many historians of religion, anthropologists, philosophers, and sociologists have been and are still guilty of many confusions and errors.

Must we say it at last? If we turn our gaze from the primitives and ancients to the present world, we have no difficulty in finding in China and Japan, in India, Arabia, America, Europe, in the Buddhist, Shintoist, Taoist, and Mussulman religions and even alongside of Christianity some living traces of that strange and persistent old dualism. In our great capitals of the twentieth century, at Paris, London, Berlin, New York, natural and supernatural magic has its representatives and followers who make fetiches and amulets and talismans, have charms, are in relation with the powers of the other world; there are sorcerers and sorceresses, there are secret societies, there is spiritism, occultism, masonic and gnostic initiations. Religion and magic are inseparable.

Even where religion seems to be in eclipse, superstition advances with singular vigor. Berlin recently announced the formation of a school of sorceresses. At Paris, there is no freethought journal that does not contain announcements recommending sibyls, cartomancians, seers, mediums, talismans, checkered playing cards, Georgian secrets for succeeding in everything "not only inflicting evils, but for everything that concerns life, disagreements, reconciliations, intimacies of the heart, success at lottery, and at the *tirage d'obligations.*"[58]

[58] Announcements taken from *Le Matin,* the daily chronicler of which professes to be an absolute materialist.

Behold "Argine," a statuette-fetich under whose patronage a player must place himself or herself to have luck at bridge, the clover leaf of Argine having four petals. Argine "can also make a charming seal that will bring happiness to a letter-writer and to the one who receives the letter."

Argine is manufactured at Paris and sold for twenty dollars!

CHAPTER IX

CONCLUSIONS

I. THE END OF AN INQUIRY

Some one has said:

"Do you wish the explanation of religions, of their teaching, of their rites, of their precepts? Go back to their origin. You will not find the origins of these religions such as they are commonly represented; nor can they be discovered in the monuments of ancient civilizations as these do not represent the earliest state of mankind; nor can they be reached by reasoning on the data furnished by the natural sciences or philosophy.

"Better than these as a source to explain religion are the present savage populations, who have halted at a lower stage of social and religious evolution; who very nearly represent what all humanity primitively has once been.

"If, then, the explanation can be found in these uncultured natures of their religious conceptions and of what is connected therewith, you will have at the same time the explanation of the religions that to-day present themselves to us as the most perfected. Christianity, for example, in its most complete and most clearly defined present form, which is Catholicism, by the path of a long and imperceptible evolution, has come from these humble religious forms which have swaddled humanity in its cradle, from which humanity tends to free itself as it gets its growth.

"In those remote epochs, religion was mingled with everything, as it was 'the expression of the need which men have of uniting to live the same feelings and to exalt the collective soul.'[1] Then, as each social fact became detached from the mass to develop by itself, religion established itself in a separate domain, more and more narrow.[2] Thus it comes to pass at the present time that morality is separating from religion and tending to form one body with the civil law, as expressed by the codes: so that *evil* is what the government forbids, *good* embraces all the rest. The 'myths,' in turn, 'the myths by which religion explained the universe,' are replaced by science. There survives the organization of the churches, an institution that corresponds to nothing since it contains no living principle, which may, however, continue into a more or less distant future as a survival of a long past.

"These conclusions, which sum up the history of religions, you will arrive at," we are told, "by the study of the primitives. Go to the primitives."

We have gone to them. That our study might be conducted under unimpeachable conditions, we chose at the outset as our field of study those primitives whom long personal association enables us to know the best; we have accepted only facts and

---

[1] F.·. Lahy, *Manuel de l'histoire des religions*, p. 32, project presented to the Masonic General Assembly of 1907 and approved upon report of F.·. Sembat.

[2] The thesis is borrowed from Durkheim and Reinach; the latter develops it at length in *Cults, Myths, and Religions*.

the views of men well known for their competency and impartiality; we have deliberately avoided *a priori* judgments and prejudiced statements, and we have examined the natives themselves, their languages, their practices, what they think, what they believe, and what they are.

Then we have compared the data thus gathered with data obtained among other similar populations of the globe, data furnished by prehistoric men, and data that can to-day be gathered from the earliest monuments of ancient civilizations.

And it is under these conditions that we are about to set down our personal conclusions.

Yes, the reader will perhaps say; but your "primitives," as you have described them, are not at all the primitives that we need for our theories. The primitives that our theories deal with are barely disengaged from animality, they have no idea of a personal God, no moral notion, no sense of shame, they scarcely distinguish the animate from the inanimate, they are naturists and adore anything at all.

And we reply: "But these primitives or savages that your theories require do not exist anywhere and perhaps never have existed; at any rate it is impossible to discover them either in the present world or in the past."

In reality, the picture that has too often been presented as the portrait of the savage is a fantastic portrait: the real savage is a man like every one of us, with his conception of life, his manner of conforming to his environment, his civilization, and his philosophy.

If he could free himself from the tyranny of certain practices or customs most often inspired by magic, reducing his needs to the minimum, this primitive would have found the means to be as happy as the members of our most civilized European societies, and often happier. Such, no doubt, was quaternary man. Let us cease pitying him: he may have been less delicate than are some of his descendants, but how much more vigorous, stronger, and freer.

Another standpoint is taken by an opposite camp. Might not these primitives or supposed primitives be degenerates; and then what value would their testimony have?

It is certain that the savage populations still spread over the face of the earth have not always been what they are to-day. They have traveled, they have changed their country and manners, perhaps their language, perhaps their religion, they have experienced prosperity, then misfortune and dispersion. We know, for example, that when the Portuguese navigators of the sixteenth century descended on the coast of western Africa, they found in many places organized kingdoms that to-day we look for in vain. In the Zambese valley the extraordinary ruins of Zimbawe make us likewise suppose that there also was formerly at least a powerful colony with a civilization already developed. Some tribes are certainly in decay, while others show remarkable vitality and power of expansion.

It is the same in Oceanica where the natives, on most of the islands, are the first to acknowledge that their ancestors were much superior to them; and some vestiges of a higher civilization found in Polynesia point the same way.

In America the Incas of Peru and the Aztecs of Mexico, at the period of European discovery, had reached an imposing state of culture.

But all in all we can affirm that the populations which to-day present themselves to us as uncivilized have always been such, or very nearly. In Africa, save for the ancient colony of Zimbawe and certain points on the eastern coast, we find no vestige of monuments, no trace of writing, not even a tradition that allows us to suppose an ancient civilization. It seems to be true that what the Black is to-day, he has always been. He was so represented on Egyptian monuments that take us back to 2000 years before our era. The Ctesias (fifth century before Christ) gives a description of the Pygmies as exact as that furnished by Stanley, when he found them in the great forest of Itouri.

We must, then, admit that, if the primitives of to-day do no longer represent the primitives of the prehistoric times, of the great dispersion, either as regards their type or their social condition or their religious and moral ideas, they are, nevertheless, of all these races, the ones that at present give us the most faithful idea of them.

Let us, then, frankly accept them as our sources. Guided by the information we have sought in their midst and responding to the invitation of our adversaries, let us formulate certain questions and draw the required conclusions.

1. From the special point of view that interests us, what is the character of the "religious phenomenon" and what place does it occupy in the life of humanity?

2. What human needs does it answer to? As mankind progresses, can not, must not religion be replaced, its morality by the civil law, and its dogma by science?

3. Of what does the religion of the primitives consist—what is it, and what is it not?

4. Can we construct the primitive religion from the religion of the primitives? What relation does it bear to these present religions? In that immense religious ocean in which all humanity moves, is it possible to discern a current of doctrine, substantial, coherent, invariable in its essence, but capable of evolving in intensity, extent, and depth, which would be the one and universal religion, that is to say, the true religion?

Our reply to these questions must be very short, but of what great interest and importance are the subjects with which they deal!

II. CHARACTER OF THE RELIGIOUS PHENOMENON

The first conclusion that we draw from our inquiry is the fundamental universality, permanence, and identity of religions.

This great fact is no longer disputed by any one, it is one of those matters classified as "definitely settled."

"The statement that there are nations or tribes which possess no religion," says Tiele, "rests either on inaccurate observation, or a confusion of ideas. No tribe or nation has yet been met with, destitute of belief in any higher beings; and travelers who asserted their existence have been afterwards refuted by the facts. It is legitimate, therefore, to call religion in its most general sense a universal phenomenon of humanity." [3]

[3] Tiele, *Outlines of the History of Religions*, p. 6.

With Quatrefages we may add that

"without doubt this religion will be rudimentary, often puerile or bizarre to the eyes of the enlightened European; no doubt we shall find absurdities and contradictions in it; but for all that, it does not lose its essential character any more than a physiological function, breathing for example, loses its character when performed by lower animals in a different and more obscure fashion than among vertebrates. All religion rests on the belief in certain divinities. The ideas that different peoples have formed of these beings they venerate or fear, evidently can not be the same. For the savage, as for the Mohammedan, Jew, or Christian, the being whom he addresses is the master of his destinies; like these others he prays to him in the hope of obtaining some blessing or avoiding some evil. To remain in the domain of facts, this being is indeed a *God* for him, and we must accept him as such." [4]

Let us credit this result to the activity of our new science of comparative religions. The investigations instigated by it, as by history, anthropology, archæology, etc., demonstrate in opposition to Lubbock, Spencer, and all their disciples by countless, authentic, and irrefutable testimonies that religion is a universal fact.

But this demonstration at once suggests certain corollaries.

If all men of all countries and all times, whatever the diversity of appearance, color, habits, or speech, have the same physical nature and the same moral nature, if all have the same rational and perfectible intellect, the same free will, the same sense of morality fundamentally, if all experience the same religious need and have satisfied that need in a manner essentially the same, why not admit that they have a common origin?

Let us suppose that the men actually dwelling on the earth had made their appearance on different planets and afterward, all at once, were gathered together in a general assembly at some one place in the universe. Noting their absolute resemblance from the triple point of view, physical, mental, and moral, when they try to account for their origin, they will find no satisfac-

[4] Quatrefages, *The Human Species.*

tory explanation outside of one which assigns them a common Author. This conclusion will be all the more patent since they have all, with an identical physiognomy, appeared on this same little point of the universe, which is our earth.

The same conclusion is set forth in other words and for other reasons by the great scholar whose authority we have frequently invoked. "The application of physiological laws to anthropology," says Quatrefages, "leads us immediately to recognize the unity of the human species." But we will not stop longer over this question, which only indirectly enters into our study.

Another consequence of the fact established above is this: If mankind universally has felt the religious need, it is because religion is essential to the nature of man. It is, then, true that this need must be satisfied, that it corresponds to something real and objective, that somewhere there exists a true religion. When the magnetic needle turns on its pivot until it has found the north, we judge that, for it to turn invariably in that direction, there must be a pole that attracts it. It is not otherwise with the human soul.

With the same comparison, Albert Réville in one of the best passages of his work, makes a like observation, although from another point of view. We have so often had occasion to quote for the purpose of contradicting him, that this time we can not resist the desire to ask his support.

"Through all its aberrations," he writes, "the human spirit has always turned towards the Divinity. From time to time attempts have been made to force it in the contrary direction. It has always resisted and, as soon as it could, it has resumed its constant direction. Like the magnetic needle, it would say to us: Such is my nature!"

So "religious history has not only superstitions, follies, and ugliness to record. It includes also things noble and splendid. In it we meet majestic conceptions and sublime aspirations. We hear accents of a purity, accuracy, and charm so mysterious and powerful that we are involuntarily led to believe that they come from above the earth. The religious inspiration in its great hours yields to no other in grandeur and fecundity.

Morality has had to suffer from religion; it has also enormously profited from it, and to-day religion is still the only serious support for conscience in the immense majority. Art has for a long time owed its finest works to it, and it is not saying too much when we affirm that without it philosophy would never have been born." [5]

Will you say that is all only illusion and deception? With one of our adversaries, will you say that the thought of man is afflicted with an incurable infirmity, that the history of religions is only the history of the necessary errors of humanity?

In that case man would be the most unsuccessful of all creatures, since the good to which he aspires, which he regards as his very *raison d'être,* his life's aim, and his ultimate purpose, would be only an illusion; his very stretching toward the desired goal would be a constant self-deception; and during all the centuries of his existence on the earth, he would have been continually advancing towards nothingness!

This would be a strange mystery, one more intolerable than all the mysteries proposed by religion

It can not be so. If religion is not merely a psychological phenomenon, but a psychic necessity, the result of a uniform mental activity which clings to the feeling that the experimental world is incomplete, if it appears to be an essential element of our nature and an irresistible inclination, this is because man has been so constituted with a higher end in view, another world, "which alone contains what man desires, that is, the full satisfaction of the intellect by truth, of the conscience by holiness, and of the heart by happiness.

The true religion is nothing but the true means for attaining that higher world: it is the route that leads man to his destiny." [6]

It is toward this end that humanity tends to steer itself, with the uncertainties, gropings, and weaknesses of an unbalanced nature, but with a really eager cooperative effort and an invincible persistence.

This point is, moreover, one which this new branch of study

[5] Réville, *Prolégomènes de l'histoire des religions,* p. 90.
[6] De Broglie, *Problèmes,* etc., p. 383.

will make clearer by a keener light. L. H. Jordan, of the University of Chicago, in his remarkable work, goes so far as to say:

"It is simply folly to attempt to write a Philosophy of Religion without first acquainting oneself with those mental tendencies and processes with which the New Psychology deals. . . . It is no exaggeration to affirm, with Professor Paterson, that the Materialism and Agnosticism of the nineteenth century have been completely undermined, and that the dominant philosophy of to-day is one that 'finds in spirit the ultimate reality. . . . The world of thinking men is becoming increasingly convinced that mind is the key to existence and that the processes of the universe are a revelation of thought and a pursuit of rational ends.' " [7]

The same spirit is manifested by one of the greatest scholars who have honored England in recent years, Lord Kelvin, who wrote in 1903:

"While 'fortuitous concourse of atoms' is not an inappropriate description of the formation of a crystal, it is utterly absurd in respect to the coming into existence, or the growth, or the continuation, of the molecular combinations presented in the bodies of living things. Here scientific thought is compelled to accept the idea of Creative Power. Forty years ago, I asked Liebig, walking somewhere in the country, if he believed that the grass and flowers which we saw around us grew by mere chemical forces. He answered, 'No; no more than I could believe that a book of botany, describing them, could grow by mere chemical forces.' Every action of human free will is a miracle to physical and chemical and mathematical science." [8]

With an intuition less reasoned out but like in tendency, humanity, in its humblest as in its most distinguished representatives, save rare exceptions, ever turns towards the Divinity, as the object, purpose, and end of all religion.

[7] L. H. Jordan, *Comparative Religion*, p. 291.
[8] Quoted by Jordan, *op. cit.*, p. 490.

III. Necessity of Religion

Without denying this surprising attraction, but rather affirming it, since it is no longer subject to dispute, there are some who pretend, however, that it represents only one phase of humanity. A day which has already dawned will come, when morality will be replaced by the law and dogma of science. What they grant—and we must thank them for it—is that it is proper to treat these two great forces, which are two great fictions, with some consideration because of the services they have been able to render humanity in its infancy

We are told that at first there must have been confusion between things different and differently founded in reason: moral precepts and religious precepts. But as society organized, a work of selection and specialization must have followed. To quote the words of Reinach,

"Man starts with a mass of prescriptions and proscriptions, the disregard of which is accounted crime. . . . Experience, however, quickly shows that some of his prohibitions do good service to the order and security essential to every organism and—for that reason—to all human society. Conversely, others are seen to wear that stamp of social inutility which characterizes the purely religious taboo." [9]

In time these latter are got rid of and only the others remain, transformed into laws resting on the instinct of solidarity, the eternal basis of all morality.

"For morality," he says, "is either social, or the shadow of a dream: there can be no question of a discipline of custom, save for the man who lives in a society. It is, therefore, the fact of social life, not the arbitrary behest of godhead, that is the well-spring of moral obligations." [10]

Then, too, all morality has its expression in law.

With what art or what inadvertence are these things recounted, and upon what confusions are they based!

[9] Reinach, *op. cit.*, p. 205.
[10] *Ibid.*, p. 206.

1. That in former times as also to-day religious, moral, and social laws are found mingled together, is quite true since morality has always been united, in some way or other, to religion. That certain of these prescriptions are legal prescriptions, which can and must be separated and distinguished from religion and even from morality in more perfect societies, is equally true. But that *all* the religious prescriptions in all religions must disappear as so many "useless taboos," so as to leave the civil "taboos" as the only necessary ones because the only social ones, is precisely what must be demonstrated by proving that all religions are equally false, and that all the prescriptions of all these religions are "useless" as a support for morality. This is what is not proved, and for good reason.

2. If we rightly understand, morality that is not social is declared to be only an appearance: so that individual morality can be what each one may wish, provided social morality remains, that is to say, provided the law is respected.

Forsooth, an extraordinary theory! Evidently morality must have a social tendency, but it will have this social effect only if it is at first imposed upon the individual conscience This is precisely what St. Paul wished to establish in the passage of his Epistle to the Romans to which Reinach refers:

"Owe no man anything, but to love one another. For he that loveth his neighbor, hath fulfilled the law. For *Thou shalt not commit adultery; thou shalt not kill; thou shalt not steal; thou shalt not bear false witness; thou shalt not covet:* and if there be any other commandment, it is comprised in this word, *Thou shalt love thy neighbor as thyself.* The love of our neighbor worketh no evil. Love therefore is the fulfilling of the law."

All these precepts, according to the mind of St. Paul, must be accepted by the individual conscience first of all, and on this condition alone will they be respected in the law.

3. Let us suppose the theory put into practice: the "religious prescriptions and proscriptions" are ignored as useless, and also the ancient "taboos" and the vain "scruples" and the inexpli-

cable "modesties." Man remains alone, man *sine verecundia,* with the law alone.

Let us suppose that law perfect, just, equal for all, anticipating everything, applied to everything.

Let us also suppose it put into practice with all desirable intelligence and impartiality.

Let us suppose, in fine, that it is accepted in part and in whole and that, with nothing but the law for their morality and religion, all citizens, reasonable men although without shame or scruples or superstitions, are disposed to observe it exactly now under the watchful eye of the policeman, instead of the eye of conscience and the eye of God.

Do you not see outside the law, in a domain that is foreign to it, a domain that it can never enter, room still for the exercise of all man's evil passions, all his baseness, all his meanness, all his treachery, all his selfishness, all his vice? What law, for instance, will prevent a citizen from being proud, jealous, wrathful, avaricious, envious, gluttonous, lewd? Who will rule over the human beast within him? What guaranty will this man give his country, society? And what hope is there of forming a good social organization with individuals who will no longer recognize any restraint outside of the law, i.e., practically outside of force?

No. Human law does not suffice to discipline man, to maintain him, to elevate him, to civilize him. He still needs a morality. And for this morality to stand firmly, it needs religion for its basis.

We may say the same thing of science. "Science," we are sometimes told, "is destined to explain the universe to us, to replace all the myths, and to make all religions disappear."

Here we find the same confusions.

1. It is really an indication that we know nothing of religion if we represent it as charged with the duty of explaining the universe to us and trying to do so by means of various myths, more or less childish, which disappear one after the other like so much thin vapor before the sun of science, rising above the horizon.

That legends, attempts at cosmogony, myths, relating to the origin of things, of men, and of the "gods," form part of the religious domain of savage or civilized people,[11] is an incontestable fact that nobody dreams of disputing. But it is to misunderstand religion entirely, as many have done, if we make it consist of these ornaments that sometimes pretend to enrich it, to adorn it, to transform it, while really falsifying, concealing, compromising it, and disfiguring its beauty.

The purpose of religion is to connect man with the invisible world, not to explain the secrets of the visible world. This connection is accomplished by the faith it offers to the believer, by the morality it imposes, by the worship it organizes. Thus religion resides in a sphere inaccessible to experimental science which, on the other hand, has full liberty to work at the methodical exploration of its own vast domain and will only suffer loss by departures from these bounds.

No doubt, religion is often deceived, or rather men are often deceived in religion; this one point at least it has in common with science. But religion and science, which may meet on the frontier of their fields of activity, at times aid, at others attack each other and exchange rude remarks, answer to two distinct needs, so that they can not replace each other. But there is nothing in them opposed finally to a definite and cordial agreement.

These general principles, however, apply only to what is true in religion and true in science. But that portion is all that counts: the rest may disappear, the sooner the better.

But if we descend from these heights to particular applications, we will be embarrassed.

"Although faith is above reason," says the Vatican Council, "yet there can never exist any real discord between faith and reason because it is the same God who reveals the mysteries and communicates the faith, who gives to the human soul the

[11] For what particularly concerns Christianity, read: J. Guibert, *Les croyances et les sciences de la nature.* You will see there that if the Biblical authors have spoken of science, conformably to appearances and in the scientific language of their time, they have simply been reasonable. "In this hypothesis, neither religious sincerity nor scientific truth is endangered." (P. 259.)

light of reason. But God can not contradict himself, and the truth can not be in contradiction with the truth. The vain appearance of a contradiction of such a kind comes from this: that the dogmas of the faith are not understood and set forth according to the mind of the Church, or because some erroneous opinions are taken for the certain teaching of reason." [12]

Thus in mathematics, astronomy, zoology, physics, chemistry, biology, linguistics, and in the other fields of human knowledge, the Catholic scholars that we find in these branches can move at their ease in the passionate search for truth. Religion claims the right to reëxamine, not science, but such particular opinions and provisional hypotheses as she finds contrary to her faith.

This is why, under the protection of these explanations and these reservations, we can subscribe and gladly do subscribe to the declarations that terminate Réville's *Prolégomènes de l'Histoire des Religions.*

"On the condition that they be well understood, religion in itself and independent science should never be hostile to each other, because as a matter of fact they do not answer the same needs and can not be substituted for each other. If science springs from the intellectual need of knowing the real and the true in all things, religion satisfies aspirations of another sort which are not less natural nor less inherent in the human spirit. Science proceeds methodically, using a hypothesis only provisionally, always subject to experience. It is essentially analytical and can never arrive at a universal synthesis which, however, the mind desires. No, even were no longer anything hidden from it in regard to those matters of which it treats, even might it pass without a moment of doubt from understanding the formation of the nebulæ to understanding the formation of the least infusoria, all that would make only a sum after all, that it had obtained; and the universe is more than a sum, it is the infinite.

"How, then, would science proceed to divide experimentally the unity that binds together the totality of beings? How would it determine the entire course of a river whose source and mouth are both beyond its observation? Science, sovereign mistress in the domain of the finite, can not pass beyond it

[12] Constit. dogm. *Dei Filius,* cap. IV, *De fide et ratione.*

without contradicting herself. Her best qualified representatives, dominated as they are by exclusively analytical habits of thought, sometimes imagine they have made the synthesis solely because they have carefully enumerated all the facts, little and big, whose series forms an object of study. Let us suppose it has been demonstrated that in the living body there are only mechanical, physical, and chemical laws in action, and that men of former times were dreaming when they spoke of vital force or of animal spirits; that all the compartments and circumvolutions of the human brain have been labeled and the rôle of each in the mental operations precisely determined. That would be marvelous; but do you think, for all that, the slightest shadow of an explanation of life and thought has been given? Where is the central, the directive cause, the source of harmony and permanent coördination? It eludes you; nevertheless, it is there. This difficulty would be multiplied indefinitely if the synthesis of the universe were the issue.

"Religion, not in one only of its traditional forms, but in its fundamental and persistent claim, has this word to say: 'I do what you can not do; I proclaim what you dare not utter; I fill the immense void that your finest researches leave unexplored. I am the indestructible aspiration of the human heart. I am the voice from the depths of the soul. I am the bond uniting human dust to absolute thought; in this unfathomable abyss, the edge of which you are fated to reach by the very momentum of your activities, I sound the sovereign reality, that which really is; I perceive in the bottomless gulf a voice that calls me and I discern a light that draws me on. Perchance I deceive myself in the ideas I form of it. It may well be that I possess only some approximations, symbols, and reflections.

" 'What does that matter? You men of science are not quite sure that you know exactly the nature of the sun, and yet does that hinder you from living in its light and heat? In the same way, I dare to affirm the reality of my object, independently of the ideas I endeavor to form of it, and that is sufficient for me. Continue your useful, admirable works. You adore the Eternal while seeking its truth in the world: let me seek in it the complete ideal, the presentiment of which raises me above the earth and whose foretaste brings me ineffable delights; and let us live in peace!' "

With still greater precision and with Christianity especially in mind, Brunetière said: "Science and religion are separate[13] domains, as Claude Bernard wrote, in which everything should keep its place. It is the only way of avoiding confusion and of assuring progress in the physical, intellectual, political, and moral order." It is to the "intellectuals" and against their views there is need of showing that science has neither suppressed mysteries nor has the immutability of nature's laws closed the world to the action of the supernatural. There is need of showing them that the immutability of dogma, far from opposing the development of religious progress, is its condition; that such immutability of dogma is the sole foundation of morality, since there is no morality without an *imperative* to command it and a sanction to assure it; that this morality, the morality of the Decalogue and the Sermon on the Mount, is the common, indivisible, universal, inalienable good of all humanity; that true progress, perhaps the only form worthy of the name, would be to succeed in engraving on all hearts the prescriptions of this morality; and that, in fine, Christianity alone is capable of preparing and consolidating that progress—I mean Christianity purified from all party spirit and restored, so to speak, to its universality.[14]

IV. THE RELIGION OF THE PRIMITIVES

Let us return to our primitives.

If they have a religion—and we think we have proved that they have one—what name are we to give it? What is its origin? From that origin can we conjecture with probability the origin of all religions? And lastly, what is the position of Christianity in regard to the primitive religion?

To answer these different questions, we must first eliminate mythology, superstition, and magic. We thereby free religion from what forms part of it in the eyes of many, but which in reality burdens it as with a parasitic growth, conceals it, impoverishes it, discredits it, and compromises it.

[13] "Distinct domains" would be more just.

[14] F. Brunetière, *Discours de combat* (New series, p. 119). Quoted in *Revue d'apologétique*, March 1, 1908.

Mythology is the collection of legends relating to the gods, the origin of the world and what it contains, the first accounts of the tribe, the marvels of nature. It may pass for an ornament with a religious appearance; doubtless it contains interesting and curious information, reminiscences, allusions and data, but it is no more religion than it is history.

Nor is superstition. Superstition, made up of vain observances, is an aberration or a deviation of religious sentiment. As the fruit of ignorance, credulity, imagination, and the ardent desire to attain certain effects, like a parasite it grows on all religions and even outside all religions, with this difference: some religions perpetually strive to free themselves from it, others tolerate it, and still others nourish it.

Magic includes incantations, conjurations, charms, witchcraft, "envoutements," sorceries of all sorts, with the constant support of the secret societies. It is also found everywhere, and everywhere is very nearly the same: in the savage tribes actually existing in different parts of the world, in the great civilizations of ancient Chaldea, Egypt, Greece, Rome, etc., among the developed peoples of India, China, Japan, as well as in the most cultivated European and American societies. It is a fact.

Not only is magic not religion, it is the conscious counterfeit and decided enemy of religion. Its avowed and universal claim is, in fact, a claim to accomplish its purpose *in spite of religion,* to force the activity and secrets of the invisible world to its service, to use them, and to use them against God.

Two German ethnologists, Preuss and lately Vierkandt, place magic at the origin of religion. Before them, J. H. King[15] had maintained the same thesis, and to a certain degree, J. G. Frazer.[16] A like tendency is noticeable in France,[17] in H. Hubert and Nauss as also in A. van Gennup.[18] Perhaps both magic and religion made their appearance in the world at about the same time. But from the purely historic point of view we can not say that one is the origin of the other. What seems

[15] King, *The Supernatural: Its Origin, Nature, and Evolution.*
[16] Frazer, *Golden Bough.*
[17] In the *Année sociologique,* 1904, pp. 1-146.
[18] *Revue des traditions populaires,* XIX, 1904, p. 553.

now to be ascertained is that magic, natural or supernatural, clings to the side of religion and strives to turn it from its object. In studying the beliefs and practices of savage or civilized populations, their mythologies and history, if we wish to avoid exposing ourselves to numerous and regrettable blunders, it is necessary to hold constantly before our minds this fundamental distinction.

As sharply as possible, therefore, the religion of the primitives should be separated from magic, mythology, and superstition. We are then able to see that it consists in a recognition of the manes, of tutelary spirits, and of a sovereign Being, the master of nature and father of men, with moral observances and the practice of prayer, offering, and sacrifice.

This religion is not idolatry. Idolatry in the strict sense of the word consists in the *adoration of images considered as the representation of a divinity;* which does not appear in the primitive religions. We detect it only later on among nations already cultured, with dispositions more or less artistic, that seem to have been led little by little to confound spirit with matter, the element with its symbol, the god with his image. Let this term be retained, if you like, to designate the religion of the Romans and Greeks; it does not belong to our primitives.

Their religion is not fetichism, by which we mean that *fetichism is not their whole religion,* but an element of religion among some of their number. We do not find it, for example, among the most primitive savages, the San, the Negrillos, and the Negritos; we do not find it anywhere in Africa, Oceanica, or America. Moreover, fetichism implies the existence and action of a spirit under the material covering to which he has been called; by this very fact it supposes an anterior animism. It is, therefore, not a primary fact "even though everything leads us to believe that it is extremely ancient." [19] This enables us to see "how little scientific strictness governs the successive categories which the school of Comte applies to religious development." This is Réville's reflection, a surprise coming from

[19] Réville, *Prolég. de l'hist. des religions,* p. 80.

the pen of an author who himself has not failed to establish "successive categories" which the facts do not justify.

This author thinks he can show, under the name of naturism, that the "worship of visible nature" has preceded all others. Many other ethnologists follow this view, some considering the stars as the object of the first adorations, others the animals, plants, or inanimate objects: such are Goblet d'Alviella in Belgium, Tiele in Holland, S. W. Powell in America, Frobenius, Usener, and Siebeck [20] in Germany. According to Frobenius, "animalism" names the period when man had not yet grasped the difference separating him from the beast.[21] According to Siebeck, in the beginning there was a period in which "there is no very clear difference between what is personal and what is natural, between the living and the non-living, between the psychical and the corporal." [22] In reality all these assertions are perfectly undemonstrable hypotheses. What can be said with the greatest certainty is that the most attentive examination of present savage populations proves that this pretended naturism, in the sense given it here, does not exist and that there is no reason to suppose it ever did exist. It would be useless for us to repeat our previous discussion of this subject.

Of totemism, given a position of honor in England by J. G. Frazer, F. S. Jevons, and W. Robertson Smith, and in France by Solomon Reinach especially, we have made a particular study. It is simply a more or less magical pact attached to the organization of the family which must be very ancient: but it plainly presupposes a belief, and is, if you like, a preëxisting religion.

This religion must be animism, according to Tylor, whom we have so often had occasion to quote. Assuredly this term might seem a happy one to designate the religion of the prim-

[20] W. Schmidt, *L'origine de l'idée de Dieu* (in *Anthropos*, no. 1, 1908, p. 12).

[21] *Ibid.*, p. 250.

[22] *Ibid.*, p. 252.

itives and, in general, would suit it very well. But the precise meaning given it by Tylor, Tiele, and their school, a meaning we can not admit in all its details, is such as to make us abandon it in order not to fall into disagreeable equivocation. This system is based on the hypothesis that an extensive religious evolution has taken place in the sense that the crudest first ideas were little by little elevated and perfected; hence the conception of a superior, personal God, the author and master of the world, must have arisen only in religions already advanced, among cultivated peoples, in the bosom of more or less elaborated civilizations.[23] But how, then, does it happen that the China of to-day, for instance, has a less precise knowledge of God than ancient China possessed? How explain the same phenomenon in India? Whence does it come that the Romans and Greeks, with a mythology much richer and more abundant and more poetic, had a religion less pure than that of the negroes of Africa? And what happens to the theory when we observe that these negroes are religiously and morally below the Pygmies and Negritos, who are, in other respects, the lowest of men?

As D. G. Brinton remarks,

"This universal postulate, the psychic origin of all religious thought, is the recognition, or, if you will, the assumption *that conscious volition is the ultimate source of all Force . . . that man is in communication with it.*" [24]

But that conscious will is precisely the Being whom we call God. Tylor's system, then, turns against its author; making use of the same facts, we can legitimately put at the base of his edifice the Spirit whom he reserves for its crown.

Animism, if it keep to the restricted and systematic sense commonly given it, is not the religion of the primitive.

Manism is an expression more correct in certain respects; but it seems to have too narrow a significance.

[23] That there has been a religious evolution, we consider certain, but not in the sense here intended. See the remainder of this study.
[24] D. G. Brinton, *Religions of Primitive Peoples*, p. 47.

Finally, the purest religions rest first of all on a belief in God and the homage due to him and since, in all the others, this first plane is occupied by the worship of the dead and of spirits, while the idea of God is never completely absent, it seems that we might group the totality of beliefs into two great classes:

Deist religions, including Christianity, Judaism, and Islam; *animo-deist religions,* which would include the paganism of savage races, along with the national religions of the Chinese, the Japanese, the Hindus, etc.

But in proposing this division and these names, we wish to state that we attach to them only a relative and provisional importance; for, on the one hand, it is really difficult to include under precise appellations a collection so complex as that of the religious beliefs of mankind and, on the other hand, in the succeeding pages of this study we may be able to propose a more correct classification.

V. From the Religion of the Primitives to the Primitive Religion

The names and systems we have just mentioned are not the only ones that have been imagined during these recent years to explain the "religious phenomenon." Their very multiplicity proves their fragility. It is a simple fact that not one of them all completely satisfies minds most desirous of being convinced.

We do not mean to say that there is nothing in them but error. There may be in each of them, there certainly are in several, exact observations, very just appreciations, ingenious remarks, indisputable but incomplete theories, and especially a number of facts that may be regarded as settled; these are to be found in Tylor, in Frazer, in W. R. Smith, even in the frankly partisan works so blindly materialistic of Girard de Rialle, A. Lefèvre, and Dr. Letourneau. These men's theory loses its value when it pretends to set itself up as a universal system which comprises the religious development of the human race in the past, the present, and the future.

Whatever be the particular and varied systems by which one

attempts to explain the genesis and development of religions, one always returns to the theory of evolution, which dominates and rules them all.

At the beginning of this study, we mentioned it [25] and we must return to it. In a general way the doctrine of evolution considers everything that exists as belonging to an autonomous and necessary process, passing from the simple to the composite. In religious matters, for instance, evolution, in the materialistic sense commonly given it, endeavors to show religion arising and developing in the spirit of man, and successively creating all the objects of belief, from the personified or animated nature of the most rudimentary religions to the supremely perfect God of the highest religions.

The exposition of this doctrine as ordinarily presented wears an air of plausibility that astonishes and seduces. But when we examine it more closely, weak points appear in great number, and already many objectors have abandoned it. To the general objection already stated,[26] we will content ourselves with adding a few reflections.

1. In the first place, according to the words of John Morley, "evolution is not a force, but a process; not a cause, but a law."[27] But, since religion, like civilization, is a living organization, we need not ask that evolution shall have created it, but only that it shall have presided over its development: this we gladly admit along with St. Vincent of Lerins and the whole Catholic school. The two greatest English representatives of this evolutionist school, Charles Darwin and John Fiske, gradually reached the conviction that there exists "a supreme and infinite Intelligence" behind the forces of nature and that the existence and activity of this Being must be frankly recognized as the basis of every system attempting to explain the plan of the universe.[28] Evolution, then, does not replace God: it presupposes him, as a law presupposes a legislator.

2. We have already said that the evolutionist school, by

[25] See Chapter II (*Evolution and Religion*).
[26] *Ibid.*
[27] John Morley, *On Compromise*, p. 169.
[28] Jordan, *op. cit.*, p. 231.

attributing very crude ideas to religions at their origin, committed an *a priori* blunder. That these first notions must have been very *simple,* little complicated, and few in number, we believe and, in fact, everything seems to indicate that it was so. But what is *simple* is not necessarily *crude,* shapeless, and miserable. The idea of a substance distinct from matter, which is our reasoning power, as also that of a sovereign Being, author and master of the world, is quite natural, reasonable, and at the same time very simple; the proof is that our poor Negrillos have these notions, perfectly clear. Religion, instead of progressively arriving at these concepts, may quite well have started with them.

3. Moreover, there always remain various obscure points that evolution never succeeds in clearing up. Why, for instance, does the human being show himself religious to such a degree that religion is a psychological necessity for him, while no animal manifests a like tendency in any of its representatives? If religion in man is only the simple product of evolution, how does it happen that this evolution does not germinate at least the first stages of a religious and moral disposition in those animals which are the closest to our species?

The comparative study of religions shows us that men in general have always had some knowledge of the Invisible and the Infinite: this argues religion to be a need of nature. Evolution gives no explanation of this psychological necessity.

Evolution does not explain the idea of God in the most primitive races, the least advanced, the nearest—if we may say so— to animality. Strangely enough, the idea is clearer, simpler, freer from mythical conceptions, as we penetrate more remotely into the past history of nations, as among the Indians and the Chinese, or as we descend lower on the ladder of civilization, as among the Pygmies.

Evolution does not explain the numerous cases of religious retrogression, at least as frequent as the cases of progress, in the entire universe. If there is any ascertained fact, it is the perpetual tendency of peoples, even the Semitic peoples, to polytheism, fetichism, and idolatry: which is altogether contrary to an evolutionary march toward the most perfect.

Evolution does not explain the presence of the religious instinct in man, nor of the moral conscience. As the biologist sees himself obliged to refer the origin of life to a power completely surpassing the limits within which his examination is conducted, the evolutionist is likewise forced to suppose these two fundamental bases of all religion and all morality as preëxisting before the action of his doctrine began its work.

In short, "evolution in religion is not now held to have produced religion; it is rather regarded as having merely given to religion a factor which was already in existence—its form and impulse and direction."[29] What has yet to be established and what we will later on examine is the part taken by nature and the supernatural in this very direction.

Whence, then, comes religion, and whence comes magic?

Let us leave Christianity aside for the time; we will come back to it presently. Aside from Christianity, then, we observe that the human race, at present and in the past, obeys various institutions of a special nature, called "religions." If we successively eliminate what distinctively characterizes each one of them, we shall arrive at a common basis where they all meet: a first observation, both interesting and precious.

Let us take Islam, the most recent of the great religions; let us subtract what is special to it, what specifically distinguishes it. Let us do the same for modern Judaism, for Mazdaism, Buddhism, Brahmanism, Taoism, and Confucianism.

Following the same process, let us pass to the ancient civilizations of Rome, Greece, Phœnicia, Chaldea, Assyria, Egypt.

Continuing to eliminate what distinguishes them, let us take up the rudimentary religions of the more or less primitive populations belonging to the white, yellow, black, brown, red, or mixed races, in the different parts of the world.

What do we find beneath all these religious strata which like geological deposits have been superposed, unequally indeed but constantly, in the course of ages upon the bare surface of the human soul?

We find a small number of beliefs, precepts, practices, and in-

[29] *Ibid.*, p. 338.

stitutions which, as they are at the base of all the rest, may reasonably be considered as the primary elements of religion and of its counterfeit, magic. These elements are found everywhere, here more effaced, there more distinct. They are approximately as follows.

Religion	*Magic*
1. Distinction between the visible world and an invisible world.	1. Distinction recognized.
2. Feeling of man's dependence in the presence of this higher world, particularly in the use of nature.	2. Dependence not accepted.
3. Belief in a supreme Being, creator, organizer, and master of the world, as well as father of men.	3. Belief, but not practical recognition: magic leaves God to religion.
4. Belief in independent spirits, some tutelary, the others hostile.	4. Same belief, with the special purpose of maliciously winning the influence and activity of the spirits.
5. Belief in the human soul, distinct from the body, conscious, surviving.	5. Same belief, with the same purpose of employing and compelling its services.
6. Belief in a world of the beyond, where the spirits live, where souls survive.	6. Same belief, with the same purpose as above.
7. Universal moral sense, based on the distinction between good and evil: a sense of shame, justice, responsibility, liberty, duty; explicit or implicit recognition of conscience.	7. Remains outside the preoccupations of magic, which aims only at the utilization of the invisible forces.
8. Prescriptions and proscriptions with a view to a moral purpose or one reputed so; notion of sin, with a sanction applied by the authority of the invisible world or its representatives.	8. Prescriptions and proscriptions with a view to the utilitarian purpose to be attained.
9. Organization of worship: prayer, offering, sacrifice, rites, ceremonies, symbols, etc., as an expression of submission, thanksgiving, or supplication.	9. Magical organization, with practices of a liturgical character, generally occult, bizarre, immoral, or cruel.

Religion

10. Priesthood, at first represented by the head of the family, then by ancients or priests especially charged with the sacred functions, then by an organized body.

11. Distinction between the profane and the sacred, and affecting persons, places, objects, words, etc.

12. Establishment and organization of the family, as religious and social center, seeking to conserve the purity of its blood, imposing laws on itself, distinguishing itself by special marks, and strengthening itself by alliances.

Magic

10. Isolated magicians or sorcerers; organized secret societies, with initiation, ordeals, ceremonial, occult rites, degrees, etc.

11. Same distinction, but relating only to the things of magic.

12. The individual, secretly initiated in the magical beliefs and practices. Totemic alliances relating to the family.

Perhaps this list might be lengthened to the extent of a few additional articles; but we would not be justified in suppressing anything in it. All of these elements, in fact, are common to all religions and all magics, of all times and all peoples.

No one of the numerous investigators who have treated the matter of primitive religions, at least to our knowledge, has thought to group them in this way; but we find them pointed out and recognized at the period of dispersion by all, and we think that no one can seriously question them.

The same question again presents itself to us, but this time more precise and more clearly circumscribed: whence come these essential and fundamental elements in primitive humanity?

Whatever be the explanations furnished as to the origin of religions, they all come to one of these answers: that these primary elements, observed in humanity prior to all history, either have been revealed to it by a supernatural intervention or are the spontaneous product of the human spirit which, as it is everywhere the same, has everywhere formed the same religious conceptions. Or else, admitting these two natural and supernatural forces, we make them coöperative so that, far from excluding each other, they wonderfully unite in a necessary accord: the human spirit acting in the fulness of the faculties that have been given it, and divine Providence enlightening, fortifying, sustaining, and directing it in the course of the ages, directly or indirectly, despite all the sources of trouble, error, and perversion that surround it.

The materialists and with them all who dislike to meet the supernatural on their road, are necessarily bound to the second hypothesis.

Spiritualists have more liberty, and with the spiritualists the Christians. For no one of the three hypotheses mentioned is forbidden them, not even the one which takes no account of divine revelation. According to the Bible, which they would like to have become involved in this question, the first couple was supernaturally enlightened on the subject of its duties, and probably their first children had their share of that revelation. By the same authority we are informed that the original fall obscured not only their intellect and conscience, but the intellect and conscience of their descendants; we know they were scattered over the earth, which became hostile to their labor; we can suppose their first tribal aggregations, doubtless during long ages, were not more elevated in civilization than the most primitive men of to-day. It is with these ancient and humble human strata, traces of which are from time to time brought to light, that religious evolution must have begun.

Furthermore, the traditionalist and fideist school, which restricted the power of human reason in the conquest of truth and ended by placing certitude solely in the revealed word of God, has been condemned by the Church, which it pretended to serve.

In this matter the most orthodox Catholic has an open field before him. Under the favor of this liberty Abbé Bros, in his book already referred to, thought he must ask of psychology alone the explanation of the origin of "the religion of non-civilized peoples."

"Putting aside revealed religion whose origin, reported in our sacred books, is quite different," he writes, "all the forms of religious activity, imperfect or coherent, are the product of emotions, of collective or individual feelings, of social states that explain them and whose history we can trace. All of them express the way that humanity, abandoned to its own powers, according to its greater or lesser capacity, in the different circumstances of time, place, and culture, has found to answer the insatiable aspiration to the divine which it feels ever living in its very depths." [30]

Developing these ideas, Abbé Bros at the end of his interesting work adds the following considerations, which strengthen those positions.

The savage, endowed with reason, is aware of the need of living, at the same time that he recognizes obstacles which hinder the satisfaction of that need. Death, with its precursor, pain, is met at every step he takes in the world; the mystery of the world, its crushing force and visible immensity fill him with terror.

But by a profound instinct man feels that he can do something to save himself, and the conception he forms of the world gives to this *vouloir-vivre* an altogether religious orientation. Pondering on beings and things, he projects his own personality upon them. Thus he animates all the forces of nature, and for him everything becomes living.

But if these beings are like unto men, they are, like men, accessible to presents, to gifts in food and clothing, to delicate attentions, to prayer. Religion is born. The necessity, joined to the anthropomorphic conception of the universe, has begotten it solely. Man had need of warding off pains and death, of acquiring what is useful. Religion gives him the certitude of attaining these two ends.

However, the savage does not live isolated: his social instinct urges him to join in common his dangers and hopes, emotions, habits, and consequently his religion, which becomes better organized, more enduring, more intense and thus assumes the character of a social institution.

Reason, with its need of explaining and classifying is heard and, no less than the instinct of sociability, influences the devel-

[30] Bros, *op cit.*, p. 11.

opment of religion. Whence comes death? What is the origin
of the world? Whither goes the spirit of the dead? Whence
come the gods? To these questions the savages reply by invent-
ing religious stories and by forming myths.

Thus,

"Necessity of living, anthropomorphic conception of the
universe, social instinct, need of explaining and putting in
order, such are the psychological elements of which the religion
of the savages is composed. Under the form of myths, of worship, or of feelings, the consequences of these principles are
diversified in time and space. Adapting themselves to the
environment, incorporating themselves in a race, progressing
with time, these diverse instincts have here and there found
outlet in different manifestations. Each of them has not always
had the same relative importance in a particular country or
at a particular period. But they have existed everywhere and
it is only by taking account of the progress of the sum
total, as of the proportional or relative development of each
of them, that we can explain the religion of any particular
savages." [31]

As Réville says, the only factor that could well explain the
genesis of religions and most of their common traits, if not all,
would be "the unity of the human spirit striving to solve the
same questions with the same elements out of which to make
their solutions." [32]

To these reasons must be added the difficulties in the way of
taking a primitive revelation as the starting point.

"This explanation is to-day ordinarily rejected," says Abbé
Bros, "first because of the improbable faithfulness of memory
that it supposes in these decayed races. We know that in the
sixteenth century the Blacks of Congo included ten million
Christian souls; when we see that nothing has remained of
Catholic beliefs among the present natives, we can not help
concluding that they must have been no less forgetful of the

[31] Bros, op. cit., p. 313.
[32] Réville, Proleg. de l'hist. des religions, p. 71.

more ancient teachings.[33] On the other hand, if some similarities exist between certain of our beliefs and those of savage peoples, they are not numerous nor of great importance. It often happens that some of their legends partly resemble certain accounts that are dear to us, but might that not be a simple coincidence, the spontaneous creation of the human spirit? And if we saw in the conservation of these recollections an intervention of Providence, we would be no less embarrassed. We could not well understand why, for example, the account of the deluge would alone have survived in the memory of men, while its importance and dogmatic significance do not at all appear to them and are even subject to discussion among Catholic exegetes. On the contrary, the essential institutions which the savages have in common, possess little connection with the primitive religion. Totemism, for instance, which is the most widespread of religious customs among savage peoples, can not have any Biblical origin; we are, then, forced to shift the problem to another ground, and to ask other explanations for these analogies." [34]

In referring to this question, Father Prat says:

"The fact of a primitive revelation is in no way an unreasonable supposition; we unhesitatingly admit it on the authority of our Sacred Scriptures. But it is now so remote from us in time that it may have become obscured or even quite obliterated. It is doubtful whether any evident traces of it can still be found in this human world of ours, a world more ancient than we have hitherto been inclined to believe. Should there still be some vestiges of such a revelation, how are we to-day to distinguish them from the spontaneous product of man's spirit?" [35]

In the presence of these declarations, if Réville still lived, perhaps he would hesitate to write that Catholics base their

---

[33] This figure of ten millions has always been considered as greatly exaggerated. Most of these Christians were such only by their baptism: as they had no instruction, it was easy for them to forget their Christianity. The relatively small number of real Christians, on the other hand, has been well maintained until our own day without priests, notably in Ambaca (near Loango), where the Blacks have handed down religious teaching and writing.

[34] Bros, *op. cit.*, p. 7.

[35] Prat. S. J., *La Science de la religion et la science du langage.*

stand in this matter on the reality of a primitive revelation
because, "guided by a visible theological interest, they hope
thus to lay the foundation stone on which later to erect
the dogma of the infallibility of the Church." [36] We note, in
passing, that the dogma of the infallibility of the Church has
no pertinence in the present question. If Réville can not resolve
to accept the hypothesis in question, it is because of its improbability when compared with all we know of the distant past of
our species and of the wretched state in which it has lived,
without considering, he says, that Genesis is concerned only with
a rather limited group of peoples who can trace their origin
to the three sons of Noe, namely Sem, Ham, and Japheth.[37]

Must we accept these conclusions as the only ones that are
"scientific," reasonable, tenable?

Despite the proofs employed to support these conclusions,
proofs which we have reproduced to the best of our ability,
many will agree that, at any rate, the discussion is far from
being closed.

1. Let us begin by answering the chief concern of Réville.
"The hypothesis of a primitive revelation of religious truth,"
he says, "clashes with the totality of all we know about the
extremely uncultured and pitiable state of humanity prior to
history." [38] That is an illusion common to all those who make
evolution, and evolution magnified according to their fashion,
into a dogma whose authority must rule every question in all
its details. In accordance with this principle, the religious
development of a people must necessarily be parallel to its
social, political, literary, artistic, and other development. If,
then, mankind has been in a state of wretched external civilization at a given moment, which may include several centuries,
wretched also must have been its religion.

The answer is before our very eyes.

The wretchedness of the first men does not seem to have been

---

[36] Réville, *Prolég. de l'hist. des religions*, p. 51.

[37] *Ibid.*, p. 67. Popular tradition which regards Cham (Ham) as the
father of the black race, is nowhere taught in the Bible. The Hamitic
peoples spoken of in Genesis, ch. 10, are not the negroes.

[38] *Ibid.*, p. 57.

lower—no matter how low it is put—than that of our present Pygmies. But it is clearly proved that these poor people, though in a very low social state, have religious and moral ideas relatively pure, doubtless very simple, but free from many superstitious encumbrances; and they are consequently found to be superior not only to the black populations in whose midst they are scattered, but even superior to the Greeks and Romans of the "best periods," however unlikely the assertion may appear. In fact, religion and morality are one thing, and a very different thing are wealth, industry, art, science, and what we have come to call "civilization." The simple but pure religious elements which we have found constitute the universal and common foundations of early religion everywhere, can be perfectly well conceived in men deprived of the material improvements that progress has later brought to life.[39]

2. What influences Abbé Bros is the improbability that poor savages would possess the retentive memory necessary to retain the lessons of divine revelation during an unlimited number of centuries. Granted. But have we not fallen into an improbable anthropomorphism when we represent revelation thus? We would seem to argue that to instruct the first men, God had to deliver a series of conferences under the banana trees of Eden, then, after finishing the lesson, return to heaven with his catechism under his arm.

Let us be serious. St. Paul states the matter otherwise. *God, who, at sundry times and in divers manners, spoke in times past to the fathers by the prophets, last of all, in these days hath spoken to us by his Son.* (Heb. 1:1.) It is, then, in several parts, in numerous fragments, and in "divers manners" (implying articulate words, visions, dreams, inspirations, interior illumination, and natural lights fortified and directed) that the revelation or rather the revelations have been made, not only to the direct ancestors of the Hebrew people, but to all the children of Adam and Eve who had a soul to save, so that all had the necessary means at least to attain their salva-

[39] The same remark might be made concerning the Jewish people, superior to all others from the religious point of view, inferior to many from all other points of view.

tion; for it is certain that God wills the salvation of all men.

We must add that none among the elementary gifts of primitive religion and morality appears in itself beyond the reach of the human reason and conscience. It would be sufficient if this reason and this conscience had been maintained and directed by ordinary supernatural help in all "men of good will."

Moreover, there can be no question here of lessons transmitted by a faithful and uninterrupted tradition. The truth is that from the beginning these primary elements of religion and morality seem to have been, as it were, deposited and socialized in an institution so general, so simple, so necessary, and so natural that the human race truly exists only by that institution: I mean the family. The primitive family, receiving these elements, assimilated them to such an extent that it seems as if it could not have maintained itself without them and they could not have been maintained without it. These elements are its internal sap. Wherever it has sent forth its shoots, this sap has made them live and multiply even to our own day. It is true that parasites appeared and covered the human plant with their growths, their leaves, and their flowers, hiding it from the eyes of the passer-by, sucking its life, and almost stifling it under their weight. The totems belong to these parasites, so do also many taboos, initiations, superstitions, and myths, in short everything connected with mythology, magic, and their inspirations. But the primitive tree ever remained, living on even with impoverished sap. This tree we have tried to disclose to our readers.

3. We are told that, "if analogies exist between certain of our beliefs and those of savage peoples, they are neither numerous nor important." Not numerous? We have pointed out a dozen, and no doubt it would be possible to indicate still more. Not important? They are the very basis of all existing moralities and religions. The religions of uncivilized peoples are in a state of confusion which may be lacking in the precise theological knowledge of the authors who have studied them, as Spencer, Tylor, Frazer, Rialle, and so many others; they may even lack the purpose intended by them. All this has caused

us to mistake their myths, legends, superstitions, and their magical proceedings for the religion of these populations, all that which is, in short, the counterfeit only or deformation of religion. Consider these, if you wish, the spontaneous product of the human spirit, which has so often gone astray in bizarre vagaries, in extravagant conceptions, in ridiculous, obscene, or cruel practices. But besides all that, there are very pure and beautiful gifts scattered everywhere, as we have shown, which constitute religion.

4. Abbé Bros confides to us "that he would feel embarrassed in attributing to a special act of Providence the conservation of these memories, whose importance and dogmatic significance is by no means evident." And by way of example he cites the deluge, recollections of which are found in many countries. We are heartily of the same opinion concerning the deluge and traditions of that sort: no special interest for man's salvation is attached to their conservation. But we are sure he would be the first to agree that this can not be said of the primary elements of religion we have cited. The explanation for the error here is that we too readily rely upon the scholars already mentioned to form for us an exact and complete idea of primitive religious beliefs. Certainly these scholars have discoursed long and brilliantly on myths, taboos, totems, naturism, fetichism, animism, and the little episodes inspired by them, all secondary matters. But, while doing this, they have completely forgotten to give conspicuous place to what precisely constitutes the essential institutions: the general organization of the family, the belief in God, the foundations of morality, the survival of the human soul, the idea of the beyond, worship by prayer and sacrifice. And these institutions are so closely related to the primitive religion and to all religions that they form their necessary basis.

None of the objections offered against "the hypothesis of revelation" holds against the facts in the case, facts that are certain and easy to verify.

We wish to say at once that assuredly the weakness of these reasons can not be made over into positive proofs, and we have

no idea of adding that the reality of revelation is henceforth
historically demonstrated merely by the history of religions.
We will see to it that we do not fall into this other kind of excess.
Revelation is proved otherwise and by other means: Catholic
theology devotes an entire section to the question, which forms
the basis of her teaching.[40]

All we wish to say here is that perhaps we have been too
hasty in reproaching the missionaries "for having sought to
make factitious resemblances between the great modern religions and the conceptions of the savage."

On the contrary, so little does this inquiry for resemblances
appear to us as vain and useless, that a real interest is attached
to its prudent and attentive pursuit.

Will the legitimacy of this inquiry be contested because its
conclusions accord with Christian tradition? Is this the reason
why we can not be "scientific"? On the contrary, we think
that the human mind has a right to search for the truth, wherever the truth may be found, even if it offends the partisanship
of adversaries.

Let us continue our examination.

1. It is an accepted fact that, so far as can be known, humanity has never been without religion or morality. But if it were
true that all religion and all morality outside of Christianity
have come solely from the working of the spirit, there would
have been a period when the human species, at its various places
of habitation, would have been deprived of all religious and
moral ideas, precisely those qualities by reason of which man
is man. At any rate it seems difficult to admit that this state
of "non-religion" and "non-morality" has been general in mankind at any given epoch of history; nothing proves that it has
been so, and everything leads us to believe, on the contrary, that
it was otherwise.

2. On this supposition, we would have to hold that at most
diverse and distant spots on the globe all the human aggregations have agreed, by a natural use of their powers, on what con-

[40] See Tanquerey, *De vera religione*. The author gives an abundant bibliography (ed. 1901, p. 19).

stitutes the primary and essential elements of all religion and all morality.

If it happened by chance, this extraordinary agreement would only show that chance is sometimes so intelligent that it would be proper to call it by another name.

Were we to suppose that philosophers, scholars, and other intellectuals had met together at the beginning of time in a sort of plenary assembly to lay the foundations of future civilizations, we could easily and surely conjecture, judging from the deliberative assemblies of to-day, that they would scarcely agree on the twelve essential points which we have indicated above. How much more extraordinary to find such tacit agreement among human aggregations some of which have remained at the banks of the Euphrates while others wander in the forests of equatorial Africa, others at the gate of the Andes, and still others, in their frail "pirogues," touch the oceanic islands one after the other!

3. If it is true that none of the primary gifts of religion is beyond the acquisition of man's reason, nevertheless experience teaches us that it is very difficult for him to acquire an assemblage of truths sufficiently coherent to serve as a durable basis for the family, society, religion, morality, and everything connected therewith: in these essential matters we have need of aid. If God made the first men, it seems strange that He has not come to their aid and that, having given them the religious faculty, He did not give it its proper stimulus. So, at least, have thought all the sages of antiquity, from Herodotus, Sophocles, and Plato down to Cicero and Virgil, from the chants of the Vedas to the first philosophers of China.[41] Divine revelation would thus have completed and guaranteed natural religion and natural law, which man can create for himself by the sole forces of his spirit but which it is extremely difficult for him to establish in detail and preserve from impure mixtures.

4. Experience also shows us that "belief, like life, is transmitted from the living to the living."[42] Although we find no

---

[41] Victor Rondet, *Les initiations; la religion.*
[42] *Ibid.*

systematic instruction organized among savage populations, yet
instruction is imparted by institutions, ceremonies, and facts.
But even that presupposes a beginning. Thus we are always
forced to return to the necessity of a primitive teaching, preserved in some way or other through the long succession of past
ages and in the extremely varied conditions which human populations have undergone.

5. This idea naturally leads to another which it seems
essential to point out, even though we be accused of departing
from the platform on which this study has been conducted.

In spite of the religious need active in man, in spite of the
efforts of his reason, even despite the likelihood of a primitive
revelation, it seems as if the religious beliefs of the races would
have more or less quickly disappeared before a growing indifference, the necessities of life, the ardor of earthly joys, and
preoccupations of every sort, unless extraordinary, marvelous,
and supernatural manifestations from time to time had come
to reawaken and nourish his faith.

Undoubtedly illusion and fraud play an enormous part in the
interpretation of certain strange facts which both primitive and
civilized peoples are frequently called upon to witness. But
this is no reason for refusing, with prejudice and once for all,
to examine facts of that kind which come to our knowledge.
Nothing is less reasonable than systematic incredulity.

Suppose there is a place where such phenomena as the following are observed, under an influence said to be supernatural:
"Broken bones that are reunited, caries that stops festering and
disappears, injured lungs that become suddenly and perma-
nently sound, lupus of the face that heals, gaping holes that
close; children, women, young men, men of advanced years,
workmen and men of the middle classes, sick poor and well-to-
do sick, all conditions, all ages, all diseases are helped" [43] by this
prodigious influence. The crowds who see these marvels with
their own eyes and touch them with their hands will feel their
beliefs exalted. But that is what has been seen and what can
still be seen.

On the other hand, occur the phenomena of telepathy and

[43] Bertrin, *Histoire critique de Lourdes.*

spiritism, the evocation of the dead, levitation, "envoutements," conjurations, possessions, the mysteries of sorcery and magic, which, explain them as you like, are not seriously disputed by any one. They are observed in Europe and America in the twentieth century among the most enlightened populations, under the vigilance of well known scholars, in India and China, in the depths of most savage Africa, as formerly in Egypt, Chaldea, and all the ancient world. Let us concede the greatest possible part in these matters to human simplicity, to the imagination, and to jugglery: it will still be true that a large number of authentic phenomena remain, to which thus far no natural explanation has been assigned. These last manifestations, from the remotest times up to our own, taking place before the eyes of the primitives by the action of their sorcerers, maintain their faith in magic and its mysteries. In a history of religion, it is necessary to notice this factor, under penalty otherwise of wilful rejection of pertinent material.[44]

We finally arrive at this general conclusion. In this great question as it presents itself to us, *the human species migrated from the original spot where it first appeared, at a period which science is powerless to determine in a precise manner. There had been put into its possession a fund of religious and moral truths, with the elements of a worship, the whole rooted in the very nature of man, and there conserved along with the family, developing with society. Each race according to its particular mentalities, its intellectual tendency, and the special conditions of its life, gradually established those superficially varied but fundamentally identical forms that we call religions. Everywhere and from the beginning, there were attached to these religions, myths, superstitions, and magics which vitiated and disfigured them, and turned them from their object.*

[44] This idea is developed with spirit and courage by Andrew Lang in his work, *The Making of Religion*. The authority of this scholar is universally recognized; but as his observations were very inconvenient, his book has been treated with significant silence. See also: C. Godard, *L'occultisme contemporain;* L. Bertrand, *L'occultisme ancien et moderne.*

VI. CHRISTIANITY IN THE PRESENCE OF HUMAN RELIGIONS

Up to this point, conformably to our program, we have kept ourselves in the domain of observed facts; and we have avoided introducing, except occasionally, the Christian and Catholic religion. According to the loudly proclaimed declarations of her adversaries, this inquiry must turn against her. The study of primitive religions would show, they said, that Christianity there finds its origin and its explanation: that it is a repetition of these ancient formulas, organized, systematized, perfected, and disciplined so as to be adapted to the higher civilization of the peoples it had conquered and who live by it.

The moment has come for the accused to take the stand and for us to ask whether she has anything to say in reply.

Yes, she will answer.

For it turns out that this inquiry which was to have confounded her, does her a wonderful service.

The Christian religion, or more precisely the Catholic, that is *universal,* religion, calls itself by this name, not only because it addresses all men actually on earth, not only because it counts on sending forth its appeal to all those who are yet to come until the end, but also because it fixes the date of its birth at the very birth of the human race. Thus, along with affirming that the first man was "Catholic," it hopes that the last one will be so.

This idea is not new. We find it in one of the first of the most ancient Catholic writers, Hermas who, in his 'Pastor," represents the Church as an aged woman already covered with wrinkles, because her age is that of the world, and because her head bears upon it the marks of all the centuries of humanity's life.[45]

St. Augustine in a well known text says:

"What is now called the Christian religion, existed among the ancients, and was not absent from the beginning of the human race even until Christ came in the flesh: from which

[45] Prunier, *Evolution et immutabilité de la doctrine religieuse dans l'Eglise.*

time the true religion, already long in existence, began to be called Christian." [46]

"As regards the substance of the articles of faith," says St. Thomas Aquinas, "they have not received any increase as time went on: since whatever those who lived later have believed, was contained, albeit implicitly, in the faith of those Fathers who preceded them. All the articles of faith are contained implicitly in certain primary matters of faith, such as God's existence, and His providence over the salvation of man. . . . The existence of God includes all that we believe to exist in God eternally, and in these our happiness consists; while belief in His providence includes all those things which God dispenses in time, for man's salvation, and which are the way to that happiness." [47]

This is why Tanquerey, in his widely appreciated theological treatise, sums up this doctrine in the following words: "Primitive religion does not substantially differ from the Christian religion." [48]

Max Müller, taking his point of view from the study of comparative religions, states his conclusion in these words:

"Of religion, too, as of language, it may be said that in it everything new is old, and everything old is new, and that there has been no entirely new religion since the beginning of the world." [49]

Religion is essentially a "bond" between God and man, between heaven and earth, between the supernatural and nature. But if humanity has a vital interest in the maintenance of these mystical relations, it is none the less true that God, on his part, can not abandon man without denying his Providence.

From the beginning, the ancestors of the human race have had a knowledge of the Divinity and of methods to maintain the necessary communications with Him: these beliefs and elementary practices in their sum total may be considered as the equivalent of the twelve that we have drawn up. But to thwart

[46] St. Augustine, *Ret.*, I, 13.
[47] St. Thomas, *Summa Theol.* English Translation. 2a, 2ae, q. 1, art. 7.
[48] Tanquerey, *op. cit.*, p. 281.
[49] Max Müller, *Chips from a German Workshop*, I, p. x.

magic, which has always been lying in wait for religion so as to turn it aside from its object, religion, watched over from on high in order that it might retain its original purity, was finally entrusted to a family, that became a tribe and then a people, until the day when the Word, acting in the world as the regulator of truth λόγος σπερμάτικος, as St. Justin says, became incarnate among us and established religion as a special and permanent institution.

Thus from the time of Abraham and in his family, we see "El" take or retake the significance of a sole God, powerful, just, and supremely moral.[50] The sacred functions are exercised by the head of the family or the head of the tribe. The law or custom is published as the expression of the divine will; the notion of pure and impure things, i.e., things permitted and things forbidden, occupies an important place in their minds. Sin calls for a sanction.

Why has the sacrifice held the place of importance given to it? Because it is considered the natural and indispensable means of communicating with God, whether to recognize His sovereign dominion, or to ask and obtain pardon for faults committed, or to thank Him for favors received, or to ask for new graces. There is implied in it, also, the idea of concluding or renewing an alliance.

Parallel with this, we perceive traces of magical practices filtering into this primitive religion, undoubtedly from more or less vitiated surroundings: the bull, by its strength an image of the Divinity; totemistic practices that make the divine alliance sink to an animistic alliance by means of living animals; or the *teraphim,* that seem to be domestic fetiches with a human form.

All that has been pointed out, as more or less apparent among our primitives: and they have not shaken off these things. As is quite natural, pure, elevated, and moral ideas have grown weak among them, almost at times to the point of disappearance, while the invasion of magical beliefs and practices has become more and more evident.

[50] See Dufourcq, *Histoire comparée des religions païennes et de la religion juive.*

With Moses, the tradition of Abraham, exposed always to the deleterious influences of Chaldea, Egypt, and Canaan, becomes more precise and begins to develop. The figure of God, when liberated, appears simple and glorious; and Jahveh becomes thenceforth the master and patron of a chosen people: "That is for Israel, not only the sustenance of its faith and the foundation of its confidence, but also the guarantee of its future salvation." [51] The natural law is codified in the Decalogue. The old liturgical practices, ablutions, fumigations, libations, and processions, become purified and sanctified by the fact that they are related to the worship of God alone; a new spirit transfigures them.

The same is true of circumcision, which marked the removal of the prohibition in regard to marriage and the termination of the initiation of youth; henceforth it will be the mark by which every son of Israel will be consecrated to God and will reproduce life under pure conditions. The same with the Sabbath: in Babylonia it was an unlucky day, in Judea it will be the day consecrated to God by prayer and rest.

To prevent idolatry, which was ever threatening to reappear in the tribe, and yet to meet the constant desire to have God in their midst, the holy ark is constructed, where the presence of Jahveh will be manifested. About this movable sanctuary, the worship is organized, with the priesthood.

In turn the Judges, Kings, and Prophets maintain, develop, and restore the Mosaic tradition, sustaining the people in their trials, punishing them when they stray, recalling them to their duties, defending them against the contagion of idolatry, magic, and immorality. At Jerusalem, the holy city, the worship receives an ampler solemnity, and as time passes, the more majestic does God's transcendence appear.

We come at length to the time when the Word, who presided over this evolution, protecting it against impure elements, crystallizes it in what is called CHRISTIANITY, no longer to be confided henceforth to the family, nor to the tribe, nor to the head of the people, nor to a sacerdotal body organized here and

[51] Valeton (in Chantepie de la Saussaye, *Manual of the Science of Religion*).

there, but to that special, living, conquering, and universal society which is called the Catholic Church.

Unfortunately this evolution did not draw within itself the totality of the religious elements. At a period impossible to determine, a double current set in among these elements. While the primordial beliefs lived and developed, so to speak, in the direct line, under the influence of a supernatural and progressive illumination, these same elements, sojourning with numerous other fragments of the human family, underwent a deformation and received additions under which they almost disappeared. Thus,

"among the peoples where the primitive religion degenerated," writes Abbé de Broglie, "the religious instincts naturally and spontaneously created forms and institutions partially adapted to the needs of mankind, imperfectly satisfying some lofty aspirations, and lending themselves to the satisfaction of the passions. Great men appeared who felt the insufficiency and corruption of the existing forms of worship and created new ones, making use of ancient traditions but also relying on man's reason and conscience and religious instincts which their genius had divined. These imperfect works have always been more or less mingled with imposture, as communication with heaven is the only means of obtaining men's confidence in religious matters. They contained a mixture of good and evil. Oftentimes they include a rough sketch of what God is to do later on; but these elements of a true religion are found isolated, scattered, opposed to one another, powerless for good, without strength or stability. The sublimest notions are suddenly transformed into gross superstitions: the loftiest ideal often becomes, by a sort of mystical fermentation, a base and sensual doctrine." [52]

"There is no true religion," said Napoleon with his genial common sense, "but that which begins with the world and continues during the course of the ages."

The true religion indeed must be universal. It is, then, the universal religion, the gist of the beliefs of all times, that we should try to discover.

[52] De Broglie, *Histoire des religions*, p. 310.

This work we have undertaken. And we saw that the religious elements found at the very origins of humanity, which develop, or if you like, evolve regularly and always in the same direction, *in eodem scilicet dogmate, eodem sensu, eadem sententia*, in spite of countless obstacles that might have turned them aside, on from the remotest times to Christ, and from Christ to the present day, are identified throughout that long journey with the only CATHOLIC RELIGION, i.e., with the only universal religion, i. e., with the only true religion.

At its side, as the human families dispersed over the habitable earth, the primitive religious notions attached themselves to their rudimentary social organizations, burdening themselves with adventitious creations, legends, myths, superstitions, and magical practices, in which we recognize the work of the human imagination, sometimes guided perhaps by those occult powers in which these earlier men always believed and which form the various states of naturism, animism, fetichism, and shamanism of the savage populations.

At the different epochs when the great ancient civilizations flourished on the banks of the Tigris and the Euphrates, the Nile, the Ganges, the Blue River, or the Tiber, as the basis are found the same traditions, but they are now covered over with new elements the more complicated as the imagination of the people was more cultivated and more active.

Meanwhile, from the wombs of these civilizations in labor, came forth, as products of a mystical fermentation, those extraordinary men to whom history has given the title of "founders" of religions. But in reality religion has no founders among men. Those who bear this title worked upon preëxisting elements; they are reformers, reorganizers, or even makers of schisms, and they are the first to declare that religion is anterior to them. Such were Zarat-houstra or Zoroaster for Mazdaism, Sakya-Muni for Buddhism, Lao-Tseu for Taoism, Khung-Fu-Tseu or Confucius for the old reformed or deformed Chinese religion, Mohammed for Islam.

All these religions in different degrees contain portions of the primitive truth and insofar they are "catholic." But the Catholic religion alone shows that vitality which is both immutable and progressive, extending to all times and places; and this is why the eye of the believer sees therein the directive action of the Spirit that lives in it, that guards it, that sanctifies it. What distinguishes the other religions, belongs properly to them, but the rest is hers. It is the common heritage that she holds in its entirety from the heavenly Father and she is happy to find fragments of this common heritage scattered under all latitudes, in all ages, in all civilizations, and in all races.

She has often been called "proud and intolerant": "Outside the Church, no salvation."

She answers: "Granted. But where are the limits of the Church, and what man will determine them? God alone perceives them in the depths of the human soul, and this is why He *alone* can be her judge."

In short, the Catholic religion emerges from this inquiry in triumph.

She alone can give the explanation of all the problems that arise in the history of comparative religions; and where, for lack of documents, proof is impossible, her solutions appear to unprejudiced minds as the simplest, the most reasonable, and the most probable.

Far from being an embarrassment to her, the resemblances observed between beliefs, morals, forms of worship, and religious organizations form an additional title in her favor.

By way of a general conclusion, based on the recapitulation that we have just sketched, we can formulate this alternative:

Either the human species has received the fundamental bases of the universal religion as a deposit by a supernatural intervention;

Or the human species is imperceptibly led toward these fundamental bases by an irresistible inclination that is connatural with it.

In either case, the human species, in its general make-up, is essentially religious and fundamentally Catholic.

This conclusion permits us to return to the provisional division of religions that we proposed above. In dividing religions into two groups (deistic and animo-deistic), we meant to emphasize the preponderance given in one group to the idea and the worship of God, and in the other to the idea and worship of the spirits or manes.

But we possess data now that enable us to propose a more precise and more correct division.

In reality there is only one religion, there has never been but one, and there never will be but one; there can never be but one.

Its elements include all that is true, just, and good in the various religious forms of the world, to the exclusion of all magical, mythological, superstitious, or simply useless alloys. She alone has an origin coeval with the origin of humanity. The others (i.e., religions) can almost certainly trace their formation to the action of a man, philosopher, prophet, or reformer, or else to the action of a period, a political or sacerdotal group, a school, or even a race; but that one true religion goes as far back as the human species itself.

She alone from the remotest times down to to-day has withstood all the forces of disintegration and ruin, all the shafts of criticism and science, all indifference, passions, attacks, hatreds, tyrannies, and corruptions.

She alone has been able to adapt herself to the most varied civilizations, the humblest as well as the highest, to all countries, all climates, all races, all political forms, all intellects, all consciences.

She alone fully answers the needs of the mind and heart, pointing man to a line of conduct, an end, a destiny that makes life intelligible and really worth being lived.

Will you say that her proof is not convincing?

We answer with Pascal: this proof is presented with sufficient clearness to satisfy the reason in its legitimate exigencies, but it remains sufficiently veiled to make faith meritorious. It can not be otherwise with a religion coming from God and addressing free man, obliged to coöperate in his own salvation.

But this religion, having natural religion for its base, is necessarily *universal* or *catholic* and is identified with integral CHRISTIANITY.

Hence we present this more exact division of religions:

1. THE UNIVERSAL OR CATHOLIC RELIGION;

2. THE PARTICULAR RELIGIONS, which borrow their name either from their founder, as Buddhism, or from their special characteristic, as Islam, or from the country or people where they are especially spread, as the Chaldean, Greek, Etruscan, or Latin religion.

Under the African equator it often happens that the sun, rising at the horizon as if by a sudden leap, illumines with its brightness the whole expanse of sky and earth. Then, as it ascends, mists, in long trains, slowly rise from the swamps, follow along the great water courses, hang over the forests, and cover the plains. The great orb, however, continuing its course, lights up the summit of the mountain for the traveler seated there.

Now, behold the world stretches before him like an immense sheet of mist, its surface like the quiet gray of a limitless ocean. Here and there, in islands or islets, emerge groups of trees and the tops of hills, while the depths of the valley rest in thicker obscurity.

Yet at none of these points is it night: day is upon the land.

Everywhere dispersed, some in the full light, others in the semi-darkness, still others in the dense mist, insects and birds instinctively turn toward the sun, some bathing in its brightness, others scarcely perceiving it, still others merely suspecting its presence, each guiding itself as best it can, and waiting.

Thus it is with the great sun of religious truth.

When it rose upon the horizon of our race at daybreak, everything was illumined by its light.

Alas! the mists came, and often generations of men had gropingly and timidly to seek this road. The sun, however, has not ceased to shine, seen from the mountain where the Catholic Church has been seated since the beginning of the ages. From there it scatters its rays in the immense expanse: men do not everywhere clearly see it, but yet they can say that it is nowhere absent. And little by little the mist dissolves and the light spreads.

Let us wait, let us hope, let us work. A day will come perhaps, when men then living, escaped from the deceptive vapors in which their fathers have sadly and painfully walked, will at last be able to raise their heads towards a cloudless sky, and the sun will shine for all!

GOD in the Bantu Languages (Equatorial Africa)

This table, founded on data furnished by Father Sacleux, C.S.Sp., shows:

1. The original and identical sense of the name of God in a great number of Bantu languages.

2. The wide diffusion of this word, since it extends from Zanzibar to Fernando Po, from the Victoria Nyanza to the Herero country, from Natal to Gabon.

We beg to recall that in the Bantu languages the noun is composed of an invariable radical and a variable prefix that determines its meaning and agreement.

From the primitive words

ULU (Kamba), high, elevated, heaven, and ILU (Mbundu), heaven; IYU (Swahili of Amu), on high, and YU (cf. Fan YO), same meaning, come the following derivatives:

M—ulu	(Bemba)	heaven
Om—uru	(Herero)	heaven
Mu—uro	(Lunda)	heaven
Li—ulu	(Kimbundu)	on high
I—ulu	(Luba)	heaven
E—ulu	(Kwanyama)	heaven
Di—ulu	(Luba)	heaven
Lu—ulu	(Nywema)	on high
Li—ilu	(Kote)	heaven
W—ilu	(Luyi)	heaven
L—ilu	(Ngangela)	heaven
Mte—ulu	(Makua)	on high
Y—ulu	(Tege)	heaven
I—dj—ulu	(Tonga)	heaven
E—yuru	(Herero)	heaven
I—yulu	(Subiya)	heaven
E—guru	(Ganda)	heaven
N—guru	(Nyungwe)	firmament
N—gulu	(Zigua)	mountain
N—kol	(Fan)	hill
I—gulu	(Karagwe)	heaven, on high
E—gulu	(Ganda)	heaven, on high
Lu—gulu	(Sumbwa)	on high
Dji—kulu	(Kota)	heaven
I—ku	(Mbuti)	heaven. Etc.

From which:

Mu—gulu	(Tabwa)	God, literally Mu (he) and gulu (of heaven)
Mu—kuru	(Herero)	God, literally, he from on high
Kuru	(Temne)	God, literally The High
Goru	(Bubi)	id.
Nkulu-Nkulu	(Zulu)	God, literally The Very High

And the following derivatives:

Dyu and Dyuu	(Swahili)	on high
Dyo	(Fan)	heaven
Dzu	(Nzuani)	on high
Dzuu	(Pokomo)	on high
Ku—dzuru	(Nyungwe)	on high
Dzulu	(Nika)	heaven, on high
Nzulu	(Sena)	in the air
U—dzulu	(Makua)	on high
I—dzulu	(Tusi)	on high
E—dzulu	(Congo)	heaven
Zulu	(Tebele)	heaven
Di—zulu	(Sorongo)	heaven
I—yu(b)u	(Rega)	heaven
Ru—(w)e(h)u	(Tchaga)	heaven
I—guu or *Igu*	(Nyamwezi)	on high
Ku—guu	(Teita)	on high, the high
U—(w)i(n)gu	(Swahili)	heaven
Yu—(w)i(n)gu	(Pokomo)	heaven
Hw—i(n)go	(Kamba)	cloud
Hu—u(n)gu	(Kikuyu)	cloud. Etc.

From which:

M—ngu	(Swahili)	God, literally the heavenly
M—ungu	(Swahili, etc.)	he of the heaven
Mu—ungu	(Pokomo)	he from on high
Mu—lungu	(Swahili)	id.
M—lungu	(Teita, etc.)	
Mu—rungu	(Rundi)	
M—pungu	(Guha)	
Mu—luku, M—luko	(Makua)	
Huku	(Nyaneka)	
Suku	(Mbundu)	

INDEX